EARLY FISHING PLUGS
OF THE U.S.A.

by

Art and Scott Kimball

A COLLECTOR'S HISTORY

Post Office Box 252
Boulder Junction, Wisconsin
54512

TO ANNIE

Contents

Introduction

Much has happened since we first published this book in 1985. Little did we realize how much was still out there. New discoveries of pre-1930 plugs came in from all over the United States. Some of these are true surprises.

Interest in old fishing plugs, in general, has risen greatly and is still doing so. More and more people are taking note of the importance of fishing plugs to our American heritage.

The scarcity and desirability of old fishing plugs has become evident with reports from auction sales of individual plugs sold for thousands of dollars. The sale of a Haskell Minnow for over $20,000.00 was rather startling to say the least.

The basic theme of this book is that every fishing plug has its own story. The term "fishing plug" needs to be defined here. Fishing plugs have been historically made of numerous materials such as rubber, hollow metal, plastic and, of course, wood. The fishing plug usually has some sort of built in action, or can be activated to attract and hold fish. A fishing plug is not a spoon or spinner, but might contain one or both of these concepts in its construction. A fishing lure is described as any artificial bait, including plugs. A second and perhaps best definition is that if you are a fisherman or a plug collector, or bought this book, you probably already know what a plug is. It is a word we accept and use. It has appeared unqualified in articles and court cases as early as 1916. The word plug appears in U.S. patents earlier than that. The dictionaries are just getting around to it. A plug is a plug.

As the authors of this book, we have combined all the information we could find, and tried to at least reconstruct the basic elements of the history of the fishing plug in the U.S.A. We fully realize there are gaps in the text you are about to read. These are areas where we simply have not been able to find out the who, where, what or when of a certain plug. Please help us fill in these gaps by identifying some of the unknowns or "who dunnits", as we sometimes refer to them. We also need to fill in the history itself: facts, legends, fish stories, dates, key connections between people, ads, old catalogs, instruction sheets, and most frustrating of all, patents before 1852. It's up to all of us to continue in the endless search to identify all of the early fishing plugs of the U.S.A.

There is a lot of turf to be covered in the pages that follow so we will make this introduction short. What you are about to read and see is generally presented with chronology in mind. In every case we go from the earliest to most recent dates covered within each chapter in this book. It is important to remember that "EARLY FISHING PLUGS OF THE U.S.A." deals with approximately the first hundred years. Most plugs in this book are at least 50 years old.

We sincerely hope you enjoy what you will be reading as much as we have in researching, writing and publishing it.

Acknowledgements

"EARLY FISHING PLUGS OF THE USA" would not have been possible without the help and encouragement of many people. We sincerely hope we have not overlooked anyone. If we did, we apologize. This is a long list. We had a lot of help. Our sincere thanks to the following for sharing their information and their help. Jim Anderson, John Anderson, Chris Balazs, Ray Bangs, Frank Baron, Leon "Bart" Bartosic, John Beck, Walter Blue, Chuck Borst, Jim Bourdon, Bruce Boyden, Dave Bronk, Larry Bryant, Dan Butts, Phil Byrne, Jim Cantwell, Arlan Carter, Raymond Carver, Malcolm Clark, Jim Colgan, Martin Copp, Joe Courcelle, Jim Daniel, Phil Dawson, Bruce Dyer, Rick Edmisten, Bob Essick, Bob Falkenstein, Neal Federle, Tim Fehlandt, Howard Fortune, Jim Frazier, Ron Gast, Joe Georgetta. Harold Gerstenberger, Earl Glasshagel, Bob Gorashko, Robert Gustafson, Clyde A. Harbin, Sr., Peter Haupt, Emerson Heilman, Dave Hoover, Don Janick, Bill Jones, Earl Knudson, Frank Koffend, Don Kramer, Bob Kutz, Paul Lindner, Willis Logan, Jim Lone, Jack Looney, Trig Lund, Allen and Charlotte McCord, Greg Mackey, Dave McCleskey, Russ Mumford, Al Munger, Dudley Murphy, Jerry Myhre, Joe Naylor, Cliff Netherton, Tom Newcomb, Jeff Nieman, Carl Nisen, Steve Ongert, Dennis Pederson, Tony Przybylo, Tom Reimer, Bill Renneisen, Randy Rhoderick, Phil Robbins, John Romero, Gaylor Ropp, Paw Paw Ruck (deceased), John Scarlet, Conrad Schornhorst, John Shoffner, Larry Smith, Steve Smith, Tom Steele, Bill Stoetzel, John Stowell, Dick Streater, Terry Strutz, Jack Swedberg, Louie Tate, Henry Taylor, Rich Treml, Al Tumas, Bob Vermillion, Tony Waring, Ed Weston, Bill Wetzel, Karl White, Bruce Wilsie, Dick Wilson, Marc Wisotsky, Tom Winter, Dennis Wolfe, John Woodruff, Clarence Zahn.

In addition to the above, we would like to thank Rusty Anthony, Bob and Liz Bulkley, Wayne R. Chapman, Dr. Harold G. Herr, Leo Hummel, Don Ludy, Todd Powell, Drew Reese, Keith Tompkins, Nick Torella, Dan and Judy Basore.

We want to especially thank Clyde "The Bassman" Harbin for allowing us to publish the important material in Chapter Eleven titled "Hidden Heddon History"! This information is the product of Clyde's sharing knowledge he gathered through difficult and dilligent research into Heddon history.

Certain individuals mentioned above deserve the special thanks of all of us for sharing in the areas of their expertise. These individuals will be acknowledged in the following text when their particular field of interest is discussed.

A select bibliography of books in and out of print is presented here. We recommend all of these publications.

Bourdon, Jim - The Bomber Bait Company - 1983 - Jim Bourdon. Nordica Drive, Croton-on-Hudson, NY 10520

Bourdon, Jim and Barzee, Ray - The Water Scout and Other Clark Baits - 1984

Bourdon, Jim - South Bend/Their Artificial Baits and Reels/As Reflected by the company's catalogues between 1912 and 1953 - 1985

Boyden, Bruce - Members of the Creek Chub "Pikie" and "Surfster" Families - 1984 - Bruce Boyden, P.O. Box 752, Annex Station, Providence, RI 02901

Dickert, Harold - A History of The Erwin Weller Co. - 1984 - Contact NFLCC - book may not be available to general public

Fox, Charles K. - The Book of Lures - U.S.A. - 1975

Harbin, Clyde A., Sr. - James Heddon's Sons Catalogues - CAH
    Enterprises, Memphis, TN - 1977

Henshall, J.A. - Book of the Black Bass

Kimball, Art and Scott - Collecting Old Fishing Tackle/A Guide to
    Identifying and Collecting old Fishing Tackle - Aardvark
    Publications, P.O. Box 252, Boulder Junction, WI 54512 - 1980

Lind, James A. - Musky - McCormick & Henderson, Chicago, IL - 1964

Liu, Allan J. - The American Sporting Collectors Handbook -
    Winchester Press, NY - 1982 - Revised Edition

Lone, Jim - A History of the Pacific Northwest Salmon Plugs - 1983 -
    Jim Lone - 11740 Greenwood Avenue, Apt. 207, Seattle, WA 98133

Luckey, Carl F. - Identification and Value Guide/Old Fishing Lures
    and Tackle - 1986 Second Edition - Books Americana, Florence, AL

Melner, Samuel et al - Great American Fishing Tackle Catalogs -
    Crown, NY - 1972

Metcalf, Rich - Chas. W. Lane - Watchmaker, Tinkerer - Rich Metcalf,
    112 Sutton Dr., Syracuse, NY 13219

Munger, Albert J. - Those Old Fishing Reels - 1982 - Al Munger,
    2235 Ritter St., Philadelphia, PA 19125

Munger, Albert J. - Old Fishing Tackle and Tales - 1985

Netherton, Cliff - History of the Sport of Casting/People,
    Events, Records, Tackle and Literature - Early Times - 1981

Netherton, Cliff - History of the Sport of Casting/Golden Years -
    1983 For both these books contact Cliff Netherton, 448 Springvale
    Rd., Great Falls, VA 22066

Pinkowsky, Bob - Muskie Fever - A.S. Barnes, NY - 1961

Smith, Larry - Great Tackle Advertisements/Book I/1882-1930 - 1984

Streater, R.L. - Streater's Reference Catalog of Old Fishing Lures -
    1978 and 1982 - Mercer Island, WA

Wetzel, Bill and Harbin, Clyde A., Sr. - A Collector's Reference
    Guide to Heddon Fishing Plugs - 1984 - Contact Bill Wetzel,
    107 Tanglewood, Bamberg, SC 29003

Wetzel, Charles M. - History of Angling and Angling Literature in
    American - Charles M. Wetzel, Newark, DE

White, Karl - Fishing Tackle Antiques - Reference and Evaluation -
    available from National Fishing Tackle Museum - P.O. Box 169,
    Arcadia, OK 73007

Frazier, Jim - Al Foss, A History of the Company and Their Lures - 1985
    available from Jim Frazier, 312 N. 46th Avenue, Hollywood, FL 33021

Fishing Lure Videos

Harbin, Clyde A., Sr. - Volume 1: Overview, Volume 2: Over 40 of the
    Rarest, Volume 3: Heddon, Volume 4:Heddon/Stockes Heritage -
    VHS Tapes, P.O. Box 154987, Dept. NFLCC, Irving, TX 75015

Anyone interested in purchasing plugs should contact John Shoffner, 17201 Hanna, Melvindale, MI 48122 periodic lists.

Other Sources of Information

Other sources valuable to collectors and historians are old fishing tackle manufacturers and distributors catalogs and flyers, old magazine advertisements, U.S. and British patents, lawsuits over patents, newspaper articles, letters and documents, the plugs themselves, and most important of all, direct information from fellow collectors and historians.

Magazines and periodicals, both in and out of print, that have been particularly helpful include Fur, Fish and Game, Hunting & Fishing, Field & Stream, Outdoor Life, Sports Afield, In Fisherman, Outdoor America, Gray's Sporting Journal, National Sportsman, Outers' Book, Outing, Hobbies, The Sporting Goods Dealer, Forest & Stream, Sporting Classic, Annual Reports of the U.S. Bureau of Ethnology and Oliver's Auction Gallery catalogs.

Many of the people who helped us with this book are members of a national club which is a "must" for anyone interested in old plugs. The name of this group is the National Fishing Lure Collector's Club (NFLCC, as it is generally referred to). The membership is currently $15.00 per year and includes a subscription to a very informative quarterly publication called the "Gazette". New material, club news, members' wats and all sorts of pertinent material is published in the "Gazette". The NFLCC has their own regional shows. (If you want to learn about plugs fast, go to a regional show, or better yet, go to the annual national NFLCC show.) Probably the best way to gather knowledge and/or information is to attend a plug swap meet, especially one of the larger meets. The activity at these shows is hard to comprehend unless you are there to experience them yourself. To someone who has never attended one of these shows, the amount of plugs can be overwhelming. Some plugs are for sale or trade, others are "Show and Tell" only. The action at these shows is fast and furious. They are usually one day shows - on a Saturday. (Some of the trading goes on before the show, usually the night before.) Most collectors try and stay at the same motel so they can get together and swap plugs. This is all part of the fun and comraderie which accompanies a plug show. If you want to know "prices", join the NFLCC and do your homework. Invest the $15.00 - it's worth it. Currently the person to contact to join the NFLCC is Rich Treml, NFLCC, P.O. Box 1791, Dearborn, MI 48121. The NFLCC also has a library which contains tackle company catalog copies, patent information, advertisements, etc. valuable to a collector. Overall, members of the NFLCC are interested and involved in more than one facet of collecting old fishing tackle. These people include collectors of reels, rods, bobbers, flies, boat motors, sporting books, catalogs, fish decoys, tackle boxes, histories, fish stories, plug stories as well as, or instead of plugs.

Museums, Displays, Etc.

It is almost unbelievable there aren't more public displays of early fishing plugs of the USA. It seems that most museums, wherever they are, have, for some mysterious reason, overlooked the great importance of our fishing heritage. Plug collectors should have a right to see some plugs if they have to look at old dolls, glassware, duck decoys, beer cans, guns, swords, old clothes, arrowheads and the like. It is hopeful that as museum curators across the United States recognize the great historical significance of the history of fishing plugs that it should become more important to Americans than it is than it is right now.

The finest collections in the world of early fishing plugs of the U.S.A. are in private hands. There are some developing collections that are on public or semi-public (fee) display. Some of these are very good. In certain cases, what they lack in sophistication they make up for in numbers. Fortunately for all plug collectors certain carefully developed private collections are going on display soon! THE BEST WAY TO LEARN PLUGS IS TO SEE THE PLUGS THEMSELVES.

Discovery Hall Museum, South Bend, Indiana
   The hometown of the South Bend Bait Company which is featured when
   it comes to plugs.

Vilas County Historical Museum - Sayner, Wisconsin
This museum is open daily in the summer and recently features a fishing guides display with all sorts of equipment used by famous northern Wisconsin fishing guides. This display has a selection of old fishing plugs used by these guides.

The National Fres Water Fishing Hall of Fame, Hayward, Wisconsin
This is a great place to take the family. There are a lot of plugs and other things related to fishing.

The Founders Traveling Museum of Fishing History, Springfield, MO
This extremely fine collection includes some of the rarest and finest plugs you will ever want to see. It is basically the carefully compiled collection of Dudley Murphy (Founder of the NFLCC) of Springfield, Missouri who was a pioneer in plug collecting.

The Michigan State University at Lansing, Michigan
They have peiodic showings of plugs. It is probably better to check with them because some of their displays are not permanent.

The Wolf Lake Fishing Hatchery, operated by the Michigan Department of Natural Resources (DNR), near Kalamazoo, Michigan
They have an interesting permanent display. Many of the articles here were donated by Michigan collectors who are members of the NFLCC. The museum is near Kalamazoo, Michigan, a town dear to the hearts of all plug collectors.

National Fishing Tackle Museum, Arcadia, OK
Karl White's museum is one all looked forward to. Karl worked hard for years developing what is thought of as one of the most comprehensive collections. The amount of items and sophistication of this collection will be an education to all who view it.

Undoubtedly other important museum displays will be coming along as this hobby increases in intensity. People simply must begin to appreciate the beauty, collectibility and fish catching ability of the plug. It would be a good idea if anyone hears of a worthwhile museum or other public display to contact the editor of the NFLCC Gazette and let him know when and where a display will be. Plug collectors will go out of their way to get there.

Chapter One

COLLECTING
OLD FISHING PLUGS

The Hobby

It is not fair to compare collecting old fishing plugs with other hobbies. Plug collecting stands on its own two feet more than other such pastimes. Once you start collecting plugs you usually get hooked on the hobby. It can go from an attractive but nondescript wall hanging to a sophisticated, specialized, historically important, scarce and valuable collection. There are some catalogued, patented and/or advertised plugs out there that major collectors haven't found - YET! There is a good chance they are all out there. Wonders never cease in this hobby. Plug collecting can get quite complicated. When you think you have seen them all, you simply haven't.

Good advice for a new collector who is serious about collecting old fishing plugs would be to go slow. Don't be over anxious to own every old plug that is new to you. If you go too fast, you will probably end up with plugs you don't want and are literally untradeable. It is easy to accumulate plugs by the hundreds. This type of plug could remain in your basement, attic or garage for a long time, not doing anyone any good. The fish themselves are the only parties involved who might benefit from this situation. Some of these plugs may become more collectible as time goes by. The common plugs could become scarce, the scarce rare and the rare about impossible. A lot depends on how many collectors there are out there.

The second thing a new collector should do is to study the hobby. A great deal of homework is a prerequisite to learning to identify and evaluate a given plug. As we shall see, certain variations of a given item are much scarcer and more desirable than others. There does not seem to be a "rule of thumb" on this. Wood plugs with glass eyes have been used as a general criterion for what's good and what is not. This is not a good rule. There are rubber plugs, plastic plugs, metal plugs and wood plugs with no eyes at all that may be scarcer and more desirable to an experienced collector. Age is an important factor in the scarcity and value of a plug. However, age alone does not necessarily indicate scarcity or desirability. Most of the major plug manufacturers, such as Heddon, South Bend, Moonlight, Pflueger, Shakespeare and Creek Chub, were organized to make and sell a whole bunch of plugs. The number of certain plugs produced in their peak years is staggering. On the other hand, production runs were relatively small in some cases, especially in the early days of a given plug. Any fisherman will understand why a few plugs have been hot over the years. They caught fish.

Most collectors eventually concentrate their efforts in a given area - on companies such as Heddon, Creek Chub, South Bend, Shakespeare, Pflueger, Moonlight, Jamison and Keeling.

Heddon baits have been popular to collect for some time. Creek Chub has become increasingly attractive to numbers of collectors. The rest will follow. Generally, there seems to be an emphasis on individual small companies that produced relatively few plugs. There is a lot to be said for "Miscellaneous" collecting. It is quite varied and can prove to be very exciting at times.

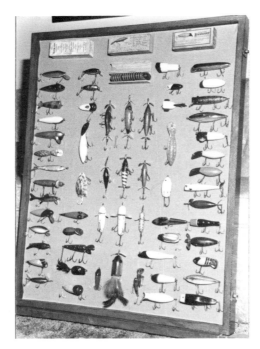

As specialized collections grow they open up areas of scarcity that are not readily apparent. There is a rapidly increasing interest in certain colors and various hook and line-tie variations of certain plugs. Certain variations are scarcer than others.

Some collectors "type" collect, which means trying to get one of each of a plug made by a certain company. Many collectors are color orientated. One of each plug in a certain color (paint job) is a very interesting display. For example, all possible Heddons in green crackleback or plugs of all types that are redheads. There are many fine collections of "critters". Frogs, mice, bugs, crawdads and fish with tails are a joy to behold. Some people collect odd or comical plugs. An interesting collection is plugs which were made to catch a certain type of fish. It's all up to the individual collector in what he wants to specialize.

Plug Terminology

There are an almost abstract number of nicknames and numbers used by collectors for old plugs. It is often amusing to watch someone's reaction to it. Imagine hearing one side of a "plug hotline" phone call. Something like this - "Yes, I have a #1700, strawberry, L, side, in decent condition, and I'm looking for a Humdinger, but it has to hang near excellent on one side and face to the left and not be a redhead". What kind of talk is this? It is, of course, "plug talk". What might seem to the average non-plug collector as mildly humorous jibberish of some sort is actually like shorthand talk. Talk isn't cheap in plug collecting. The phone company gets its share of a serious collector's hard earned dollars. The quicker you can say it, the better. As in everything else worthwhile, study and patience are a necessity. If you want to collect plugs you have to know them. Collector's talk is a language all its own. This presupposed know-ledge is at least a certain facet of plug collecting.

　　We will be referring to component features of plugs in this book. Plug terminology is sometimes confusing and misleading. If we look at a plug through the eyes of someone reading a patent it becomes clear that not only have plugs themselves been called many things other than plugs, but the parts that make it up sometimes also have diverse titles.

　　Perhaps the best example of an important U.S. patent for a plug was, and is, Fred D. Rhodes' brilliant Patent #777,488, granted December 13, 1904. We will hear more about the "Perfect Minnow" later. In the meantime, we will discuss its features as they are typical of most plugs in general.

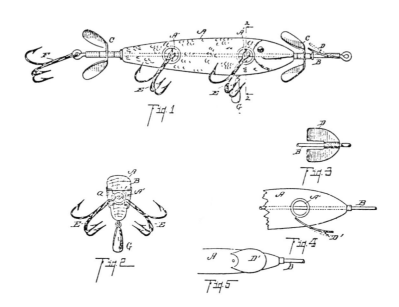

　　We have not enhanced the original patent drawing. It is exactly as it appears in the records of the U.S. Patent Office. Let's start with Figure 1 which is a "side elevation view". It is made of wood. The patent states, "The object of this invention are, first, to provide an improved fish bait or lure which is adapted for use as a surface or as a casting bait and also as a deep-water or as a trolling bait". This covers a lot of territory.

　　Item A is the body itself which is designated as follows, "an improved bait or lure is preferably shaped like a minnow and may be suit-ably painted or decorated as desired". Item B is a "rod" that runs

through the body. It serves as both a line tie on the front and looped
in back to provide the rear hook hanger. The rod which also runs through
the split rings (Item a[1]). These split rings accomodate the four hooks
positioned side by side, end to end. This construction is know to collectors as "wired through, end to end". The "rod" or wire involved also
acts as a shaft for the "suitable spinners (Item C) which are attached to
a hollow tube and fits over the wired through wire. These "spinners" are
usually referred to as props by collectors. This is a typical 5-hook
underwater minnow construction. Remember, the plug in the patent also
floats or sinks at will. The external belly weight (Item G) is enough
lead to take the "Perfect" down, which without it might float. It is interesting to note that the external belly weight on production models is
secured rather permanently. Figures 3, 4 and 5 are generally referred to
as diving lips. The patent states, "The guiding blade or fin D is also
adapted to keep the bail in an upright position in the water and should
the same strike up on its side will turn the same to the upright position".
You could alter the fin so the plug would dive at whatever depth you
wanted. "The greater the angle of the blade, the deeper the bait will
run in the water". D in Figure 3 - the lip is on the wired through shaft,
in front of the prop as it is in the patent model. Figures 4 and 5 -
this lip is on the body of the plug itself.

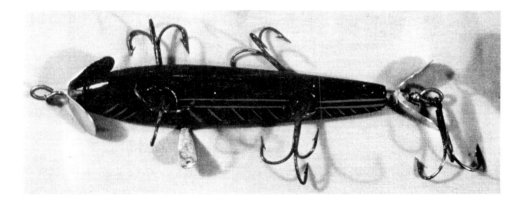

The Rhodes' Perfect Casting Minnow Production Model

That's about it. Put this together and you have the most versatile
plug in town.
Plug terminology is so vast and complicated that it is quite like
learning many foreign languages. Each company has its own numbering systems
and terminology. These will be discussed individually in the text where
they are pertinent.

Condition

Condition is important to plug collectors. Condition determines
values sometimes where age or rarity doesn't. There are collectors who
specialize in plugs in great shape. This means it has to be in very near
new shape. New plugs that are old are generally rare. There are exceptions.
The exceptions are usually new plugs in a box found in dealer lots, such
as a carton of 24, or in one interesting case, a whole production full.

Collectors seem to set their own condition requirements. Generally speaking, condition seems to get less important with age, rarity, desirability and current popularity. Sometimes it's just better to get any example you can get of a plug such as a Henkenius/Kane plug, a Schoonies Scooter or a Wilcox Wiggler. Hopefully you can upgrade at a later time. However, it is important to remember condition is extremely important to certain collectors. Some collectors simply won't hang up a plug unless it is in excellent or new condition. Top condition is a new, unused plug in its original box, preferably with the instructions or pocket catalog which were often inserted with the plug. Value wise it means any plug in excellent condition is worth a lot more than the same one in Fair-Good condition although both are considered collectible under certain circumstances.

There are various methods of describing the condition of a plug. Some collectors prefer a number system, others use abbreviations. Unfortunately, this is not more standardized. It seems up to the individual collector which system works best for him.

The following is a typical grading system:

Mint - In original box with instructions or pocket catalog.
   Mint - new, unused, unblemished plug
Excellent - Near new, shows slight use but no abuse. May
   be unfished but shop worn.
Very Good - Shows some use but no abuse unless minor and
   noted. No major parts missing or replaced.
Good - An average plug showing use. Good is generally
   considered to be a very acceptable collecting condition.
Fair - Needs work, finish is rough, badly chipped, etc.
Beater - Good for parts only
Parts missing or replaced should always be included in the
   plug description.

Many older plugs show "age cracks" in the painted/varnished finish. As long as all the paint and varnish are intact, this is O.K. This condition should be noted when describing a plug for trade, especially in the case of a scarcer or rare plug. "No paint" describes a plug down to the wood. A "repaint" is a plug painted over the wood. An "overpaint" is a paint job over the original paint.

Overpaints have promise and can sometimes be saved. There are several methods of removing an overpaint - all are dangerous. A lot depends on the type of paint originally used on the plug and the type used to "improve" it. Careful scraping with a fingernail or credit card works especially well when the overpaint comes off in chips. Using an extremely fine abrasive sandpaper can work also, but in either case, you must go slow, be patient and careful. Remember, sandpaper is only for overpaints and some barn paints. Other difficult paints to remove are aluminum, silver and gold. One method that seems to be a short cut can work miracles sometimes. This is the use of ammonia - not "sudsy", but the plain household variety. This doesn't take long usually - no longer than 3 or 4 minutes. Get ready to rinse it in fresh water fast. Look out for the original finish, and good luck! Don't ever use fingernail polish remover, varnish or paint remover of any kind. No matter which chance you take, don't ever use an abrasive on original paint or metal. Leave well enough alone. When in doubt, good advice is don't!

Make sure a plug is repainted before attempting to "restore" it. Some early plugs (such as the Moonlight Zig-Zag) were painted very crudely in their early production. For example, the earliest production Moonlight Zig Zags were painted with white coach paint which bubbled and ran. There are other similar examples such As Fred D. Rhodes' Perfect Casting Minnow which were hand painted. So make sure that plug is definitely a repaint or overpaint before jumping to conclusions. Seek advice before making a mistake you might regret for a long time.

A problem collectors sometimes run into is what to do with a plug that has 5% to 15% of the original paint intact. If we are to follow the trends set in duck decoy and gun collecting, even a small amount of original finish is more desirable than restorations of any type. This rule is especially true with scarcer items.

Once again, the best advice as to cleaning up a plug is don't. If you must, a mild soap and water on a soft rag should do it. Be careful about getting a plug wet that has any kind of paint or varnish chipping problem. Water gets underneath and expands the wood. This can make the original paint chip more. Even the mild abrasives make a plug look "cleaned up". These are definitely not recommended. Even worse is the insistence of some collectors on varnishing or using polyurethane, etc. on a plug. If you must tune up your plug, a good wax such as Johnson's Paste Wax (or any good brand of paste wax) may be O.K. Please be careful here. Some waxes could ruin a great old plug. Some collectors don't like "cleaned up" plugs, period! I have also heard of good results on chemically impregnated "cleaning rags", but it's still better, in the long run, to be safe rather than sorry. We do not recommend any type of cleaning!

Professionally repainted plugs, restored plugs and fake plugs are problems that are likely to grow unless they are stopped now! A professionally repainted or restored plug should be identified as such. In all fairness to collectors, they should probably be branded deeply on one side in fear that such a plug could fall into dishonest or even unknowing hands. This may seem like a rather drastic way of doing things, but consider how reproduceable paint jobs and even plugs themselves are. Remember some of the toughest plugs are just a piece of wood, a line-tie and some hooks. There are some great looking Heddon Black Suckers, Slopenoses (Dowagiac Experts), and worse out there right now. These are all expensive plugs in original form. Plugs can be copied or altered to look like the real thing. Some are not always marked as "fakes". If the plugs were made differently from the originals it wouldn't be such a problem, but in some cases, these plugs even have the right type of glass eyes. The only way to stop fake plugs is to make it rough on the counterfeiters. This is an area in which to be vigilant. There are usually ways to tell if a plug is fake. The best way is to get a consensus of opinion from experienced collectors, especially those who fall into the specialty area of the plug in question. In fairness to collectors anyone making a replica of an old plug should alter it slightly so it could not be mistaken for the real thing.

Displaying Your Plugs

There are many ways to display a collection of old plugs. When properly presented a specialized display can be both strikingly colorful and extremely interesting. The way you hang up your plugs varies with your "Show and Tell" needs. Some displays are portable so they can be shown at plug shows or in local displays such as a library or sporting goods store. However, most displays are more or less permanent in the collector's home. Some collections are hung up all over the house and others are carefully sheltered inside cases with glass or plexiglas covers. Never make the mistake of drilling or gluing a plug to mount it! One of the best case systems we have seen incorporated the following features:

1. Removable plexiglas cover - plexiglas won't break but scratches easily - it is rather expensive but does a good job. Glass is O.K. but it breaks.
2. A thick ceiling tile backing with a cloth cover - which will accomodate "T" shaped pins (available at most craft shops) which will put a plug where you want it. If you do it right, it will stay there.

Any variations of these themes seem to work well. Usually the glass, or plexiglas, front slides in and out. These can be made quite secure if need be. They can also be portable. One good way to have a display that can be both portable and permanent is to hinge two cases together so they fold face to face and can be latched and carried easily by attaching a handle to the top side of one of the halves.

If you want to just hang up your plugs, rows of small 1/4" dowel rods or standard furring strips work well. It is easy to get at your plugs this way.

Keelings and
Clarks

Trading Plugs

If you want to pursue plug collecting, get ahold of fellow collectors or create an interest locally. It's surprising how many people fall in love with this hobby. It's easy to see why. There is no doubt plugs are great old things to collect. Trading can be a lot of fun. It can also be very rewarding but complicated to the two or more parties involved. Most of the historically important valuable collections are the result of numerous swaps over many years.

Some collectors, especially new ones, are reluctant to swap. There are two basic reasons for this. The first is they don't want to do a trade now that they will be sorry about later. In other words, they don't want to "get taken". The second reason is that some collectors simply like what they find themselves. This is very understandable. To each his own. However, it is sufficient to say, in many cases the only way to get a rare plug you need is by trading. This is like the key coin in coin collecting - a key plug deserves a key plug. Most collectors who trade together and are acquainted, try and help each other. The most important thing about a good trade is that the participants are all happy. Plug trading is national in scope. Collectors from all over the U.S.A. get together on the phone, exchange letters and have swap meets, shows and get-togethers.

Plug swapping is recommended. Please be careful. It's better to take your time. It's even good sometimes to get some expert advice. Good luck!

<u>Values</u>

Sooner or later a collector of old fishing plugs comes up against the question, "What's it worth?". Why is one old fishing plug worth more to a collector than another? A good question, but a tough one to answer. The best recommendation to anyone who is interested in values is to study available material. This is very important because values vary with the times. Sort of like the stock market. Some plugs that were worth $20.00 a few years ago are only worth $5.00 to $10.00 now. The other side of the coin is certain plugs that have proven themselves rare have become quite valuable.

It is important to remember the rather recent status of the hobby. Plug collecting, as well as most tackle collecting, generally speaking, is just now gaining in popularity. There is a great likelihood that the numbers of collectors will grow rapidly soon. There are many collectors and fishermen who are not serious collectors now but will probably become so as they get deeper into the hobby. Whatever happens only time will tell. The one overriding factor is that extremely large numbers of plugs were made. The more collectors, the more plugs. The future of values will depend on how many of which plugs turn up. It is not unusual for a whole batch of a previously rare plug to surface. When this happens, it is great because more collectors will have a crack at hanging a real classic on the wall without the price being too prohibitive.

There are many sale lists sent out. Some of these have the plugs priced. Others are open to bids. Sometimes the bid results on this type list are available. The sale lists are first come first served. The auction or bid lists have deadlines when the highest price prevails or is occasionally rejected. It depends on the rules of the auction. The best way to receive these lists and other material is to join the NFLCC (National Fishing Lures Collectors Club - see Acknowledgements for details). Reading these lists is one of the best ways to learn values.

Plug prices have been surprisingly high in certain individual cases. Generally, these investments are warranted, but be careful. There are not many plugs that will bring hundreds of dollars and more. These plugs are worth that because they are extremely rare, at least at this time. High priced plug investment is very speculative. It requires studied judgement. Once again, it is deceiving to compare plug collecting with anything else.

Rarity will be indicated in the text by individual comment. In the case of larger manufacturers, we will point out some of the scarcer plugs and variations. The reasons for this system of comparitive scarcity is to at least give the new collector an idea of some of the plugs that have proven to be either hard to find, or for some reason or other, are in high demand. Usually it's because they are rare - hard to find. Some of these plugs were made for just a few years. The fact they <u>didn't</u> make it for long in a given manufacturer's line is because the plug was not popular. It didn't work right, no sales, no fish, patent infringements or whatever. These are the ones that are tough to get.

There are plugs illustrated in the text that are unknown to us as to who, what or when. These will be designated. The final category of plugs is the one patented or advertised but to the best of our knowledge have not shown up in collections. It seems plugs show up faster after they are identified. In some cases it's possible that some plugs are not out there at all.

Generally speaking, scarcer production (catalogued or advertised) plugs are worth more than experimental "prototype" (a word often misused), homemade plugs or unknowns. Watch out when an unknown becomes known. It is at this point when collectors find out they should have one!

Exact plug values are very difficult to determine. Much has to do with supply and demand. A vast majority of plugs are worth less than $5.00. There are a few worth more. Certain plugs have sold for hundreds of dollars. There have been a select few that have been reported to have sold for over $1,000.00. These plugs are indeed rare and desirable. They also represent the exception. Most plugs, including the few highly desirable ones are affordable. The best way to find plugs is to "kick them out of the bush" so to speak.

Finding Old Fishing Plugs

Part of the fun of this exciting hobby is the thrill of finding a great old plug. There are many ways to go about this. Undoubtedly the best place to look is inside an old tackle box and one of the best ways to find these is through advertising. Collectors advertise locally and nationally for plugs. One of the best ways to present a local ad is to give your name, address and phone number. Some people will prefer to contact you by mail rather than calling. A good inexpensive way to advertise is to put up a "Wanted" poster in the local supermarket or shopping mall. Laundromats usually have bulletin boards.

Local displays in sporting goods stores, libraries, museums, schools, etc. can bring plugs to the owner. A small "Wanted" sign next to the display works great. Another good source of plugs is to display at sporting goods/outdoor shows. A colorful presentation usually draws a lot of attention. If anyone says they have old plugs make sure and get their name, phone number and address. Don't wait for them to contact you. It's better that the collector follow up the lead.

If a collector wishes, he or she might consider giving a speech or slide presentation on old plugs. Many fishing clubs, local historical societies and service clubs welcome a good program. Many people will want to help you in your collecting.

Flea markets are good. However, it is getting so you will have to get up early in the morning to get first crack. At least earlier than the next guy.

Garage sales are great. Most collectors have some great "garage sale" stories. Make sure and ask for tackle. One should be a little careful here. I heard of a woman who sold a collector her husband's tackle box. If you do this it is sometimes best to be prepared to get out of town fast.

Antique and resale shops are O.K. Dealers sometimes simply are not interested in fishing tackle because they don't know the values or don't, as yet, have the interest. When they do price them, it is likely you will find common items at too high a price. However, you might be fortunate enough to find a rare plug at the same "high" price as its everyday neighbors.

Many plugs are still on the bottom of the lake or floating on top. These are usually beat but interesting. While fishing, do a little looking around. You can "get eyes" for plugs - just keep looking. The best plug we ever found was a Moonlight #1 Bass Bait.

There is nothing more that can be said here without taking up unnecessary room. Please walk with us through the world of early fishing plugs of the U.S.A. We hope you enjoy this book. Happy collecting! Remember one thing - there are still a lot of old fishing plugs out there.

Chapter Two

THE EARLY HISTORY

When Europeans came to the United States they brought, at best, the fishing equipment they had used in their native lands. Explorers, traders and settlers had to forage for food. They not only found new fish such as the black bass and musky, but also found new and unusual fishing habits and habitats. The U.S.A. was a wilderness inhabited by people of diverse history.

The Prehistory

Native Americans were and are excellent fishermen. Pioneers found they already had pluglike items used to catch fish. The use of the artificial lure was widespread among the prehistoric inhabitants of the U.S. Fish of various kinds were an important food source for many of the tribes and some ingenious and effective "fish lures" were devised.

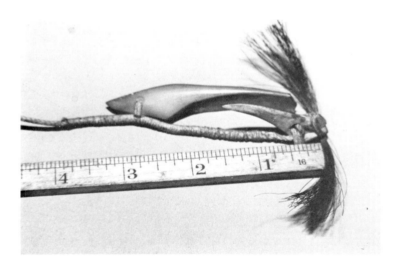

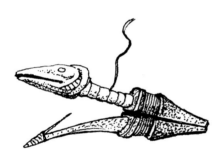

Northwest Coast
Halibut Hook

Artificial lures used for trolling for bonito were used in Hawaii. Bonito was one of the most significant sources of protein available to them. The use of this type of lure was widespread.

23

These composite fish lures vary substantially only in their raw
materials. The basic design was similar throughout - the barbless point
made of bone, mother-of-pearl or tortoise shell. The long shank being
made from mother-of-pearl. All these were typical features on this type
of "plug".

The Great Lakes Indians used wood lures carved into the shape of
various fish prey. The lure was fastened with twine or leather and
attached to a stick or canoe paddle which when moved would cause the lure
to dart around, hopefully enticing a large fish within spearing range.
This method was most popular for northern pike and muskellunge.

The Upper Mississippi people made use of shells for a fish shaped
lure, with possible hook attachment, that was presented in the water to
attract fish to strike.

Point Barrow, Alaska Eskimos used an artificial bait made of ivory
and sometimes known as a "squid" which was attached to a short line made
of whalebone. The lure was meant to represent a small shrimp which was
kept moving and the fish bit at it. The body of the lure which was made
of walrus ivory was sometimes decorated with beads used for eyes, etc. The
hooks were made of brass or copper.

Undoubtedly there were more "plugs" made of wood, leather, feathers
and other degradable materials. Unless ancient wood has been under water
it probably rotted out a long time ago. Collecting artifacts of prehistoric
fishermen is a fascinating hobby. Good examples are quite difficult to find!

The American Angels

There is a history of pluglike things that came from Europe, generally speaking, England. These are called Devons, Angels, Phantoms,
Caledonias and other names strange to the ear.
    "Angels" or "Devons" are so identified in Patent #272,317 granted
to Mr. Ernest F. Pflueger of Akron, Ohio on February 13, 1883. Figure 2
(B), in the patent drawing is described as a Devon in the text of this
important patent and is used as an accepted term rather than the name of a
locality in England which is known for its fishing and called Devonshire.

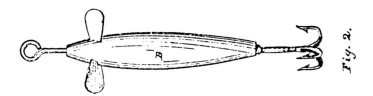

The Angel seems to be named for Mr. Angel reported to have been born in
1800 and lived until around 1875. Mr. Angel's Angel was apparently
never patented. The "Devons" or "Angels" mentioned in Mr. E.F. Pflueger's
patent were to be different from their British ancestors because they were
luminous - they glowed in the dark. The important part here is the apparent
acceptance in the U.S.A. of the word Devon and Angel. The patent sort of
Americanized the British Devons and Angels.
    The only reason we are briefly discussing lures from England is
that they were adapted and perhaps less importantly, imported for use in
this country. We are really only concerned with the American Angels and
Devons. Nevertheless, a brief history of the origin of British Angels
would be appropriate here. Mr. Angel developed his lure over a long
period of time. Perhaps as much as forty to fifty years were spent in
making, testing and improving an artificial lure that apparently caught
enough fish to count. There were many versions of the Angels and Devons.
All fundamentally built on the same principle. A principle of a spinning
minnow imitation. Mr. Angel had help in this development which included
his son who carried on the business for a short time after Mr. Angel passed
away. In the early 1880s the Angel business changed hands. We do not know
much about it after this time. The traditions carried on. Some over to
the U.S.A. which included improved Angels and Devons called such unpluglike
names as Silk Phantom, Caledonias and Double Devons.
    Although the Angels, etc. are not exactly plugs they lead to the
development in the U.S.A. of competitive products which took over the
previously imported product sales. Some English made products were stamped
with their U.S. distributor's name or trademark. It is not uncommon to
find British lures in an American tackle box. They are worthwhile collecting and sometimes surprisingly old.
    One of the earliest U.S. patents we can find is for a Devon type
artificial bait by Mr. Archer Wakaman of Cape Vincent, New York. It is an

improvement in trolling hooks. A method for better hooking a fish, known later as the Breakless Devon by Pflueger. Another acceptance of the Angels made in U.S. sales.

    Angels were and are fish catchers. They were not made for the bait caster. Most American collectors don't collect English lures and vice versa. The interesting thing about Angels or Devons is the sort of constant recurrence of the principle in plugs made in the U.S.A.

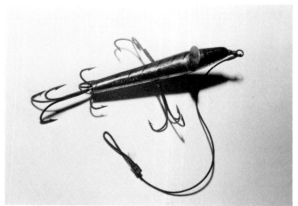

Thousand Island Bait by
Archer Wakaman, New York

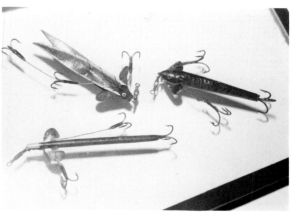

Made in England

Made in the U.S.A.

    The development of plugs in the U.S. eventually relates to bait casting. Still fishing, spinning, trolling and skittering had already been tried and proven to work. Bait casting was an innovation. The idea of getting a bait out or in there with a certain degree of accuracy was important to catching fish. Different types of fish offered new challenges to the incoming and west going Americans. Different fish and different fishing conditions required new techniques - the highly perfected quadruple multiplying reels with their matched bamboo rods, small diameter lines that could hold sufficient pounds of fish under pressure of a fight or current. A job that only a bait casting outfit could handle. The principle here is that a combination of the weight of the plug and the ability of everything from the plug back to the fisherman himself counted. If everything was in tune and you could do this with an artificial bait, look out! The guys who carved the first plugs found out rapidly just how successful a properly designed and used hunk of wood (or other suitable material) could be.

    From the earliest days, it became quickly apparent to the inventor/ maker of wood plugs that they not only caught fish but under certain circumstances a whole bunch of fish.

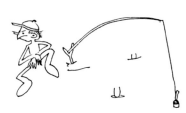

At one point there was talk of making plugs illegal. The fish were taken
by surprise. It almost seems the fish got smart fast. Otherwise why have
plugs constantly evolved into something new. There is always something
new to offer the fish, fishermen, and it seems the collector also. That's
what it's all about.

    The earliest hand carved, barn painted classics were rather simply
made. The originals were sometimes fashioned out of a piece of wood or
metal originally made for something else. Many items have been altered
into plugs through the years. An old tin sign or tin can could supply plug
parts. Perhaps an actual wood "bung" (a tapered object to stop a hole
leaking such as in a wine casket - it "plugged" the hole) could have been
used to make a plug. Maybe that's where the word plug originated. Who
knows? A plug had to work. "Props" had to spin, hooks and line-ties had
to stay put. All problems to a designer of new plugs.

Harrison Sutherland's
"Wooden Minnow" -
Date unknown.

    Before we go to the meat of the book, let's take a brief look at
what a plug is from a plug maker's standpoint. It is important to both
historians and collectors to remember there were a great many plugs made
of certain types. Many of these were made/manufactured over a very long
period of time mainly because they caught fish. Plug patents started as
independent inventions of fishermen or people who wanted to make and sell
plugs. If the first ones caught fish this usually meant making a few
more for yourself and your buddies. If it went beyond that it became a
business. Once your fishing friends start telling their pals about a hot
new plug, that's it. The next thing is production.

    Basically, if you carve a plug out of a piece of wood you need to
attach hooks and a line-tie to it. You might want to paint it, weight it,
put eyes on it or embellish it in any way you wish. If this sounds easy,
it isn't. You don't just paint a plug - you must use the right paints in
different combinations and in different layers to make a plug that will
last. Painting a plug was a big problem in the early days of plug making.
To be done correctly, it takes many processes. When wood soaks up water
or is banged or scraped, the paint might come off and the plug will probably quit doing what it was supposed to do. A plug made to float might
suddenly sink! Some of the most beautiful and desirable of all early
U.S. plugs had poor paint jobs. There are certain old plugs that are

very difficult to find in any condition. Certain ones are almost impossible to find with 100% of the original paint, even if they are unused.
It took some time to develop decent priming and painting techniques.

The finishes on early Heddon plugs were carefully spray painted over a secure
primer and then varnished. Old Heddon plugs are known for their beautiful
and sturdy, high quality paint jobs.

     Other plug making techniques also took time to develop. The body
had to be turned or otherwise shaped for wood plugs, including cork. A
plug body had to be molded for rubber, guttapercha, isinglass, plastic
wood, solid metal and numerous plastics and other materials. Other metal
plugs were soldered, hammered and otherwise crafted. Every plug maker
has their own idea about how to make plugs. To make a good one is difficult. For example, at the peak of its production, there were 37 individual steps in the making of the famous Pflueger Globe. Plug making requires precision, patience and a technique. As a matter of fact, every
step in plug making should be a trade secret. It was difficult to perfect manufacturing techniques that worked.
     Many plug companies or makers bought component parts on the out-
side. Salesman offered entire lines of metal parts. Metal workers could

supply the metal components and the rubber molder could mold the rubber. If someone was handy with paint, their talents were called on - sometimes in the factory or garage or basement. Sometimes in someone else's paint shop. In many cases, the wooden bodies for plugs were contracted on the outside by plug manufacturers. Sometimes this was done locally as in the case of the Clarks and Keelings, and some Moonlights. In many cases where large amounts of finished shaped bodies were required they were jobbed out to large converting firms such as The Artistic Wood Turning Works of Chicago, Illinois which was used by Heddon, Moonlight and probably others. Plugs that went into production had to be assembled, painted, packaged and labeled. This work required time, materials and people. It is interesting to note that women did a lot of this meticulous, exacting and sometimes highly artistic work. Plug collectors and fishermen owe these ladies a vote of thanks.

Inside the James Heddon's Sons factory. It is our <u>guess</u> that this photo was taken in June 1924. What do you think?

        The history of manufacturers of fishing plugs made in the United States of American goes way back. How far back is something we will perhaps never know but endeavor to find out.

Early U.S. patents for fishing plugs have been the primary basis of dating in "EARLY FISHING PLUGS OF THE U.S.A.". It is reasonably safe to assume that plug inventors who were granted patents discovered and developed their particular "flash of inventive genius". They field tested and perhaps gave away some of their plugs to fishing friends before the patent date, even before the patent applied for date. How many months or years before is hard to say, since it varied. It took anywhere from a few months to a couple of years and sometimes more to get a patent after the patent was applied for. The main importance of the patent themselves is the dating. At least this part is accurate. It is not to say the patents themselves are not accurate. They are, in fact, so accurate as to occasionally be misleading. The patent search for fishing plugs has been exciting and in certain cases it has been very disappointing. There appear to be patents missing that are critical, especially certain early ones.

Patents were first granted in the U.S.A. in 1790 at which time they were under control of the Attorney General, the Secretary of State and the Secretary of War. The President's O.K. was needed on patents at this time. By 1794 this granting authority was reduced to the Secretary of State. The Patent Office itself was formed on July 4, 1836 at which time they started the present numbering system. In 1849 there were some improvements in the system. The Official Gazette was started in 1872. This was a listing of all patents in brief form. The patents before 1849 are very hard to find. Sometimes they come up blank. It is possible some were destroyed. Some old patents could be gone forever which accounts for some of the difficulties that have arisen in research for this book. It is possible, but sadly not probable, that copies of these old patents are still in family or company records somewhere. All we can do is hold out and hope they will surface someday. We are looking for such patents or information on anything that could possibly indicate American fishing lure production especially before 1852. Even stories and legends would help here. If there are any still out there, please let us know. It is the wish of all of us that this vital information is not lost forever.

Most plugs came and went. Some lasted a long time. Today, as always, it is hard and expensive to make a good plug. It is also not easy catching a decent trophy native fish. It never has and it probably never will be. You probably will always be after "Old Mamoo" (the exalted one) unless you are there at the right time, in the right place and with the one plug that works.

Three basic types of plugs evolved in the U.S.A.

Surface Plugs

Plugs that float and stay on the surface are called surface plugs. They were appearing in numbers around 1900, but were around before that.

Henkenius/Kane Plug
Fort Wayne, Indiana
Patented 1900

Underwater Plugs

Underwater plugs sink. They are generally found in the form of "Underwater Minnows", and are sometimes referred to as "Experts". They are usually made of wood weighted with enough lead to make them sink.

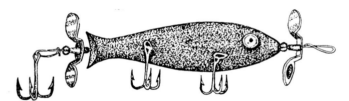

Double Spinner
Artificial Minnow
by F.A. Pardee
Kent, Ohio
Circa 1902

Floating Divers

The third type of plug and the most recent is the floating diver. There are two basic types of floating divers. The first has a planed front end that makes the plug dive upon retrieve in a current or trolled at the proper speed. There was quite a bit of patent controversey over this type of plug.

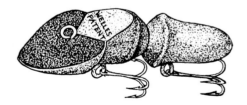

The Welles Patent Plug
1914 Patent

The second type of floating diver has a lip on the head or tail (as is the case of crawdads). One of the earliest patents to clearly illustrate this principle was the important Fred D. Rhodes' patent of 1904 discussed on page 15. For some reason this principle did not become popular until much later. One of the most famous patents covering type two floating divers is the Henry S. Dills' patent granted in September of 1920 - the patent stamped on the metal lip of Creek Chub Bait Company's long lasting and fish catching Pikie Minnow - perhaps the most prolific plug of all time.

Fishing plugs were produced all over the U.S.A. However, it is interesting to note the main flux has followed a pattern. We have named this area "Plug Alley". During approximately the first hundred years it included the homes of most of the major manufacturers as well as many important smaller plug makers. It also includes a great deal of area pertinent to the development of the metal lures, spinners and spoons, rods, reels, etc. A great deal of fishing tackle was developed in "Plug Alley".

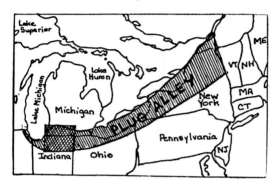

A great many early fishing plugs of the United States that have been near and dear to collectors and fishermen alike were made in a specific area of "Plug Alley". This area covers two states - Indiana, and perhaps most important, Michigan. The square area designated in the "Plug Alley" map is enlarged in the drawing below to show the intense concentration of the plug industry. William Shakespeare, Jr., Messrs. Rhodes, Moonlight/Paw Paw, James Heddon's Sons, Creek Chub, Worden, South Bend, Lockhart and Coldwater to name a few. Millions of plugs were made here. As collectors all we can do is hope there are still a few around.

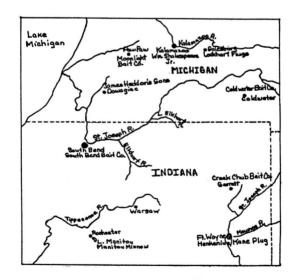

BRUSH'S TROLLING SPOON
Patented August 22, 1876

LOU RHEAD'S NATURE LURES

LANE'S AUTOMATIC MINNOW
Patented July 29, 1913

CHRISTIANSEN FROG
from Minnesota

Harkauff Assortment - Note two Trout Minnows
Circa 1903 - Harold Herr

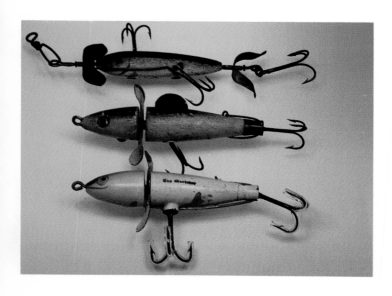

Top plug probably by same maker as the
Manistee Minnow below (C.R. Harris?)
Bob Bulkley

The "Ultra Casting Wood Minnow"
distributed by Norvell-Shapleigh
Hardware - St. Louis, MO - Bob Bulkley

Probably a
very early
South Bend
(Worden?)
Surf-O-Reno
- Keith Tompkins

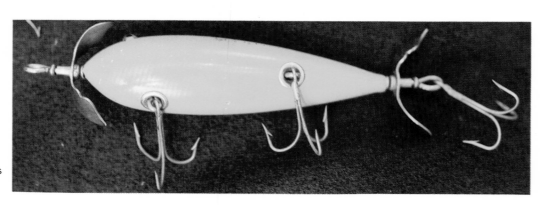
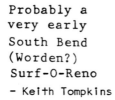

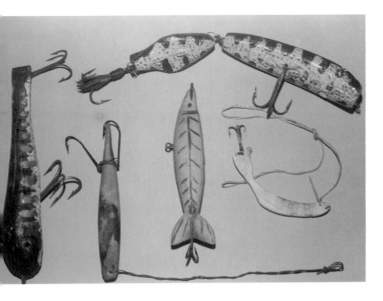

The Haskell Trolling Bait - Pat. Sept. 20, 1859
Bob Bulkley

Fishing Plugs made by Native Americans
Kimball Family Collection

Shakespeare Tournament
Casting Frog - circa
1900 - Harold Herr

Pflueger Trory Minnow - Circa 1899
Drew Reese Collection - Arlan Carter Photo

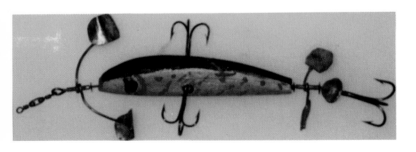

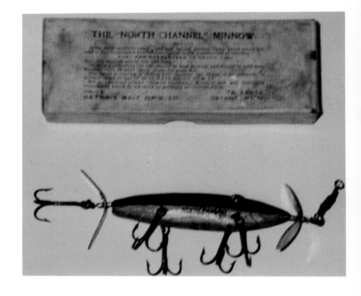

Old surface plug - circa 1900, possibly earlier
Found in Fred Rhodes' cabin in Michigan
Rus Anthony photo and collection

The North Channel Minnow - Detroit Bait Co.
Detroit, Michigan - Circa 1904
Wayne R. Chapman

PIKEROONS BY MOONLIGHT

ATTRIBUTED TO MYERS & SPELLMAN
Michigan

BITE-EM BATE COMPANY

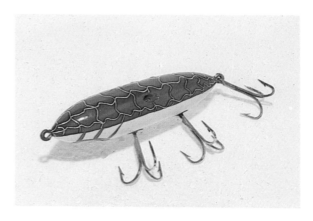

EUREKA WIGGLER
Patented June 9, 1914

JAMISONS

CLARK ROUND EXPERT

SOUTH BEND
BASS ORENOS

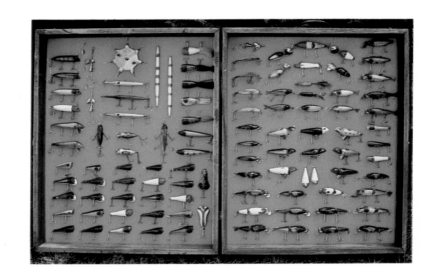

CREEK CHUBS

CREEK CHUB
PIKIE MINNOWS

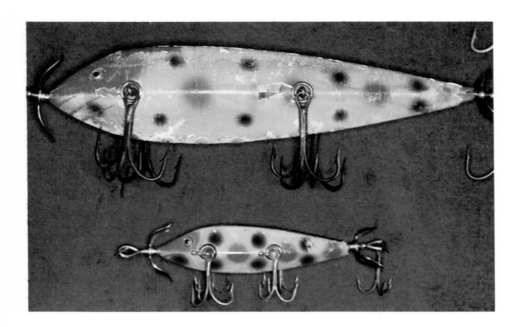

The Heddon "Big O" above, # 00 below
Arlan Carter Photo

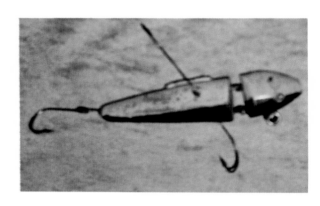

The Jim Tracy Plug - circa 1918 (Streater)
Dave Hoover

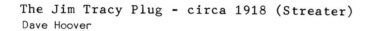
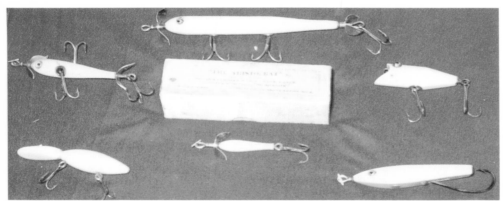

Nixon Aristocrat Plugs - circa 1918
Dave Hoover

The Blodget Hook #1 - Milwaukee, WI

Pepper Baby Bass Bait
Bob Bulkley

Horan Weedless Rubber
Bulb Bait - circa 1912
Jack Looney

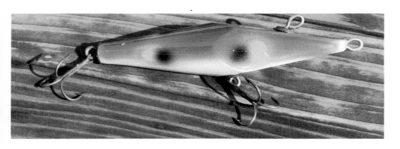

The Fish Spear in frog finish
Bill Stoetzel

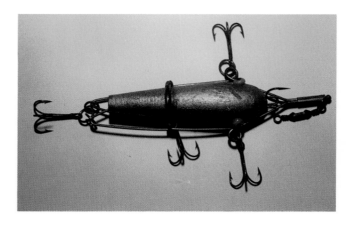

Ketchum Plug, Portage, WI
Art Kimball Photo

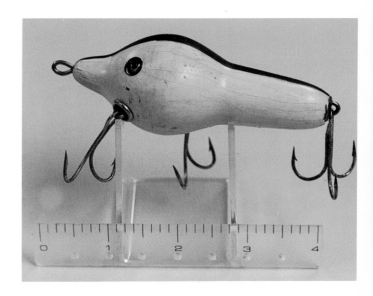

Baby Heddon Night Radiant - circa 1913
Karl White

Paw Paw Underwater Minnow - circa 1914
Bob Bulkley

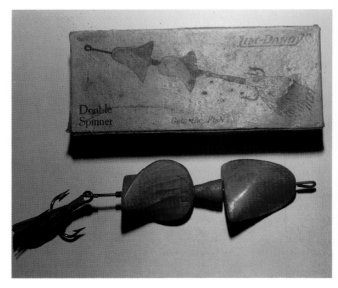

The Jim Dandy Double Spinner - circa 1914
Don Ludy

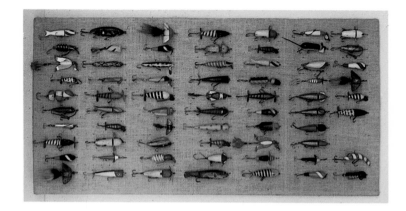

PLUGS THAT SPIN ON AN AXIS

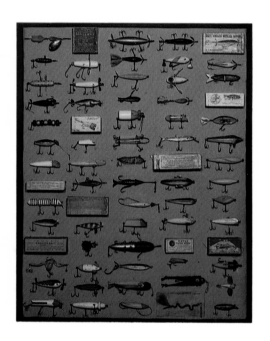

MISCELLANEOUS OLD PLUGS

CHIPPEWA BASS BAITS
Patented November 1, 1910
and May 2, 1911

SHAKESPEARES

SHAKESPEARES

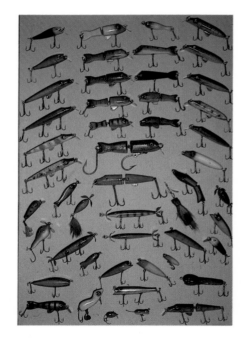

LAUBY WONDER SPOONS
   (wooden spoons)
Company started in 1933

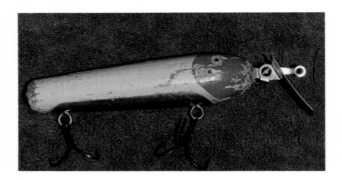

Fred Paulson Plug - circa 1927 - Illinois
Jack Looney

"Minnie the Wiggler" and Friend
Dan Basore

Keelings with tails
Jack Looney

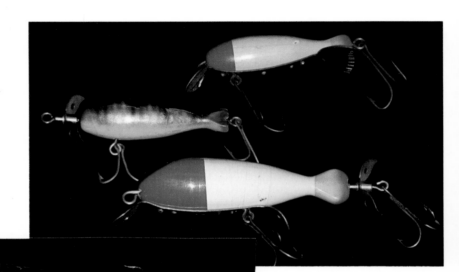

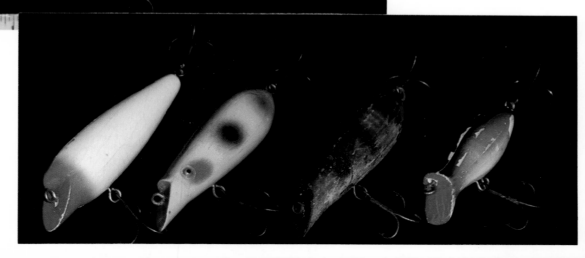

Flat side Keelings
Jack Looney

Keelings
The two center plugs
are mice
Jack Looney

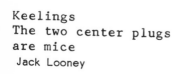

Possible Jones Plug - Pat. 1923
Jack Looney

The Bug Minnow - Pat. 1923
Bob Bulkley

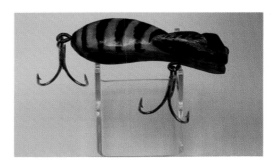

Plug by Oscar Peterson - circa 1924
Famous for his fish decoys - for
more info see "Michigan's Master
Carver Oscar W. Peterson" by Ron
Fritz - Bob Bulkley

Tuttle Muskrat Plug
Lou Eppinger Collection
Arlan Carter Photo

Tuttle Duck Plug
Lou Eppinger Collection
Arlan Carter Photo

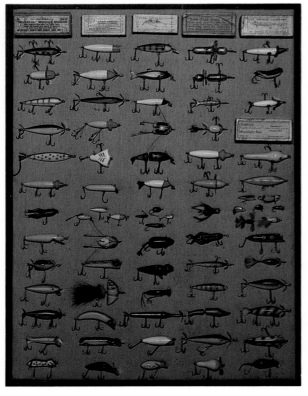

MISCELLANEOUS OLD PLUGS

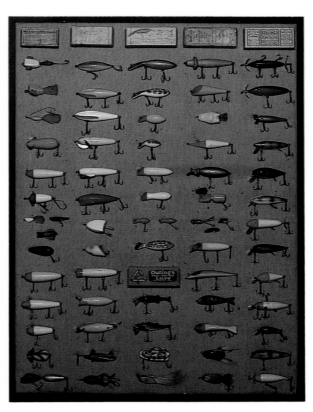

MISCELLANEOUS OLD PLUGS

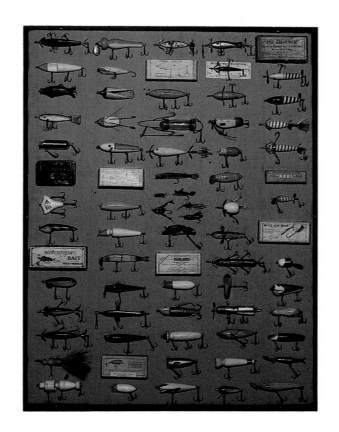

MISCELLANEOUS
OLD FISHING PLUGS

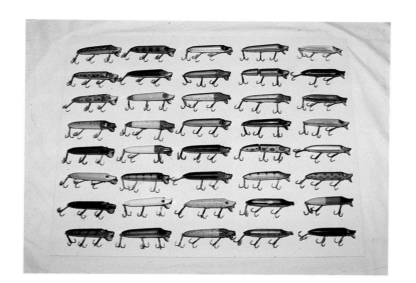

VAMPS BY HEDDON

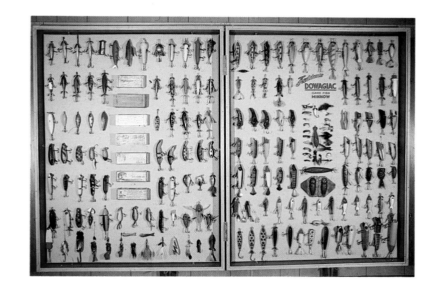

HEDDONS

BLACK SUCKER BY HEDDON

Wright & McGill Squid
Don Ludy

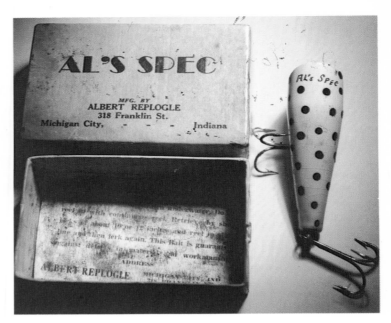

Al's Spec - Michigan City, IN
Bob Bulkley

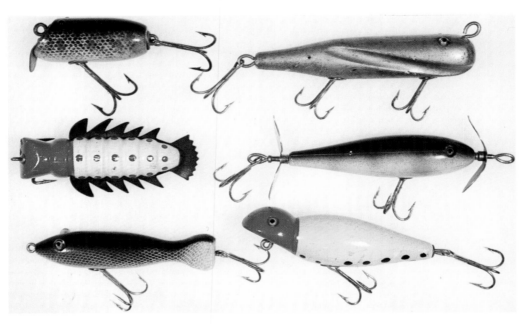

Various plugs by Strikemaster, Versailles, OH
Jim Bourdon

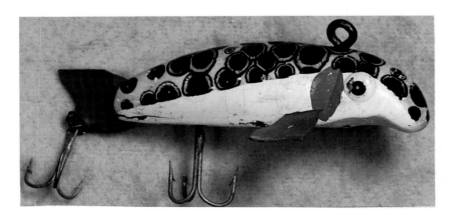

Bud Stewart Plug - an early example
Ray Carver

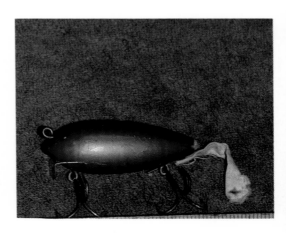

Florida Flapper - circa 1930
Jack Looney

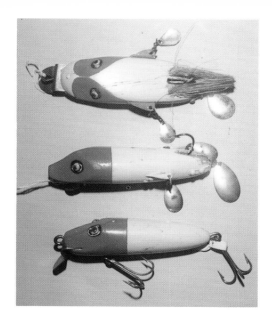

Plugs by Hans G. Wethall
Pat. 1929 - Minneapolis, MN
Jerry Myhre Collection

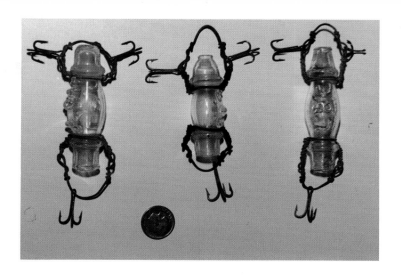

Glass Bait Holder Plugs - 2" and 2½"
Al Munger Collection

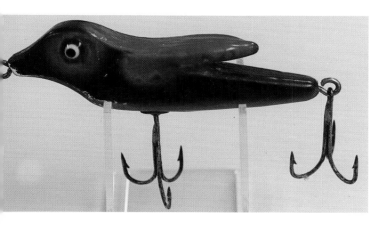

The Kinney Bass Bird - made in Florida,
Painted by Heddon - Karl White

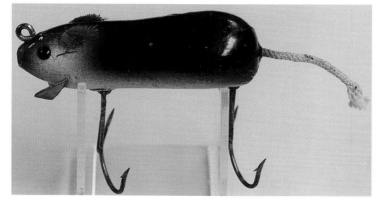

Reported as "The Mack Mouse" - nothing
more known - Karl White

J.K. Seymour Angle Worm - Elyria, OH
Entered in Pflueger files in 1929
possible an earlier lure - Dan Basore
Photo & Collection

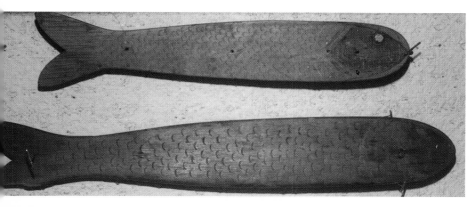

Pop Dean "Shingle" Musky Plugs
Sayner, WI - These are Pop's
oldest plugs - circa late 1920s
Kimball Family Collection

ENTERPRISE MANUFACTURING CO.
        (Pflueger)
TRORY MINNOW

PFLUEGERS

ELECTRIC MINNOWS BY PFLUEGER

Chapter Three

MISCELLANEOUS

"Miscellaneous" plugs will be the longest chapter in this book. The data is developed chronologically from the earliest date we can prove until a period approximately 50 years ago where we must end.

Major manufacturers of plugs will be discussed in separate chapters following this one. Where the important name first arises historically in the events to follow we will refer it to its particular chapter. We will generally be referring to company or plug maker's names. There are a few cases where the plug name itself is better known to collectors, in which case we will use the actual name where it's more appropriate to do so.

Julio T. Buel - Whitehall, N.Y.

The earliest patent we have seen for a plug made in the United States is Julio T. Buel's Patent No. 8,853 of April 6, 1852 which is for an "Improvement in spinning bait for catching fish". Julio Buel's patent was for a hollow lure that would resemble a "live fish or fly". The material suggestion in the patent is metal (hollow). However, it mentions "other suitable material". The structure of this important "fishing bait" is a floater or a sinker. There were stoppers in the air chamber that could be used at the discretion of the fisherman to make the lure sink or float. According to the patent, this lure could "be made to float on the surface of the water for catching certain kinds of fish by closing the aperture. It can be made to sink to any desired depth by opening the aperture and allowing water to take the place of air", etc. According to the patent paper, J.T. Buel's invention would probably have looked something like this.

As far as we know this version of this famous patent has not been found.

The intriguing problem with Patent No. 8,853 is that is has historically been attributed to the original "spoon bait" or "trolling spoon", when in fact, Mr. Buel makes it a point in the text of the patent to deny this. J.T. Buel states, "I wish it to be clearly understood that I do not claim what is called a 'spoon', 'minnow' or the common 'fly', all these having been used before". He goes on to add, "I do not claim passing the line loosely through a cork or float that the float may move freely upon the line. Neither do I claim attaching a spinning bait to the line by means of a swivel". This indicates a previous claim of some sort for all of these things. These non-claimers cover a lot of ground. They can also cause some problems. There is a distinct possibility of an earlier U.S. patent by J.T. Buel and/or others.

J. T. BUEL.
MODE OF TAKING FISH.

No. 8,853.   Patented Apr. 6, 1852.

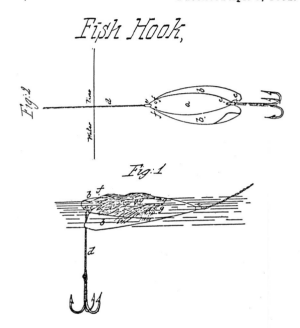

This is a condensed version of this very famous patent. The commercial version of J.T. Buel's patent closely resembles the top patent illustration. "J.T. Buel's Spinner" was made for many years in several sizes. A decent example of a J.T. Buel's Spinner typically marked, "J.T. Buel, Whitehall, N.Y." is not particularly difficult to find. Certain variations, some with different markings are scarcer.

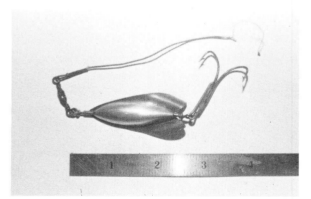
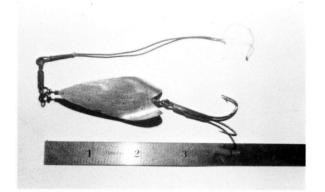

The above variation of "J.T. Buel's Spinner" is marked, "J. Warren, Sole Maker", along with the 1852 patent date. Other interesting variations are marked S. Alcock & Co. (an English company), another simply "Made in England". A version we have not seen has been referred to as "The Warren County" and was supposed to have been made by a gentleman from Lake George which is in Warren County, New York. There is another version that could be marked Bate or at least it was advertised by them in the early 1860s. This one comes in sizes 1 through 6. They were offered by the Thomas H.

Bate & Co., No. 7 Warren Street, New York City. The name Warren appears again??? In the early 1890s a version was catalogued marked "Pike Spinner". Mr. Charles Pike worked for J.T. Buel until the mid-1880s when Mr. Pike obtained the company. The "Pike Spinner" was so marked on the belly in an ad describing this lure which was from an early 1890s Thomas J. Conroy (N.Y.) trade catalog. There are undoubtedly more scarce variations of J.T. Buel's spinner. Some might be copies and even infringements, others licensed or permitted manufacturers. There is a lot of room to collect this historical plug. We will not go into further variations here because the lure that developed is generally regarded as a metal lure rather than a plug by collectors. It must be remembered that this is the earliest patent to show up. The history of fishing plugs of the U.S.A. starts here. Also, if there is actually an example of the float or sink version, made of metal as described in the patent, this would at least qualify to be the first plug.

To the best of our knowledge, Julio T. Buel was born around 1806 in East Poultney, Vermont. Julio Buel is reported to have been an observant fisherman. As a young man of perhaps 8 or 10 years of age, Julio took notice of local fishes' reactions to foreign objects being thrown into the water. He eventually fashioned a hook attachment to a piece of tin and caught some fish. This is not the most popular version of the Buel legend which appears as an incident which happened on nearby Lake Bomoseen, Vermont when J.T. Buel accidentally dropped a spoon into the water and watched a fish take a swipe at it. The result was his attaching hooks and providing a line tie to a spoon with the handle cut off. As far as we can tell, Julio was around 18 at this time. Whether either or both of these legends are true, there is no doubt of J.T. Buel's importance to the plug industry of the U.S.A.

In 1844 J.T. Buel moved to Whitehall, New York which is near his birthplace. At this time he was associated with the fur trade. By 1848 he is reported to have been in the lure making business. In 1854, two years after the famous "first" patent, he was granted another patent which involved the first use of weedless hooks. An 1856 patent accelerated this theme.

All Julio Buel's ideas have been incorporated into lure making ever since. The J.T. Buel Company has gone through many changes over many years. In 1912 Mr. Pike transferred ownership to a Mr. Fagan who called it "Northern Specialty". The business changed hands again recently in 1959 and in the 1970s it was purchased by the Lou J. Eppinger Manufacturing Company of Dearborn, Michigan. The quality carries on for 132 years.

This lure is attributed to J.T. Buel - vintage unknown - it is called "The Far Casting Bait". It was offered as recently as 1916.

Thanks to Jim Frazier for special help on J.T. Buel.

The Bates Patent Spinner

      On June 12, 1855 Charles DeSaxe of New York, New York was awarded
a patent for an "Improved Serpentine Spinner to catch fish". This wonderful patent was conceived more with the action of the plug than what it
was made of. This action was of a continual type. As long as the plug
is in motion or there is a current, it would spin on its axis. One interesting feature of this particular patent is that it states in paragraph
four that "The particular tackle to which the Serpentine Spinner is attached is not material".

      This patent was assigned to Thomas H. Bate, also of New York, New
York. By 1860 Mr. Bate was advertising as the "patentee of the Improved
Serpentine Spinner". In the mid-1860s he was selling a line of lures
which included several sizes of the Bate plug. These were made of copper
and stamped with Mr. Bate's name. They were sold through a catalog by
The Thomas H. Bate & Company, 7 or 9 Warren Street, New York, New York.
Bate's Patent Spinners are rare.

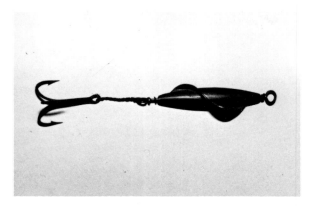

Commercial model of the Bate's Patent
Spinner.

A wood plug that meets the specifi-
cations of the patent. If this is
indeed a Bate it sure is an old plug.
It is probably something else made
later. We don't know. It is unmarked.

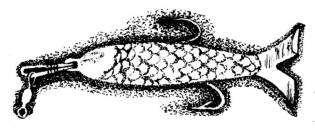

This "glass minnow" was advertised
by Thomas H. Bate & Co.

The Haskell Minnow

      On September 20, 1859 Riley Haskell of Painesville, Ohio received
a patent for a "Trolling Bait for catching fish". Haskell's Trolling Bait
was made in at least three sizes - 3½", 4½" and 5". The action consists
of a body who's main portion (front) remains stationary while the tail
end revolves. The general construction is of two thin concave hollow

metal parts soldered together. According to the patent, the upper portion was filled with cork, the bottom with lead (the first lead in the
belly plug). The metal suggested by Mr. Haskell was silver plated copper.
Other materials were listed as alternatives such as India rubber, guttapercha (a hard rubberlike substance extracted from a tree that grows in
Malaysia), and wood! We have a responsible report of an example made of
wood and painted silver. The Haskell is wired through end-to-end.

     The Haskell lure is a joy to behold. Careful attention was given
to details such as scales, fins, eyes, gills, etc. They are clearly
stamped on the side with the patent date and maker's name.

     Mr. Haskell was known for his craftsmanship. His gunsmithing had
a reputation for high quality. In 1857 he had a gun and fishing tackle
shop on House's Block (a main street) in Painesville, Ohio. In 1859
Riley Haskell moved to different quarters where he continued in business.
Riley Haskell was born in 1827 and passed away in 1882 at the age of 55
years.

     His minnow is quite rare. We only know of four specimens at this
time.

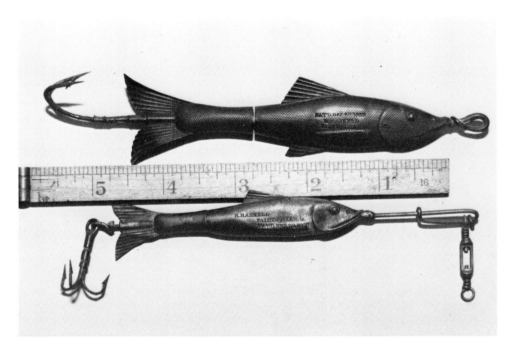

Thanks to Ray Carver (NFLCC Librarian), Dan Basore and Gregg Mackey for
specific help in researching Riley Haskell.

Munger 1862 Plug

     This wood plug was given to Mr. George Munger by his father on
November 30, 1862. It was a gift that was given along with a hand carved
duck decoy. The Munger family has a tradition of decoy and plug carving.
This plug was made for fishing around the area of Chincoteague Island,
Virginia. This information was provided by Al Munger who has maintained

a hereditary interest in sports fish and the history of the tackle used to catch them.   See "Selected Bibliography" for details on books by Al Munger.
     Plugs such as these are unique.   There are probably many plugs made by decoy carvers.   Many times this type of plug show as an unidentified (Who dunnit) hand carved plug.   A plug like this becomes extremely interesting to collectors when it can be authenticated as to maker, date and location.   The decoy carver/plug maker combination is a vast and fertile field to collectors.

W.D. Chapman & Son

     The products of Mr. William Dana Chapman of Theresa, New York must have been legendary among fishermen of days gone by.   Mr. Chapman, and later his son, developed a line of metal lures so extensive that by 1884 they advertised 80 artificial baits.   Most of W.D. Chapman's baits were spoons and spinners.   The ones of interest here are the Chapmans that are the most important in the development of the plug.
     Collectors of Chapman lures freely admit that they will probably never find even a representative "type" collection in a lifetime.   It is vast, spanning at least 41 years starting with the first W. D. Chapman patent for a "Fish Hook" May 15, 1866 which is basically for a detachable hook.   It is the spring clip hook and line-tie attachment found on many later Chapmans.
     This patent was followed by an 1870 patent for a "Minnow Propeller" that consisted of two convex plates secured (usually soldered) at the edges.   When in motion the effect is great.   It gives the impression of a three-dimensional fish flashing in all its brilliant colors.   The following illustrated lure is marked Allure on one side and "W.D. Chapman, Theresa, N.Y." on the other.   The lure itself is made of two convex pieces of metal which become fish shaped when fitted together.   Half is made of copper, silver plated and decorated with perch marks that were put on with a chemical that does the equivalent of bluing steel.   The other side is brass which is likewise "blued" to match.   Both sides have embossed eyes. The rear bearing is an opaque blue bead.   When you turn this Allure on its side there is a copper spear shaped spinner in the belly that rotates inside.   One side of the inside spinner is embellished with red spots and the other side is silver plated.   This particular lure is probably from

the 1870s although it could be more recent. It resembles a 1907 patent, however, it utilized the Chapman name alone which indicates an earlier date. This one is sort of a beautiful puzzle.

In 1871 there was an addition of a long tubular brass swivel which is seen on many Chapmans. The following illustrated lure features the clip hook and leader attachment of the 1866 patent and the tubular swivel of the 1871 patent. The lure itself is more recent because it bears the Chapman & Son, Theresa stamping. It is probably circa late 1880s or early 1890s.

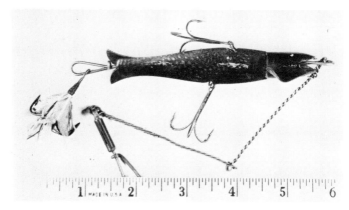

W.D. Chapman was granted another patent on March 18, 1884. This was for a scalloped edged spinner. These are probably the most common Chapmans and are usually marked Allure. Even the most common Chapman lures are scarce. Some are real tough to find. This "Allure" was made in several sizes from the small #2 size to the huge 2/0 musky size. The only reason we mention this spinner here is to clarify the multiple use of the word "Allure". Another marking seen on Chapman lures is IXL. This is actually a play on words - "I excel".

The next patent granted to Chapman was on July 28, 1885. We have seen an example of this lure - it is a nice one!

From here we jump to 1907 with a patent assigned by Mr. Chapman of Theresa, N.Y. to Messrs. Fred J. Sharp and Charles J. Smith both of Watertown, New York. It is a simplified version of the first lure illustrated in the W.D. Chapman & Son section.

W.D. Chapman went through three distinct changes in name and one in location. The earliest Chapmans are usually marked W.D. Chapman, with or without, Theresa, N.Y. information. The exact date of the change in name to W.D. Chapman & Son occurred sometime between 1866 and the late 1870s or early 1880s. The address was still Theresa, N.Y. but the name changed to Chapman & Son. This went on until the final name change to Chapman Son & Company, Rochester, N.Y. We do not know the date of this change. W.D. Chapman was still using the Theresa address in 1907.

Chapman lures vary in design and size. They went further with improving metal lures than almost any American manufacturer specializing in metal lures. There were many intriguing names attached to Chapman lures. Unfortunately we do not know to which lures belong the names like The Boss, Reversible Propeller and Spiral Spinner.

We do not know what eventually happened to the Chapman Company. All we can say is that they are very interesting and difficult to collect. It is quite possible there are a lot more out there. As more and more plug collectors turn to metal lures, we hope to see Chapmans surface. Thanks to Marc Wisotsky for his help on this matter.

Marked W.D. Chapman
This is sort of a 3-dimensional
version of the "German Propellor"

Spiral Spinner
Nickle plated over brass - has
embossed "perch" marks.

This minnow is silver plate over copper
on one side and brass on the other.
It is incomplete.

Marked Chapman Son & Co., Rochester,
New York

Rhodes/Rhoades "Improvement In Spring Fish-Hooks"

In 1867 Elias Rhodes, Jr. and James W. Rhoades of Clyde, Ohio patented a weedless spring hook with a spiral metal front end. This lure is interesting because of the names. It would be interesting to know if these Rhodes/Rhoades men were related to the more famous Messrs. Rhodes from Kalamazoo, Michigan. Much more about these Messrs. Rhodes later.

The J.E. Christian "Fish Hook"

The J.E. Christian "Fish Hook" was patented June 30, 1868. It has a body of woolen yarn or rubber. The "revolving plate" looks somewhat like the Pflueger Black Bass Spinner which came along later. It was intended to look like a worm - perhaps the first artificial worm.

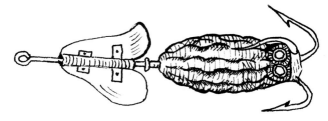

The Albee Fishing Jig

Sewall Albee of Wiscasset, Maine was granted a patent on November 3, 1868 for a fishing jig. It's not exactly a plug. Nevertheless, it appears to be the first jig. To the best of our knowledge, this lure has never been found.

The Huard/Dunbar Plug

Mr. David Huard and Mr. Charles M. Dunbar of Ashland, Wisconsin received a patent for an "Improvement in Trolling Fish-Hooks" on May 26, 1874. This is a minnow shaped single hook weedless plug. The patent calls for wood or other suitable material. This plug pulls by the tail.
Ashland, Wisconsin lies on the shores of Lake Superior on Chequamegon

Bay where there are sand spits jutting out. Inside this area huge northern
pike come in to chow down and mate. The everlasting method to catching
big northerns in these shallow weeds or sloughs is to throw out a cisco,
perch or smelt with a hook in it and let it lay there or bring it in slowly.
This plug would do the trick! This is certainly the first wood fish shaped
weedless plug that pulled by the tail. It was probably made of two pieces
of flat wood laminated vertically. We sincerely hope someone reading this
book has one of these plugs.

Brush's Patent - Floating Trolling Spoon

Henry C. Brush's 1876 patent for a "Floating Trolling Spoon" is
considered by some to be the first wood plug. It's truly one of the
first. This plug sinks slowly. It came in three sizes - #1 bass, #2
pickerel and #3 "muskalonge". It was available with "silver", "gold and
silver" or "silver plated" spoons or blades. Certain variations such as
the musky size are rare. Any Brush is scarce. If you look for one hard
enough you will probably find it. The patent date is August 22, 1876.

Archer Wakeman's Lures

On August 5, 1879 Archer Wakeman was granted a patent for a
Devon style lure. It features an improvement in hook hangers. It is
quite similar to the later Pflueger Breakless Devon. Mr. Wakeman was
from Cape Vincent, New York, in the beautiful Thousand Island area of
the St. Lawrence River. His lure was sold by a Mr. A. Able of that
town and was referred to as the Thousand Island Minnow. This lure is
realistically painted over a plated body.

A. Wakeman received another patent in 1886 covering another
Devon type lure that held a minnow. It was called the Wakeman Skeleton
Bait and was quite a contraption.

Wakemans are rather scarce and quite worthwhile.

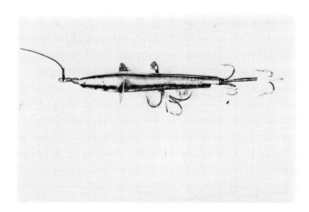 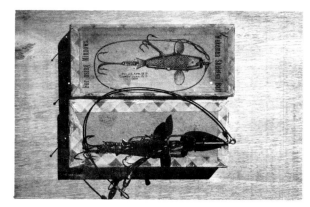

Irgens' "Crystal Minnow"

"Be it known that I, Jorgen Irgens, of Bergen in the Kingdom of Norway, have invented a new and improved fish hook attachment". This is the original Crystal Minnow - made of "silvered or gilt glass" or "vitrified pottery". The glass "may be white or tinted in a suitable color to imitate the various colored fish". This patent is dated September 7, 1880. Citizens of foreign countries could obtain U.S. patents. Historically these must be considered at least contributions to U.S. plug history.

We will later see essentially the same lure in the Pflueger Chapter. Mr. E.F. Pflueger added luminosity and catalogued it as the Luminous Crystal Minnow. He probably got together with Mr. Irgens. The plug illustrated could be a Pflueger. It should give you an idea what Jorgen Irgens' plug looked like. This is the only one we have seen without a prop.

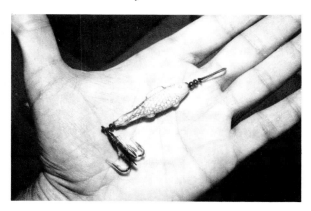

The Flying Helgramite

At last the Flying Helgramite. There are few old plugs that excite a few old collectors more than The Flying Helgramite. It has been considered the first wood body plug. Once gain, it sure is <u>one</u> of the first.

The Flying Helgramite was patented by Harry Comstock of Fulton, New York on January 30, 1883. The version pictured in the following patent picture has never shown up.

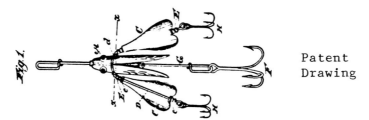

Patent
Drawing

There were three sizes of The Flying Helgramite offered by Harry Comstock in 1883 - sizes #1, #2 and #3. There were four sizes a few years later offered by Mr. E.F. Pflueger of the Enterprise Manufacturing Company of Akron, Ohio. Mr. Pflueger's Helgramites were called Luminous Flying Helgramites.

Two distinct versions of the "Helgramite" have shown up. The first or type I Helgramite is a non-luminous, wood bodied plug, 3" long (wood to wood). In both examples we have had the pleasure of studying, the wood is painted solid dark red, not maroon but close. The "fins, wings or blades" (called all 3 in the patent) were unmarked and somewhat smaller and less elaborate than the better known version of the Helgramite. Both types of Helgramites are wired through with brass rods, both ways, and have a Chapman type clip fore and aft for hook and line-tie.

The type II Helgramite is similarly structured but more finely finished. The body is painted green in the front, yellow with dark brown stripes in the center and a metal tail cap. Type II Helgramite sports glass eyes. The "wings" are longer than in type I, plated and painted red on one side. Clear red beads were used on front and back of the body and on the front of the wings. The three type II Helgramites we observed all had at least traces of luminous overpaint which indicates a later Pflueger Helgramite. At least one had a bucktail. We don't know if this was original or not. One school of thought on the two types of Flying Helgramites is that two qualities were offered - an "economy" model and a "deluxe" model. It is our opinion that E.F. Pflueger only sold one type and that was always luminous. Further, Harry Comstock's version was not luminous. We have not seen a type II Helgramite with non-luminous wings. It was advertised, so it should be out there. It is quite possible that both H. Comstock and E.F. Pflueger sold two seperate models. In that case there could be four types - two luminous and two non-luminous. We hope more Flying Helgramites show up. They seem almost prohibitively rare.

Type I, left

Type II, right

Type II Helgramites had the following clearly stamped on one wing. The stamping is in an oval pattern and reads as follows: "H. Comstock - Pat. Jan. 30, '83, Fulton, N.Y." In the case of the photo you can see this stamping where Mr. Pflueger's paint has chipped off.

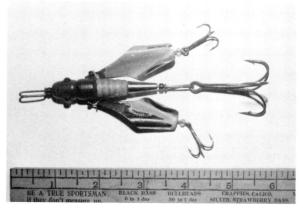

Ernest F. Pflueger (SEE PFLUEGER CHAPTER)

To the best of our knowledge, Patent No. 272,317 of February 13, 1883 was Mr. E. F. Pflueger's first patent. It covers adding luminosity to already existing types of lures such as the "Angel or Devon", "artificial minnow" and "spoon". These had already been done before. What's new here is Mr. Pflueger's lures glowed in the dark. Much more about Mr. Pflueger in the next chapter. E.F. Pflueger was the earliest of the major plug manufacturers.

Christopher Hymers' Patent

Christopher Hymers of St. Louis, Missouri patented a "Self Adjusting Fish-Shaped Fish Hook Holder". That's quite a handle. The treble shoots out of the mouth activated by a coil spring. It's difficult to tell what this plug looks like. It's probably metal. It was patented March 13, 1883 and probably looks something like the drawing. It would be nice to see a real one.

Newton A. Dickinson Patent

The Newton A. Dickinson plug was a very simple lead-head, wood bodied weedless jig from the East Coast. It was patented March 18, 1884. Materials mentioned in the patent other than wood were "rubber, horn, ivory, bone or any material". This covers a lot of jig type lures.

F.C.P. Robinson Mouse

The F.C.P. Robinson mouse is probably out there somewhere. It is for sure an old plug. The patent states it is to resemble a rat or mouse. Mr. Robinson goes on to state "The body is covered with fur or hair on the skin or otherwise", (Otherwise?) "or of material in imitation thereof, so colored and applied as to resemble the skin and hair of a rat or mouse". The patent mentions the use of "glass or other reflective material". A glass eyed mouse or rat from 1885. We sincerely hope there is still one of these out there. Check out your old mice. Frederick C.P. Robinson is from New York, N.Y. This patent was assigned to Mr. Thomas A. Conroy of Brooklyn, New York.

Patent
Drawing

Cornelius Lie Patent

Cornelius Lie's hollow metal plug works on the principle of a gorge. That is, when the fish hits it and the hooks are set, the hooks expand inside the fish's mouth or stomach. It is hard to imagine something swallowing a piece of finely crafted metal. The hooks are spring loaded. This hand painted plug is made of tin plate and has embossed scales. We do not know where it was made. Mr. Lie is reported to have been from Norway. This is the only one we have ever seen. Patent is dated November 17, 1885.

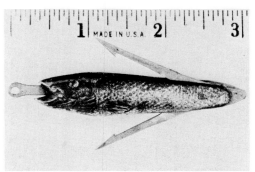

Gustav van Normann's Patent

Gustav van Normann's "Fish Hook" looks more like another weedless hollow metal plug similar to Mr. Lie's beautiful little metal minnow. We have never seen one of these. They are undoubtedly quite rare. It was patented July 6, 1886.

W.A. Cooke's Patent

The unusual feature of Mr. W.A. Cooke's patent of March 29, 1887 was the ability of the body to stay upright rather than spinning. This was accomplished by the careful use of light wood ("cork or locust bark" were recommended). The shape had to be such to stay upright. This was further helped by the use of a belly weight!

William Cooke was from Gaithersburg, Maryland. It would be great to see one of these. We bet they were beautiful little minnows complete with tin fins. It was patented March 29, 1887.

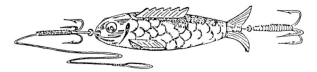

Brewster Patent

On January 1, 1889 William F. Brewster of East Orange, New Jersey patented a hollow metal weedless plug. The blades at the head of this plug are referred to as propeller blades in the text of this 1889 patent of the fish shaped lure illustrated.

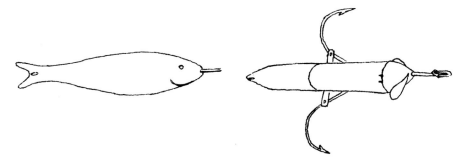

Sturrock and MacDougald Patent

James Sturrock and George Duncan MacDougald of Dundee assigned to Morris Carswell of Glasgow Scotland a U.S. patent for a "Devon" with an internal swivel. This was in 1890. In 1891 Carswell patented a simpli- fied improved version of this "Devon" - another U.S. patent, although this could have been made in Scotland. I guess we will have to call these American "Angels". Look closely at your "Devons".

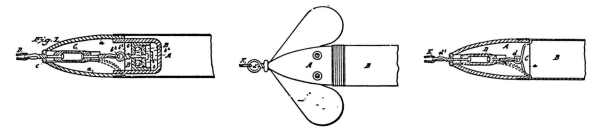

Lagerstedt Patent

This fish shaped weedless plug was probably made out of hollow brass. Please let us know when you find one. This was patented by Samuel S. Lagerstedt of Campello, Massachusetts in 1891.

Welsh and Graves

The Welsh and Graves glass minnow tube was made in Natural Bridge, New York. The name and patent date of Jan. 3, '93 is embossed on the clear blown glass tube which is meant to hold a live minnow. There is a ground and drilled hole in the nose of this plug to circulate water. The one illustrated has a cork stopper. We have heard of one with a threaded stopper. These are scarce and nice. There have been three sizes reported.

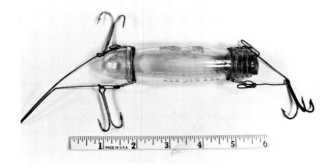

John Pepper, Jr. Patent

Mr. John Pepper of Rome, New York received a patent on May 2, 1893 for a number of wonderful ways to fool a fish. They were all made out of metal. We do not know the relationship between John Pepper, Jr. and Joseph E. Pepper. Both men were from Rome, N.Y. Certain details in John Pepper's patent indicate a connection. We would appreciate knowing more about the potential connection here. We reproduced some of the components of John Pepper, Jr.'s patent. We will introduce Mr. Joseph E. Pepper a little later (1902).

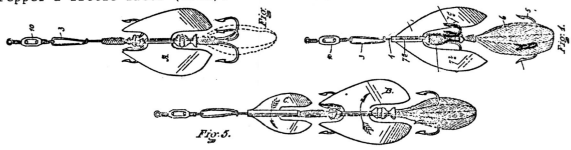

Goff and Judkins Patent

H.S. Goff of Lordsburg and A.B. Judkins of Los Angeles, California patented a weedless "Fish Hook" on May 8, 1894. Here is what appears to be another weedless hollow metal plug. There were many patents for concealed hook plugs - some were spring loaded and others worked by leverage. This one works off a cam that swings the concealed hook out. It is interesting that so few examples of this type plug have appeared. Perhaps not that many collectors pay attention to weedless plugs.

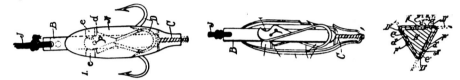

The Hastings Frog

The Hastings Frog by Mr. James T. Hasting of Chicago, Illinois was patent on February 19, 1895. This soft hollow rubber frog was extremely popular. The Jamison Company of Chicago, Illinois sold this plug for many years. The Jamison version is rather common but hard to find in decent shape. Hollow rubber plugs sometimes deteriorate faster than those made of other materials such as wood. It is quite possible that the earlier Hastings version is somewhat different. We have been unable to prove this. All Hastings frogs we could identify were in Jamison boxes. More about Mr. Jamison later. See Jamison for photo. This was one of the earliest patents for a hollow rubber frog.

The Burgess Plugs

We do not know exactly when Mr. Benjamin F. Burgess of Jackson, Michigan started making plugs. He filed for a patent in 1894 for a weedless hook. This hook appears on the Burgess 3-hook underwater minnow. The side hooks on the photo below are not correct. The wood body shows an impression of the original hooks. The hand paint job and sweeping props are O.K. Apparently this plug came with two types of props. It's an old and rare plug. Another plug attributed to Burgess is the surface plug on the right.

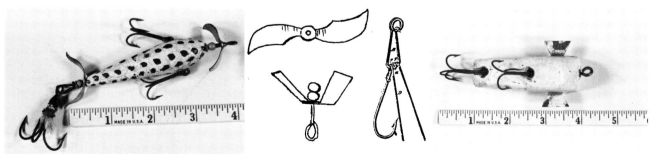

A. Kelley Patent

A. Kelley's "Artificial Fish For Bait" patented on April 23, 1895 is a hollow metal lure that spins on an axis - a "Devon" like plug. There are some mysterious Devon like wood plugs around. It is doubtful that any of these are Mr. Kelley's products.

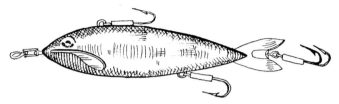 

If Mr. Kelley didn't make this wood plug (brass hardware), who did? 3½" wood to wood.

The Gaide Bait

The Gaide bait came in at least two sizes. This important September 8, 1896 patent was referred to in a later lawsuit between the Enterprise Manufacturing Company of Akron, Ohio and W. Shakespeare, Jr. of Kalamazoo, Michigan. This is a very old wood plug - perhaps the first surface bait. The two specimens we have seen so far are both painted dark red. The two in the photo are wired through both ways. Mr. Gaide mentions casting in the text of the patent and the bucktail recommended is deer hair attached to the skin. Also use of close grain wood was called for. Carl J.W. Gaide was from Fort Wayne, Indiana.

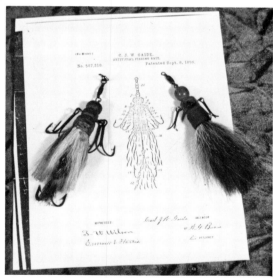

The Aluminum Fish Phantom

The Aluminum Fish Phantom is what Mr. Livingston S. Hinckley of Newark, New Jersey called his new plug. This hollow aluminum plug was

actually called the "Phantom Float" in the patent, which was dated
January 12, 1897. It was also referred to as the "New Jersey Aluminum
Phantom", "Aluminum Phantom", "Aluminum Killer", "Yellow Devil", "Yellow
Boy" and "Yellow Bird". Mr. W.A. Able & Company of Syracuse, New York
called it the "Three Rivers Minnow". The Aluminum Fish Phantom came in
four sizes - 2" with treble hook only, 3", 3-3/4" and 4-1/4". It came in
natural aluminum finish and painted solid yellow with gold dots. The
latter became a very famous and popular finish. This is an important
old plug. It was recommended for both trolling and bait casting. It is
the first patent for a hollow aluminum surface bait. Mr. Hinckley must
have made a great many Aluminum Phantoms. There are quite a few still
around. They are relatively common for a plug this old. The 2" model
with a single treble on the tail seems to be the hardest one to find.
Many plugs to follow utilize Mr. Hinckley's idea of a twirling head.

Lucky Joe's Fish Bait

The May 1897 issue of "The Osprey" (a magazine devoted to collecting
bird eggs and other popular pastimes of the day) contained a large ad that
states that fishermen of America appreciate Lucky Joe's Fish Bait. They
were 50¢. Unfortunately there was no picture so we don't really know if
Lucky Joe made a plug or something else. It could be something unmention-
able like stink bait. It could also be a plug. Lucks Joe as he was also
referred to did business from Kalamazoo, Michigan. Anyone out there know
who Lucky Joe was? He sure sold a lot of whatever it was. He received
9,305 orders in 1896.

Osborn Patent

Harmon R. Osborn's hollow metal artificial bait must have been great
looking. It was patented July 20, 1897. The hinged hollow metal body
sported the use of feathers as a weedless feature. If there is one of
these in existence, it must be a beauty!

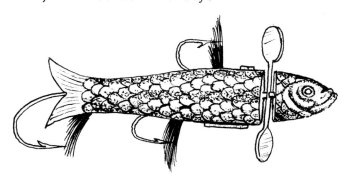

The Harris Frog
_____

        The Harris "Small Cork Frog" is extremely well made and beautifully
hand painted. It sports an outside dangling belly weight. The specimen
in our collection measure 3-1/4 wood to wood. C.R. Harris's patent was
dated August 24, 1897. He did business out of Niles, Michigan. This is
a good old frog to get ahold of. There don't seem to be many left. They
could be confused with other frogs. Look for black bead eyes and a belly
weight. Mr. Harris also offered a Devon type lure called the "Harris
Featherbone Minnow".

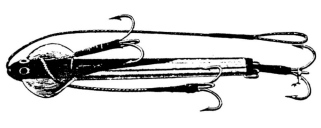

The Abbey & Imbrie "Ghost"
_____

        This hollow aluminum lure was patented by W.H. Rockwood of New York,
New York on November 15, 1898. It was distributed by Abbey & Imbrie of
New York, N.Y. under its own name. The aluminum body is made of two pieces
and folded. It is stamped, "The Ghost", Pat Nov. 15, '98, Abbey & Imbrie,
N.Y. The Ghost has a feather tail and is 1-3/4" long. It might have been
made in other sizes.

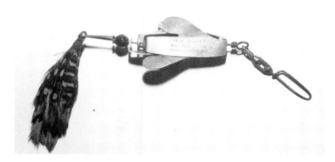

Thomas Maroney Patent
_____

        Thomas Maroney of Buffalo, New York patented this rocket/fish shaped
plug on June 20, 1899. It is another weedless spring action lure. The
head spins and the tail wags. Is there one of these still out there?

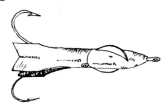

The Dixie Minnow

Mr. Edward T. Dukes of Quitman, Georgia patented the beautiful, hand painted, all metal Dixie Minnow in 1899. These are hard to find especially with the original paint still there.

Howard Squid

The H.A. Howard "Squid" was patented October 24, 1899. This plug looked something like this and could have been made of wood.

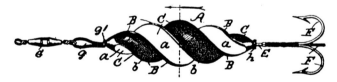

Hedgeland "Artificial Bait"

Frederick W. Hedgeland was from Chicago, Illinois. He received his patent on November 15, 1899. It appears to be a hollow metal plug. This Chicago plug has probably been confused with the next plug in this book - the Jeinings from New York.

George Jeinings Bait

This hollow metal plug by George Jeinings, Newark, New Jersey appears to be aluminum and is marked Pat. Pending on the blade. It is believed to be from around 1900. It came in at least two sizes - the #1 which was 2-7/8" (metal to metal) and the other size (number unknown) is approximately 3-1/2". This plug was distributed by Abbey & Imbrie, a large retail supplier of fishing tackle for many years. This plug is difficult to find.

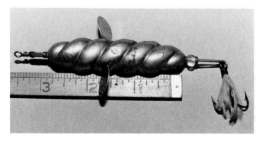

Peterson/Olson Patent

This wonderful "frog" or "a small animal" plug would be a wonder to behold. It is the first of many patents that work on the principle of a "driving wheel" which is an eight bladed prop that runs a crank shaft action that activates the four legs. We don't know what Gustav A. Peterson and Andrew Olson of Florence, Minnesota actually had in mind here. The patent date was December 12, 1899.

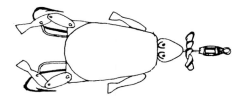

Votaw/Thomas Patent

Morris W. Votaw and Martin E. Thomas's patent of February 13, 1900 is the earliest we have seen from Kentucky, the home of fine bait casting reels. This little rubber minnow is a rare gem. Rubber deteriorates fast. It would be difficult to find one of these.

The Henkenius/Kane Plug

This important patent is for the first wood plug of a type familiar to most fishermen and collectors. The later and perhaps more famous Decker plug, Shakespeare's Wood Revolution and the famous Pflueger Globe are good examples. Peter Henkenius and James M. Kane were from Fort Wayne, Indiana. Mr. Henkenius is reported to have been a candy maker as well as a plug maker. The Henkenius/Kane plug is wood with crude aluminum "integral propellor blades" which are maked on one blade, "Pat Apl'd For" in a circle (see below). The plug on the left is a standard Henkenius/Kane plug painted silver with black dots and a keel which is wired on. The plug is wired through both ways. The plug on the right is unmarked and could be an earlier version. It is painted yellow and red. This classic plug is hard to find. Perhaps there are more out there and people have not recognized them. The patent was applied for on July 23 or 28, 1900 (the writing on the patent is hard to read as it is on so many old patents). It was granted on November 19, 1900. This indicates a pre-1900 development.

Hall Patents

The plug on the left was patented December 25, 1900 and the one on the right February 11, 1902. In both cases the hooks revolve. The idea is to make them invisible while in motion. These plugs were recommended for clear water. The material used is unknown. James Bascom Hall was from Cleveland, Ohio.

The Shakespeare Wood Revolution

Messrs. William Shakespeare, Jr. and William Locher of Kalamazoo, Michigan received a patent for the rare, desirable and revolutionary Wood Revolution. Mr. Shakespeare's plugs will be discussed in full in the Shakespeare Chapter. One interesting thing could be said here and that is that Messrs. Shakespeare, Jr. and Locher applied for their patent on July 5, 1900 and received it in February, 1901. When you compare this to the very similar earlier Henkenius/Kane patent (November 18, 1900) it becomes apparent that although the Wood Revolution patent was filed for about three weeks earlier than the Henkenius/Kane patent, it was not granted until about three months later. Why? Incidentally, the Metal Revolution patent came along a couple of months after the Wood Revolution.

Geen Patent

Philip Geen from Richmond England (Surrey County) received a U.S. Patent on August 27, 1901 for a spiral "spinning" bait. These are cast metal. I would guess that although it is a U.S. Patent, they were possibly made in England, but this is not necessarily true. Geen baits were advertised and show up in the United States. Mr. Geen also made a plug. Feast your eyes on this beauty. Need to know more here. Maybe Mr. Geen moved to the U.S. Does anyone out there know about this?

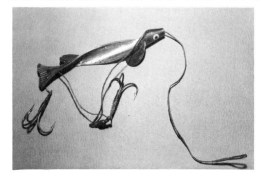

Heddon Slopenose

On April 1, 1902 Mr. James Heddon of Dowagiac, Michigan received an important patent for a surface plug which is affectionately nicknamed the "Slopenose". This introduces Mr. Heddon and his famous plugs. More about both in the Heddon Chapter.

"Who Dunnits"

      "Who Dunnits" will be presented from time to time in the text of this
book. We will fit them into an approximate time period. This particular
group could date into the last century or the early 1900s. The names, dates,
makers and other details are not known here. Some of the metal fish could
even be foreign. There is a good chance all plugs below are from the U.S.A.
Any help in identifying on "Who Dunnits" will be appreciated by the authors.

Unknown Metal

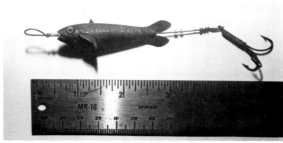
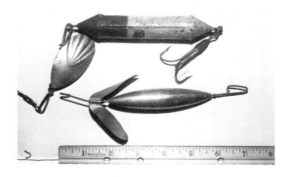

Unknown Plugs of Wood and Other Material

The next two are made of leather (left) and felt (right). They came out of
the same tacklebox, circa 1901. The felt one had a tail - we should have
taken better care of this one!

Unknown Plugs of Wood

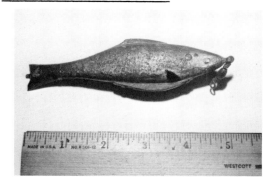

Attributed to Wright & McGill

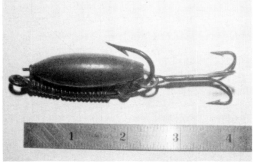

Attributed to Wright & McGill

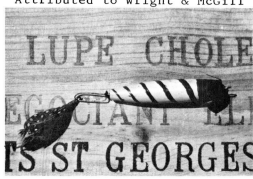

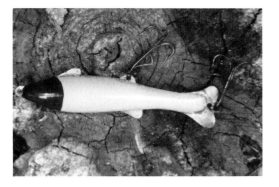

Unknown Underwater Minnows

Wood underwater minnows cause much puzzlement among collectors. The following illustrated plugs are good examples of this.

Has brass tack eyes over
a celluloid type material.

Feathers overlay the wood
on this one.

This wonderful plug could
be English. Perhaps not?

Unknown Underwater Minnows - Continued

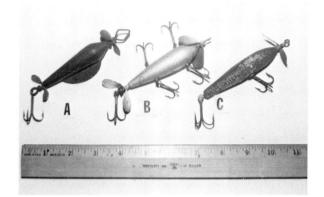

These three plugs all have metal caps on the nose. The one on the left is wired through and has brass props and inletted keel. This is an extremely interesting old plug. The center plug has a prop attachment similar to an experimental Heddon we observed. The one on the right is dark grey crackleback.

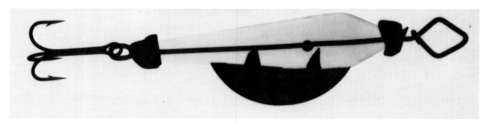

X-ray of plug on the left. This plug is maroon and has a brass screw that holds the through wire in place.

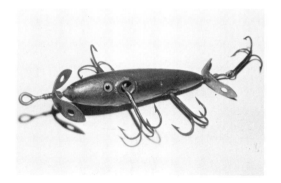

This plug is as troublesome to I.D. as any we have ever seen. The holed props are painted red. It's wired through. This is one wild unknown. Has features of Woods, Rhodes and Heddon. It also has a cap on tail and nose similar to the previous plugs.

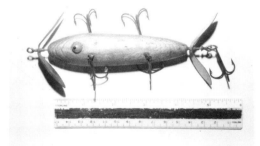

Unknown Underwater Minnows - Continued

The green, white and red hand paint job on the two plugs on the left (below) is similar to paint on what is later, perhaps erroneously, referred to as "Myers & Spellman" plugs. More about these later. The most interesting feature of these plugs is the hooks, which are of the Woods removable type invented in 1904. The top plug also has a raised wire attachment to keep the hooks off the body. This was an important feature in patents of this vintage. If you analyze these two features, it sort of falls between another Woods hook patent (1906) that combines the two features. The props are reminiscent of one type on the Burgess minnow. The two plugs on the right (below) feature the same hook features. The props are nondescript as to I.D. The top plug is red, white and blue with black and yellow glass eyes and the bottom plug is gold with red glass eyes.

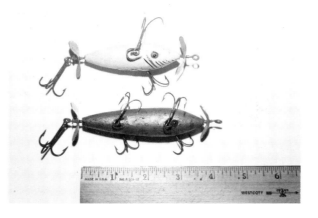

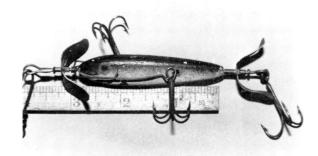

Identified as a possible
C.R. Harris

The "Big Mystery" Surface Minnows

Collectors have been aware of a cigar shaped surface minnow that occasionally turns up. These plugs confuse and mystify. They are almost all standard bass size (3-3/4" - 3-7/8"). One example of a small one around 2-3/4" has been reported but not seen. They all have a belly hook hanger that is a simple screw eye with a small concave washer soldered to it. This washer was undoubtedly to keep the hook from scratching the surface of the paint.

The problem arises in the similarity of certain other features to different products of other manufacturers. Collectors have tentatively attributed these plugs to Worden, South Bend, Shakespeare, Burgess, and the even more confusing Myers & Spellman. These theories could all be

The "Big Mystery" Surface Minnows - Continued

true or false. What we do know is that one was found in what we hope is
the original box. It is called the Ultra Casting Wood Minnow by the
Diamond Manufacturing Company of St. Louis, Missouri. That's probably
just what the plug is. The box is made of cardboard. The plug is a redhead. The prop is the one that shows up with the most frequency.

Other plugs with the hook guard have features that run all over the
board - different type props, paint jobs and eyes. The belly hook hanger
remains the same.

The props are the cause of discussion. One type prop has embossed
center reinforcement and stamped circles near the tip that are usually
painted red on the inside. The prop is similar in ways to the Junod patent
of 1903 which is the prop Mr. Worden used on his pre-South Bend Bait Co.
plugs. The thought here is that these are indeed "Wordens". The prop on
the Ultra Minnow in the box is sort of a version of this principle - the
metal in front is pressed to act as a reinforcement. Others seen have
varied props, some definitely indicate the later short shank construction
of William Shakespeare, Jr. One "prop" is definitely Burgess-like.

It could be that all opinions regarding this plug are somewhat true.
You can't always identify a plug by a particular feature. The area of
unknown early surface minnows is highly overlooked. This is just one
example.

Similar to Ultra Minnow
observed in box.

There is some thought that
this might be a Worden.

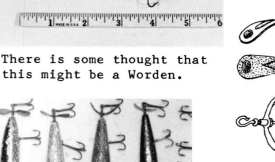

Thanks to Clyde Harbin, Walt Blue, Steve Ongert and Jack
Looney for help on this most difficult plug.

The Jacoby Novelty Company

The plug on the bottom came in
the box to the right. It is labeled
The Jacoby Novelty Co., Minneapolis,
Minn. It is made of rubber and is
the earliest "Fish Nipple" type plug
we have encountered. Inside the box
is an ad for a hook called The Jacoby
Weedless Bass Hook, Pat. Nov. 11,
1902. The top plug is very similar
but has a Pflueger type prop.

Joseph E. Pepper - Rome, New York

Joseph E. Pepper was one of the earliest plug makers. His plugs probably date to before 1900. A Mr. John Pepper received a patent for spinners in 1893. We suspect a connection. Nevertheless, we do know that Joe Pepper named one of his plugs in celebration of the 20th Century. It was called the 20th Century "Wonder" Wood Fish Spinner. It came in at least three variations, the two below and a larger 5-hooker. 20th Centuries had painted eyes and gill marks. They were silver and black.

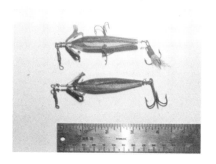

Joseph E. Pepper advertised another minnow in the early 1900s which was called the National Minnow. The ads and the minnows don't always look alike. When it comes to the Pepper underwater minnows it must be remembered that they were sold in various quality levels over a rather long period of time which ranges from at least 1902 to 1915. They were probably sold longer than that.

Pepper material is sparse. The earliest minnows seem to be finished in hand painted silver and black like the "20th Century". The props on Peppers vary a great deal. They run from elaborate creations to more regular blunt end types similar to South Bend. There are some in between.

One thing Pepper minnows have in common is the red hand painted gill marks which are slanted from the belly on the bottom toward the front. This is the opposite of hand painted gill marks found in most other company's underwater minnows.

Pepper Minnows are very diverse and difficult to recognize. The plugs in the photos below are all thought to be Pepper Minnows.

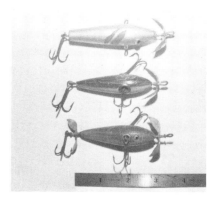
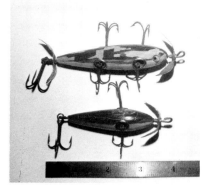

This last photo are not definitely
Peppers. The one on the top has the reverse gill marks and is in green crackleback. The bottom plug is very similar
to one offered by either Clarks Horrocks
or Horrocks-Ibbotson Company under their
own name. These particular plugs are
still somewhat of a mystery. Joseph
Pepper seems to be the best guess.

The first Joe Pepper patent was applied for in 1907 and granted on
April 28, 1908. It is for a plug he called the "Roamer" Bait. It came in
at least two sizes (1-3/4" and 3") as shown in the photo on the left. The
photo on the right represents a Roamer with replaced rubber legs (the Roamer
had string legs) on top and an unknown on the bottom. It's possible the
bottom plug is a very early Roamer or something else.

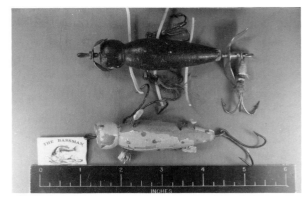

Joe Pepper produced two extremely well made plugs called Pepper's
Revolving Minnow and the Roman Red Tail Minnow. They were basically the
same. The front fins could be adjusted to control the rotation of the plug.
The Red Tail had just that - a red metal tail that made it more stable.
Both minnows were put up in fancy cantilevered wood boxes. The plugs are:
Top - Red Tail, Bottom - Revolving. The one in the box is the Revolving.
Both are circa 1911. Both plugs are strikingly beautiful especially in
excellent condition. These are very desirable Peppers even though there are
certain other Peppers that are harder to find. All Peppers are beyond scarce.
One neat feature of both of these Peppers is if you don't want them to spin
at all, just unscrew the front fins! These fins are marked and painted
bright red.

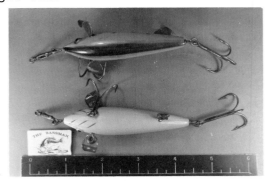

Probably the best known Joseph E. Pepper plug is the Roman Spider. It came in three sizes (photo on left). These are all hand painted and show the crackleback finish Pepper developed. The eyes are yellow with black centers - a typical Pepper feature. These were around in 1914 and possibly earlier. They are tough to find. The Spider also came in a redhead (photo on right).

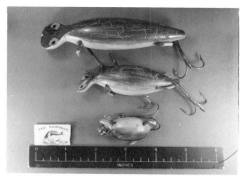 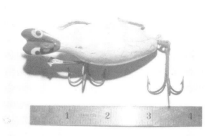

The following three Peppers are all very scarce. The plug on the left is the Roman Diving Bait, center is the Yankee Aero Bait (it also came in a jointed version), and the right hand plug is what is believed to be the Pepper's Mystic Spinner, or a plug close to it.

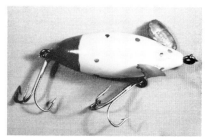 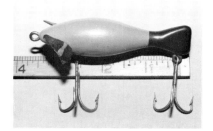 

The following two Peppers are quite rare. To the best of our knowledge Joe Pepper's Floating Minnow and Pepper's Bass Bait have not been found, as of yet. They are probably both from around 1912. There are undoubtedly more Peppers out there.

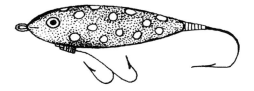 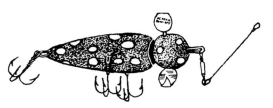

The Kent "Ohio Minnows and Frogs", F.A. Pardee (The Kents), Manco and Samuel H. Friend

The Kent type minnows and frogs could go farther back in history than we suspect. They are included here in the 1902 period as a starting point only because this is the earliest date we can prove. They could go back to 1898 and possibly quite a bit earlier than that. The information we have indicates the potential of a starting point as early as the 1880s. This can't be proven. It is possible that the start of the Kent type minnow leads back to the creation of a metal worker who made such artificial minnows to fish with based on something he had seen used by Native Americans. If this is

true, this makes the early Kent type minnows a candidate for the first wood
underwater minnows.

The earliest "Kents" were crude with relatively sloppy hand paint jobs.
The props were of aluminum and sometimes painted with a red dot on one side.
The early ones looked like the following.

This plug could be one of the old ones. It has
features to indicate early development - beads,
wired through and distinct props. If this plug
could talk, it would be informative.

It is generally assumed that the later models, as they approach production, were refined in terms of finish, consistency and fish catching
abilities. The production models of the Kent Double Spinner Artificial
Minnow were painted in an exquisite silver body, black tail and red gills
paint job. These minnows, both 3-hooker and 5-hooker were manufactured by
the F.A. Pardee & Company, Kent, Ohio.

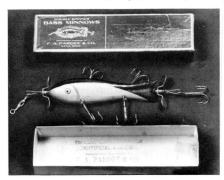

The "Kent Frog" as it is
lovingly known was actually
called the Kent Champion
Floater. Both Pardee plugs
sometimes had plated props.

Somewhere along the line both the frog and the minnow were distributed
under the name "Manco" Floating Frog and "Manco" Wood Minnow. The date involved here is unknown to us. We feel it was before Mr. Samuel H. Friend
succeeded F.A. Pardee & Company.

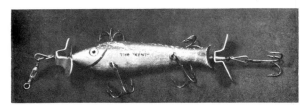

The Samuel H. Friend Kent Double Spinner
Artificial Minnow was clearly stamped
"The Kent" on the side. There is evidence of the return to an aluminum prop
here.

In the early 1900s the Kent minnow under any names was also known as
the Pflueger Trory Minnow. The Kent "Champion" Frog became the Kent Frog.
(See Pflueger Chapter) All varieties of minnows and frogs are very desirable
to collectors.

Special thanks to Dick Wilson who is the man from Kent, Ohio.

The North Channel/Delavan Minnow

This underwater minnow has been a puzzle to collectors. The name North Channel is clearly stamped on the side of the green/silver, glass eyed plug. There is a version of a plug like this that has sideways props - they are unmarked. (See bottom plug in the right photo below) This also came in a 5-hook version. We have not seen a North Channel or Delavan so marked in a 3-hooker. The North Channel Minnow was offered for sale in 1903 by the Detroit Bait Co., Detroit, Michigan. It is possible they also made them as well as sold them. North Channels are classic old minnows. There are a few around but seem to be getting more difficult to find as time goes on.

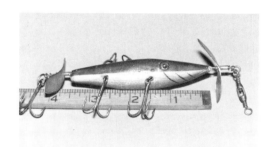 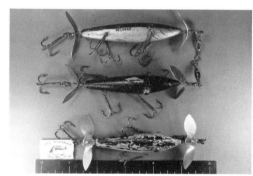

The Harkauf Minnows

There are at least four versions of the Harkauf. Perhaps the most well known is an inexpensive small 2-1/2", 3-hooker with a three bladed prop and painted eyes. Another small minnow is the Chaser Minnow. It has a hook on the tail and one on its nose. It's chasing a fly. Harkaufs were distributed by H.C. Kauffman & Co., Philadelphia, Pennsylvania. They also made a higher quality 3 and 5-hooker. The 3-hooker has a bucktail similar to Wordens. These have yellow and black glass eyes. Harkaufs were for sale from 1903 until as recently as 1930. It is believed that at one period in time they offered "do it yourself" minnows. Bodies were furnished both painted at 35¢ and unpainted at 15¢ and 17¢ respectively for 2-1/2" and 3"ers. Props and screw eyes were also available. Any Harkaufs are hard to find.

  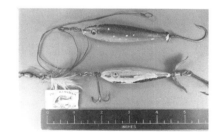

Harkauf Trout Minnow

The Experts - C.C. Shaffer and F.C. Woods

The March 17, 1903 patent granted to Charles C. Shaffer of Alliance, Ohio represents the archetype Underwater Expert. The patent drawing clearly displays all the features of a typical Expert - the prop and holes in them. All this plug needed was Woods patent removable hooks, and you have the

Woods, Clarks and Keelings Experts. The hook patents came along in 1904 and 1906. The original Shaffer Experts were probably made much before 1903. Mr. Shaffer was employed in the U.S. Railway Postal Service at the time he was working on his "Expert" idea. Realizing that perhaps it was better for someone else to market his plug, he called on a man named Franklin Woods to help him in his endeavor. Mr. Woods was possibly a relative of Mr. Shaffer's. It is quite possible the plugs below are the first plugs marketed by Mr. Woods. This could have happened as early as the late 1890s. It is more probable it was a little later around the turn of the century. This still makes it a very early plug. It is also possible that early Woods products came even earlier. Perhaps someone could help pinpoint this date. It would be appreciated. The Experts below do not have holes in the props or Woods patent removable hooks. If these are indeed F.C. Woods products, the lack of these two features indicate a date prior to 1903. The 5-hook version of this particular plug was sold under the name Holzwarth Minnow distributed by J.C. Holzwarth of Alliance, Ohio. These sometimes had diagonal "perch marks".

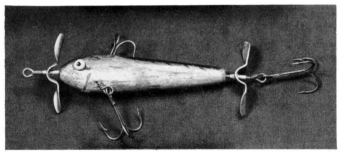 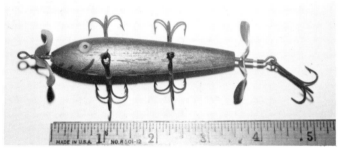

There were two quality levels offered in the F.C. Woods Experts. The shaped body minnows which had type II hooks were the most expensive - $1.00 for the 5" 3-hook, musky size #0 and 75¢ for the 3" and 3-1/2" ers (#s 1 and 2 respectively). Some of the earliest Experts had non-removable hooks and no holes in the props like the plug on the left. The plug on the right has type I removable Woods patent hooks. Most of these had type II.

 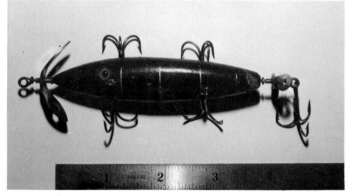

The less expensive Experts were round and generally had type I removable hooks. This version came in two sizes - 3" 3-hooker, #6 and 3-1/2" 5-hooker, #5. The plug on the left is a #5 round Expert. It looks like Mr. F.C. Woods might have made a frog similar to the Kent Frog. All features are definitely Woods. The frog on the right has type II hooks.

Photos on following page.

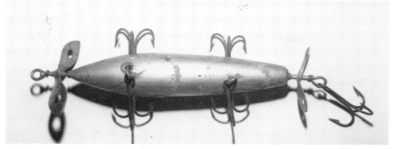

#5 Round Expert

Possible F.C. Woods Frog

F.C. Woods minnows were sold under this name until at least 1907.
Messrs. John L. Clark and Fred C. Keeling both of Rockford, Illinois manufactured and distributed Experts utilizing Woods patent hooks. There are
differences in the Clarks and Keeling Experts which will be discussed later
in the text. Mr. Clark started in the Expert business around 1905. Fred
Keeling soon took this over. In addition to the sizes mentioned above,
several others have been seen including a couple of small 2"ers. One has a
tail hook only and no eyes, another has 3 hooks and glass eyes. Two good
ways to tell a Woods Expert from a Clark or Keeling is; #1 the hole in the
Woods prop is larger than the Keeling, #2 is the gill marks (usually three)
sweep back from under the chin to eye level. The Clarks and Keelings are
somewhat different. Keelings are more like Woods and Clarks are distinctive.
Woods Experts are somewhat scarce, mostly because of their age. F.C. Wood
used both baked enamel rainbow, white and green, and aluminum with red or
green decoration, or just plain aluminum.

Top - Clark, bottom - Woods

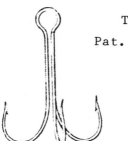

Type I
Pat. 12/23/03

Type II
Pat. 10/2/06

Bryan Patents

This artificial fish bait is
by T.A. Bryan of Baltimore,
Maryland dated April 21, 1903.
It is up to the reader to figure out what it does. It
appears that it might electro-
cute the fish. If this is so
watch out for a wet boat seat!

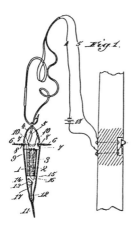

Another plug by T.A. Bryan
of Baltimore, Maryland. This
plug has a spring motor to
oscillate the fins and tail,
circa 1903. It looks about
as complicated as a watch.

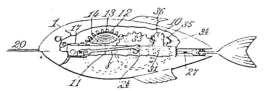

The Junod Patent - The Worden Prop

Paul Junod of Celina, Ohio filed a patent on June 5, 1903. It is for a reinforced prop. How Paul Junod and Mr. F.G. Worden ever got together we do not know. What we do know is that Mr. Worden was making a full line of wood underwater minnows starting about this time. He is credited with founding the famous South Bend Bait Co., South Bend, Indiana. Mr. F.G. "Bucktail" Worden is introduced here. We will see more of this important man and his products in the South Bend Chapter. Learn to recognize the Junod prop. If you find one on a plug, it's a Worden. All Wordens are tough to find.

The Junod reinforced prop -

The Hardy Interchangeable Casting Minnow

Patented July 19, 1904 by William A. Hardy of Monticello, Indiana. The Hardy is exceedingly rare and it's a "looker" to boot. It came in a cardboard box with a drawing of the plug on the top. The price was 75¢ for the complete plug. Extra bodies in different colors were 35¢ apiece extra. There is a good possibility of a Hardy Surface Minnow. It does not incorporate the same principle. The props are screwed in. This is not positive. The drawing is the result of an artist's reconstruction of a heavily fished repainted, cut up old plug.

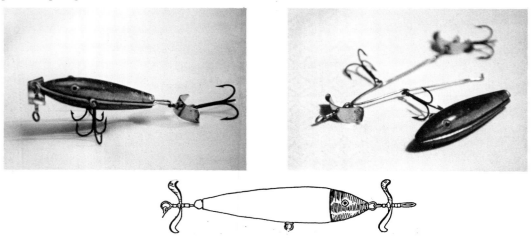

Hardy Surface Minnow?

The Kalamazoo

The Kalamazoo had a slit cut down the back to help make the hook changing characteristic of the plug easier to accomplish. The hooks hung out the side at a backward angle and were wired through by a removable brass wire. We have seen three 5-hook underwater minnows, one surface version but have not seen any 3-hookers. Each one we have seen is different in the type of hooks used, none are rigged exactly like the ones in the little ad (following page). The top plug on the left on the following page is rubber stamped "The Kalamazoo" on the side.

TWO BAITS IN ONE.
Can be changed from
weedless to plain hook
without the use of
knife or tools.

The Kalamazoo Fishing Tackle. Mfrs.,
610 Douglas Ave., Kalamazoo, Mich.

PRICES:
No. 1, 60c; No. 2, 75c;
No. 3, 85c; 25c extra each
with weedless hooks.
Write for Dealers' Prices.

The Kalamazoo Minnow was sold between 1903 and 1905 by Mr. Jay Rhodes of The Kalamazoo Fishing Tackle Manufacturers, 610 Douglas Avenue, Kalamazoo, Michigan. This most unusual minnow was an attempt by Mr. Jay Rhodes to provide a fish catcher for the then growing bait casting public. The Kalamazoo was on display and sold at the 1904 Worlds Fair in St. Louis, Missouri. Jay Rhodes' Kalamazoo Minnow and his Mechanical Frog took a gold medal at this event - the second highest award presented at this Worlds Fair. While in the area, Jay Rhodes caught so many bass on his new baits that some of the bass were placed on display in large aquariums that were built to house these captured beauties. Strong reason to own a Kalamazoo.
While at the Worlds Fair, Jay picked up a supply of wooden pencil boxes in which to package his Kalmazoos.

Jay Rhodes was known as an inventor. By 1904 he had acquired over 100 inventions, most of them unrelated to fishing. Jay Rhodes was not exactly down in St. Louis just to display and sell the Kalamazoo. At this time he was employed by the Fred Austin Company of Chicago, Illinois. Fishing plugs were a sideline, not that Mr. Austin was not interested in plugs. In fact, he had a great interest. He was the owner of Patent No. 777,488 of December 13, 1904 which was assigned to him by Fred D. Rhodes of Kalamazoo, Michigan. Jay was Fred's uncle. More about Fred D. Rhodes next.
The Kalamazoo was offered in three versions. The #1 was 60¢, #2 - 75¢ and #3 - 85¢. Weedless hooks were 25¢ extra. Unfortunately, the ad did

not say which was which.   There are two plugs shown - a 3-hooker and a 5-hooker.
It appears #3 might be a surface minnow.   The bottom plug below probably floats.
We could not convince the owner to try it in his bathtub so perhaps we will
never know.   The diagonal hole through the wood body principle in this plug
appears time and time again in surface plugs to follow.   This is a rare and
important plug.   A guess as to which plug was which would be that the #1 is
the 3-hooker, #2 the 5-hooker and #3 the surface minnow.

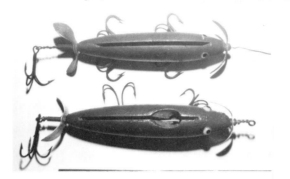 

     Jay Rhodes improved his design and incorporated a single principle which
eventually became of upmost importance in minnow development and that was to
ease in the cost of manufacture.   He internalized the belly weight and made
the bodies round.   He made hook changing easy by using long custom made screws
in the head and tail which could be removed.   Jay was going to patent this,
but was advised not to because his nephew Fred Rhodes had a patent that covered it.   This was good advice because the patent did indeed cover it.   Later
there was a major lawsuit involving this patent between William Shakespeare,
Jr. and The Enterprise Manufacturing Company (Pflueger) of Akron, Ohio.   See
the section on the Fred D. Rhodes Perfect Casting Minnow for more about this.
See page 14 for patent information.

     The pertinence of the Kalamazoo lies beyond its obvious charm and
rarity.   We do know that probably at least 1500 were made.   Perhaps as many
as 5000.   If that sounds like a lot, it isn't.   Try and find one!   The 3-hooker
represents a transition between Jay Rhodes' Kalamazoo and William Shakespeare,
Jr.s' version of the "Rhodes" Minnow.   It appears as advertised in the 1907
Shakespeare catalog.   In 1905 Jay Rhodes sold the rights and equipment for
his Kalamazoo to William Shakespeare, Jr. of Kalamazoo.   This exchange
included Jay's patented Frog, Fred's Perfect Casting Minnow and Bert O. Rhodes'
patent for a rubber Mechanical Frog.

Jay B. Rhodes also made a frog, "The Kalamazoo Frog"? The patent (October 31, 1905) is for what appears to be a wood frog. This would possibly be one of the best possible plugs to find. This should not be confused with the Rhodes Rubber Mechanical Frog.

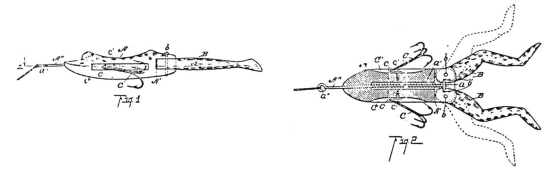

Jay B. Rhodes' name appears later on what appears to be a fish spearing decoy with hooks. The body material recommended in the patent is cast aluminum with celluloid horizontal "wings or fins". This body contained a combination of lead shot and cork so you could regulate the buoyancy. There could possibly still be one of these out there - we hope so. It was patented November 18, 1919 - a long time after Jay Rhodes made his deal with William Shakespeare, Jr.

Special thanks to John Woodruff and Walt Blue

The "Rhodes" Perfect Casting Minnow

It is once again time to talk about what is perhaps the most important single patent in plug history. The Fred D. Rhodes patent granted December 13, 1904 which was assigned to Fredrick C. Austin of Chicago, Illinois. This fine plug really started something! It involves the names of people who are legendary to lovers of old plugs. The "Rhodes" Perfect Casting Minnow was a popular fish catcher.

Jay Rhodes' nephew Fred had been fooling with plugs for a long time. In fact, by 1904 he was reported to have sold 3500 of his Rhodes Perfect Casting Minnows, a plug near and dear to the hearts of all plug collectors. The production model of Fred's Perfect was a flat wood plug that was more or less permanently wired through end to end. It had large holes drilled through the side to accomodate a protective cup and a circular split ring to which two treble hooks were attached and held in place by the long brass rod or wire. See page 14 for patent drawing. "Rhodes" Perfect Casting Minnows have strikingly beautiful hand paint jobs. One has turned up with a red, white and black finish that is a "knock out". The plug on the left (following page) is green, gold and red. The plug on the right (following page) is the patent model.

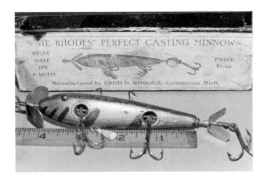

The production version of the Perfect came in two sizes - a 4" 5-hooker and a 3" 3-hooker. The 3-hooker seems to be harder to find than the larger Perfect. Both are treasures. The 5-hookers usually had a hanging external belly weight. The two 3-hookers we have seen have an external strip of lead tacked to the body - bottom left below.

When William Shakespeare, Jr. purchased the three patents, two frogs (Jay's and Bert's rubber frog) and one minnow from Jay Rhodes, part of the deal seemed to be the completion of several hundred minnows by Fred Rhodes. The plugs when delivered were unsatisfactory to Mr. Shakespeare. It is possible that the plug in photo (below right) is one of these.

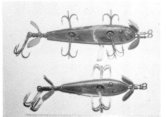
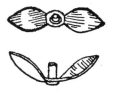

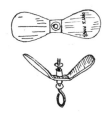

Some Perfects have turned up with the later Shakespeare, Jr./ "Rhodes" prop.

Thought to be made by Fred D. Rhodes - has the prop found on most Perfects.

There was an important, expensive and lengthy lawsuit between William Shakespeare, Jr. and the Enterprise Manufacturing Co. of Akron, Ohio (better known as Pflueger). Shakespeare won. It caused Pflueger to cancel a patent that had been granted by the U.S. Patent Office. The trouble was over the method of hanger hooks on a split ring that had a "rod" running through it. Pflueger infringed on the Fred D. Rhodes patent.

All three Rhodes men were obviously connected in the plug business. The plugs below are from Kalamazoo and thought to be experimental early products of Messrs. Rhodes. The one on the left shows characteristics of both Jay and Fred's works. The origin of the plugs on the right is speculative. Nevertheless, there is evidence to indicate a Rhodes connection. The plugs on the far right remind us of William Shakespeare, Jr.'s and William Locher's Revolution. Perhaps all these Kalamazoo men were connected in an earlier time in more ways than we realize. William Shakespeare, Jr. continued to use the Rhodes name for some time after purchasing the Rhodes plug business.

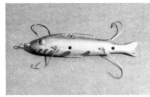
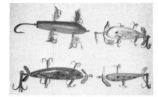
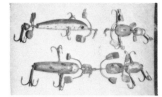

Special thanks to Jim Cantwell, Trig Lund and Walt Blue

The Bert O. Rhodes Perfect Swimming Frog

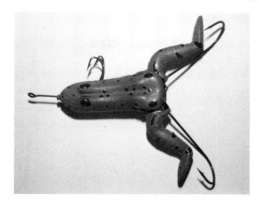

Bert O. Rhodes was marketing the rubber mechanical frog in 1905 under the name Kalamazoo Fishing Tackle Co. Jay Rhodes called his company the Kalamazoo Fishing Tackle Manufacturers. They used the same address for awhile. More about the Perfect Frog in the Shakespeare Co. section.

"Who Dunnit" Surface Plugs

There are some mysterious surface plugs that have turned up that should probably be included at this point in the text. They all have qualities or properties in common. One big thing is that they are generally found around the Kalamazoo, Michigan area. The one that is a particular puzzle is a version we have seen with a hook rig like the Turner Casting Bait. The ones in the photos following just start to show the diversity of this plug. More needs to be known here. In the meantime, all we can say is that most collectors familiar with this plug seem to think the same thing - Rhodes/Shakespeare. These are all big - 5-1/2"ers. One version has been observed with Shakespeare type short shank props.

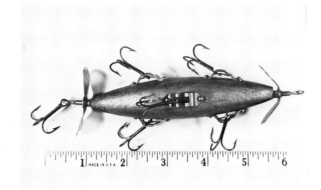

More "Who Dunnit" Surface Plugs

These are also big plugs - approximately 5-1/2". Who made them? When?

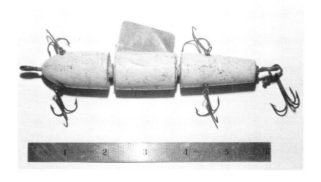
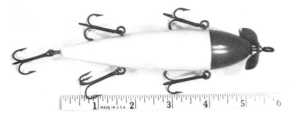

The Malcom A. Shipley Cedar Propellor/Pocono/Etc.

It is difficult to date Malcom Shipley's Cedar Propellor. Mr. Shipley
was from Philadelphia, Pennsylvania and had a retail business. It is likely
he was marketing his Cedar Propellor from the late 1890s until the very early
1900s (around 1903). It has been called the Pocono and Shipley's Cedar
Propellor and probably more things. There are various versions. We have
seen several basic models. A short (approximately 2-1/2")fat one just showed
up. The bodies are generally unfinished cedar.   Painted ones have been seen -
usually all white. 2-1/2", 3-1/4" and 3-1/2" versions have been seen. There
are varied opinions on the Cedar Propellor ranging anywhere from another
"first plug" to just another plug. It's probably neither, but perhaps deserves
more attention than it gets. They occasionally show up but not very often.
The Cedar Propellor is wired through, end to end. The ones with hanging hooks
have screw eyes. There is the possibility that the Cedar Propellor is quite
old. We would like to have more positive information on this.

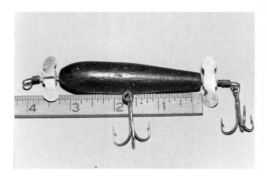 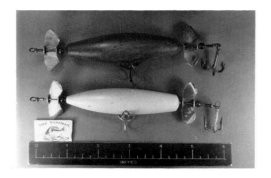

D.W. Brown's Wiggle Tail

D.W. Brown of Akron, Ohio perfected the Wiggle Tail, a chubby minnow
with a cam shaft operated tail. Some of these mechanical wonders exist. I
would think if a big fish hit this plug it might destroy it. Maybe that's
why they are so rare! Two versions have been seen based on Daniel Webster
Brown's patent which was granted December 13, 1904. Both are wood minnows
with tails made of what appears to be a tough composition material. The
Wiggle Tail is shown below. One version had a hanging belly weight. The
drawing on the right is a patent granted to D.W. Brown on September 10, 1907.
We have not seen this plug. Perhaps there is one out there someplace. It
should wiggle real well with the eccentric prop on the nose.

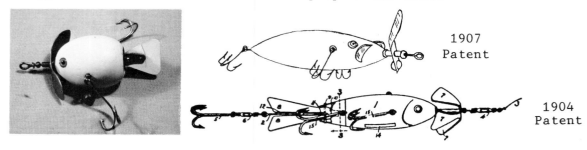

1907
Patent

1904
Patent

Here is another Wagtail - this one is by Harry C. Clippinger of
Akron, Ohio. It was assigned to Messrs. Mark E. Metzger and Daniel W.
Brown. The tail on this plug wags sort of the same way as the D.W. Brown
plug pictured previously (Patents 1904 and 1905). The movement of the rear

prop oscillates the tail by a little rod turning and banging both sides of
a U bolt type attachment to the tail. The materials are not known. The
hooks were held on the sides with a rubber band. The assignees of this
patent are both from Akron, Ohio. Patent dated Spetember 25, 1906.

Jamison

        William J. Jamison was born in Ohio in 1865. Mr. Jamison was a fisher-
man ever since he was a young boy. By 1906 W.J. Jamison was active in the
gentleman's sport of tournament casting, and he remained involved in this
sport for some years. It is interesting to look at some of the names contem-
porary with W.J. Jamison's tournament casting activities. Names such as
Jay and Fred Rhodes, William Stanley, William Shakespeare, Jr., B.F. Flegel
(of reel fame) and Robb, just to name a few. Many plug inventors, innovators
and manufacturers were active in tournament casting in those days.
        William J. Jamison's business was in Chicago, Illinois where it thrived
for many years.
        The Jamison-Hastings rubber frog was perhaps the first plug Mr. Jamison
marketed. It was a hollow rubber frog with a belly weight, and had two single
weedless hooks, one attached to each leg. The Jamison-Hastings frog is based
on a patent granted to Mr. James Hastings of Chicago, Illinois in 1895 (see
page 57). Mr. Jamison packed these individually in cardboard boxes as he did
with most of his plugs.

        On January 3, 1905, Mr. W.J. Jamison received a patent for a plug that
all plug collectors recognize. The famous and fish catching Coaxer was made
for many years in many sizes with various extra features. In 1910 Mr. Jamison
received a letter from Dr. James A. Henshall, author of The Book of the Black
Bass, praising and endorsing the Coaxer. Louis Rhead, author of Fish and
Fishing, and maker of a very unusual line of lures, also recommended it in
the text of his book. Mr. Jamison developed the Coaxer out of experiments
with pork baits and red felt combinations. He made one out of cork and red
feathers and perfected it so it would act right in the water. When he finally
fished with it he found his idea worked even better than he had dreamed.
Mr. Jamison stood behind his Coaxer. He challenged other to use different
plugs and catch more fish, but the Coaxer was the winner. The #1 Convertible
Coaxer beat the "Decker" in the "World Championship". 28 bass on the Coaxer
and 16 on the Decker. It also beat James Heddon's "Dowagiac" 29 to 8 at
Congamond Lake in Connecticut. These contests were around 1910-1912 and
were sponsored by "Field & Stream" magazine and The Congress Lake Club of
Canton, Ohio. The plug that did it was the #1 Convertible Coaxer, the version with a double belly hook and a trailing single hook attached to the built-
in single hook. The plug following on the left is one of these. The Convertible Coaxer was designed to run on the surface but not float.

        There was also an underwater Coaxer made of a combination metal and
wound body. It is thinner than the regular Coaxers. It is the plug following

in the center. The Coaxer on the right is the "Teaser" surface bait. It is
essentially two Coaxers in tandem.

 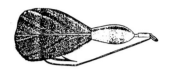 

      Another Coaxer was the tiny Coaxer Trout Fly - it can't sink. These
little plugs were available on #7 or #10 hooks. They are less than 1" long.
By 1912 the Floating Trout Fly came in 24 finishes. All Coaxers are <u>not</u> red
felt on a white body with a red feather or bucktail. Any Jamison pro<u>d</u>uct in
different colors other than red and white are scarce. Coaxers are around.
Bill Jamison apparently made a bunch of them.
      The Coaxer Floating Bass Fly was a little larger than the trout version.
It was made on a 2/0 single hook.
      The #1 Weedless Coaxer is 1-3/4" wood to wood. The #2 is smaller than
the #1 and considered by some to be a better fish catcher especially for bass
and "pickerel". The #2 is 1-1/4" wood to wood (all plugs in this book are
measured in body length, not overall). The #3 Weedless Coaxer is again
smaller than the #1 but larger than the #2. The #3 is 1-3/4" but has a thinner
body than the #1. The #1 and #3 are the same weight for casting with the #3
being recommended for smallmouth bass. All three sizes came in a version
called "Convertible Coaxers". The Convertible Coaxer differed from the standard Weedless Coaxer in that it had a removable set of double hooks on the
belly. This was for a quick change for fish either in pads and weeds or open
water. The added weight of the double hooks makes the Convertible Coaxer
run on the surface but not float. There were advertised versions of the
Convertible with bucktail instead of feather tail and luminous. The largest
and perhaps most difficult Coaxer to find is the musky size. It has a 2-5/8"
body. All musky Coaxers we have observed have had the "Convertible" feature
(a removable two point belly hook).
      There is a poem called <u>The "Coaxer"</u> in a Jamison catalog circa 1912.
The last lines say it all.
               "It can't snag and you won't lose it;
               It's bewitched as sure as fate.
               They'll believe your big fish stories
               If you use the Coaxer Bait."
It was unsigned. Another poem about the Coaxer, in the same catalog, was
signed by B. Bass. We wonder who Mr. B. Bass was?
      The Coaxer was made from at least 1905 to 1928.

      The Nemo speaks for itself. There were two sizes - the Nemo bass bait,
2-1/4" and the Nemo muskie bait, 4-1/4". The bass bait came in all white,
red, yellow, blue, green or any combination. The Nemo was a combination
surface and underwater plug, by moving the position of a round ball weight
hanging on the belly. If you put the weight on the front of the bait, the
plug would come in 15" to 18" under the water. If you stop reeling the Nemo
pops to the top. The Nemo is a classic, weedless plug that was new for the

1911-1912 season. The Nemo bass bait is rather hard to get, but the Nemo musky is worse.

The Nemo musky is a three level plug. Like its little brother it is meant to be a multiple purpose plug. If you keep the weight on the rear it runs on the surface. With the weight removed it runs 15" under the surface and with the weight on the front attachment behind the head it will run 3' to 4' beneath the surface. In all cases it will pop up if forward motion stops. The musky Nemo came in white, red or yellow or mix it up as you wish.

The Nemo was an extremely high quality plug. Both Nemos utilized a Spanish cedar body and nine coats of celluloid enamel. All Jamisons had durable paint finishes. The Nemo was named for Mr. W.J. Jamison himself. People close to him called him just that, "Nemo". He was also referred to in ads as "Smiling Bill Jamison".

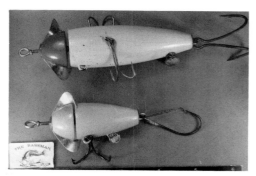

The Mascot Weedless Baits were first offered for sale around 1916. The patent for the Mascot was dated July 10, 1917. This patent covered both versions of the Mascot - the Mascot and the Winged Mascot. Both were very innovative. Two line ties allowed for two actions - on the surface or near surface. The Mascot principle is beloved by many musky and bass fishermen. It would be a heck of a jerk bait! One thing great about most of Mr. Jamison's plugs is that they were meant for the plug caster, not trolling, skittering or something like that. They are honest, durable fish fry plugs. The Weedless Mascot featured the double (2 point) upturned removable belly hooks - a great idea called ice tongs. Slide them off, turn them upside down and the plug is not as weedless anymore. The Weedless Mascot is 4". It came in redhead, or all red, white or yellow. One 5" musky size Mascot has been found.

The Winged Mascots were offered about the same time as the Weedless Mascot (1916). The Winged Mascot had nickle plated fins to allow it to be a dual purpose plug - pop it on the surface or wobble it home. The patent called it "wabbling". The Winged Mascot came in three sizes - the #1 was a 4"er, the #2 a 2-3/4"er and the third type is a big 5" musky size. The Winged Mascot also came in a deluxe version in scale finish with glass eyes. See following photo, left for #2 Deluxe Winged Mascot. The photo on the right is a Musky Winged Mascot on top and two Weedless Mascots below. The weedless part of these plugs refer to the two pronged removable hooks (see Deluxe Mascot photo). Mascots are scarce especially the Musky and Deluxe.

It is possible that the Mascot was made
with a single line-tie on the nose.
This 3-1/2" redhead could be a very
early version.

        The Mascots, both Winged and Weedless, proved successful. W.J. Jamison
offered more plugs based on the principle of the Winged Mascot. The Humdinger
came in 2-3/4" and 3-1/2" sizes. It was initially offered around 1916 in
redhead only - other finishes followed. The two Humdingers on the top of the
photo following are in frogback. The Humdinger featured non-interlocking
hooks. The plug below it followed the Humdinger. The Jamison Struggling
Mouse, 2-1/2", in mouse grey with black eyes. Notice these Jamisons are
"cup" rigged. The Struggling Mouse also came in frogback, crab and redhead.
The Humdingers seem to be scarcer than the Struggling Mouse.
        Another Mascot type Jamison that is quite hard to find is the Chicago
Wobbler. This 4-1/4"er came in all white, all red and, of course, redhead.
The Chicago Wobbler is the plug on the right, following.

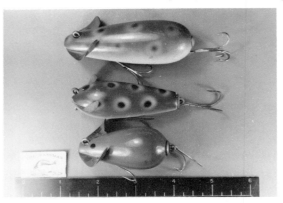

        There are two more bass plugs that deserve attention. We have never
encountered either plug. The plug in the drawing on the left is the Jamison
2-3/4" Surface Wiggler. It is suspected that this is the plug in a September
16, 1919 patent which describes a "float" with hooks. The plug on the right
is Bill's Bass Getter. It has only one line tie on top of its head and is
designed to run 9" to 12" under the water. It was advertised in 1928 and
offered in redhead, rainbow, silver, perch, white, red or yellow. Bill's
Bass Getter features Jamison patented barbless hooks. These were a great
idea for "catch and release".

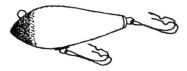

        W.J. Jamison made three fly rod size plugs other than the Coaxers.
The first is the fly rod Wiggler which came in two sizes - 1-3/4" and 2-1/8".
In 1928 the standard colors were offered along with redside minnow, golden
shiner and yellow perch. Fly rod Wigglers aren't easy to find but they are
around. They had decal eyes.

The Mascot apparently came in fly rod size. One example has been noted. This is one to look for - it's a tiny version of the Winged Mascot.

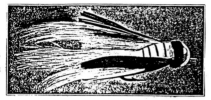

The Jamison Floating Bass Bugs came in twelve patterns. Some had great names - the Dr. Henshall, Zane Grey, Wilder's Fancy, Dilg's Gem, to name a few.

The Jamison Wig Wag is a jointed plug that came in two sizes - the 4-1/2" bass and the 6" musky. They came in redhead, black head/silver body, and yellow head and body with brown back.

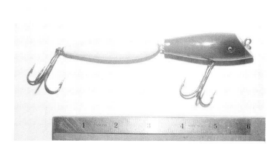
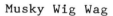

Musky Wig Wag

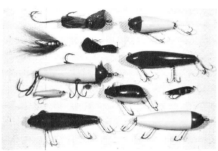

Miscellaneous Jamison

We want to thank Jim Bourdon for sharing information supplied to him by Mr. William Jamison's daughter Ethel Holmes. Also thanks to Cliff Netherton for information in his excellent books on tournament casting (see Bibliography for details).

The Snyder Spinner/Success Spinner/Mills' Yellow Kid

The Snyder Spinner had several names. William Mills called it the "Yellow Kid" and it was also called the Success Spinner. The Snyder was made of hollow copper. It is an airtight floating bait. The Snyder came in one size - 3", and six colors - yellow with gold spots being the most popular. It also came in redhead, green with gold spots, brown with gold spots, white with gold spots and yellow body with redhead. There are both two and three hookers. The 2-hookers are more difficult to find. Typical Snyders are in following photo on left. Many of these plugs have a copper tube going through the side to hold the wired through side hooks. There is some opinion that these are Shakespeares. We do not agree with this. We think they are Snyders. The other hook hanger is a wire soldered in for the hooks. There is probably more to this than reported here. As these show up in their original boxes more might be learned. The plug on the right looks like a Snyder but is embossed in a scalelike pattern. Very fancy. This is a "Who Dunnit". Snyders were catalogued and sold from 1904 to as recently as 1919. They are a good plug to own but not very difficult to find.

The "Decker" by Anson B. Decker
_____

  The Decker bait is as famous as any old plug. The Decker Surface
Water Bass Bait came in various sizes - 2-1/2", 2-3/4", 3-1/4" and 3-1/2"
have been reported or advertised. The 3-1/2"er is the easiest one to find.
There seem to be fewer 2-1/2" Baby Deckers around than any of the other
sizes. It was advertised as late as the early 1930s. Any Decker is hard to
find in excellent condition. They were fished hard and didn't have a very
durable paint job. They caught fish - especially bass. In 1911 the Decker
took both 1st and 4th prize in the "Field & Stream" contest. One of these
fish was caught right in Mr. Decker's hometown lake - Lake Hopatcong, New
Jersey (the same name as his hometown).

  Ans Decker used the Lake Hopatcong, New Jersey address until sometime
after 1911 when he used a Brooklyn, New York address.

  In 1911 Ans B. Decker advertised that he had probably spent more hours
fishing than any of his competitors. He reported he had been active for
35 years - since 1876! It is suspected that he had made and fished with his
early Deckers by the turn of the century.

  Deckers came in several colors, but white and all yellow seem to have
been the most popular. Other colors offered include all red, redhead, yellow,
mottled grey (mouse), and blue and green blend. The props on the Deckers
were made of aluminum and generally stamped with the name. We were unable
to find a patent granted to Mr. Decker. The Deckers in photos following
on left, all have the name on the prop. The Deckers on the right differ
as follows: the one on the left is a standard 3-1/2"er, the center Decker
has a slightly different prop which is straight on the edge where most are
turned up and it is also marked, the plug on the right has all the characteristics of a real Decker except it is unmarked. Many Deckers seem to have
cup rigged type hook hangers.

  There are two other Decker plugs. The Decker underwater, 3-1/4"
left and the Decker Troller, 3-3/4" right. The Troller has a feature that
allows the body part to slide up the line upon strike. We have never seen
a Decker Troller and do not know what they were made of. The Troller was
offered in colored back and white belly. The Troller looks very Devonlike.

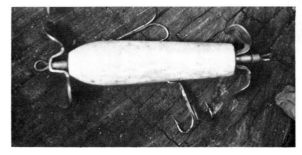 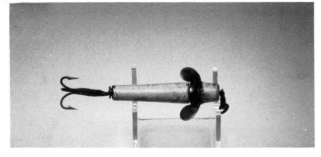

Bob Bulkley Photo and Collection

Ans B. Decker was always anxious to challenge his plug against any competitors (especially W.J. Jamison) for money in bass catching contests. Mr. Jamison's Coaxer seems to have usually won.
Thanks to Clyde Harbin and Jim Bourdon.

Decker Types

There are many Decker look alikes. Mr. Decker always warned of duplicates. Some of these are interesting as well as confusing. A round nose version of both the surface and underwater Decker were advertised as early as 1905 by Mr. Jacob Mick of Patterson, New Jersey. This is very early. These were offered in the 3-hook "Jersey" rig. New Jersey laws only allowed for 3 points on a plug - 3 singles, one treble or a double and a single. Note that these seem to be wired through, not cup rigged. Most of the plug makers made special versions for New Jersey. The plug in the following photo on the left is believed to be one of Mr. Mick's top water baits. Another early Decker type plug was offered as the Cummings Top Water Bait, manufactured by George Cummings, Dover, New Jersey. Another Jersey rigged plug. This one has thin cups (following photo, right)

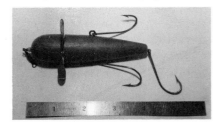

The plugs below are unknown. They both look extremely old. It would be very interesting to know their history!

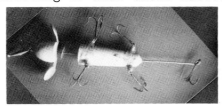

The Decker types in following photos are unknown as to maker, when, etc. The interesting thing about the plugs on the right is the keel. Perhaps these are closer to Henkenius/Kane plug patented 1900. The plug on the right looks like it was made of cork.

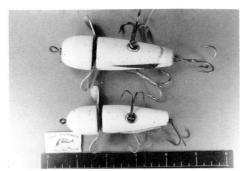

There are many "Decker" type plug. They are easily confused with the
Decker. Some were possibly earlier (see page 62 for the Henkenius/Kane plug
for the first patent on this plug as an example). The future will bring
forth such names as the Portage Reflex (Pflueger), Shakespeare's Floating
Spinner and the famous Pflueger Globe (see Pflueger and Shakespeare chapters
for more about these).

There are also more "Decker" types that are unknown as to maker. Some
might have been made by Mr. Decker for a distributor or other maker who used
his own name. We do not know who made the Manhattan Top Water Bait, the
Top Water Casting Bait (Abbey & Imbrie's name (a New York retail plug and
other fishing tackle dealer). Another version was distributed by William
Mills & Son called the "Jersey Queen". It would be nice to say these plugs
were made by Mr. Decker for these dealers. However, in the 1919 Abbey &
Imbrie catalog two separate plugs are listed - the "Top Water" and the
Decker. The "Top Water" baits appear to have a more rounded nose than the
true Deckers. Nevertheless, it is still very possible Mr. Decker, himself,
supplied these plugs. It could also be they were made by someone else. More
information is needed here.
Thanks to Marc Wisotsky and Clyde Harbin.

The Eclipse Wooden Minnow

The Eclipse is a little known underwater made by the William Stuart
& Company, Canton, Ohio. It was advertised in a national magazine as early
as 1905. It is a fine and rare minnow. The Eclipse has aluminum cups and
came in a 3-hook and 5-hook version. It came in white, green, red and yellow.
The colors are blended to a light colored belly. The Eclipse sported three
hand painted gill marks. It came in a wood (pencil type) box.

The Wiggle Tail Bait

By the LaGrange Bait Company, LaGrange, Indiana

J.D. Sherbrook Artificial Bait

Patented September 5, 1905, this mechanical wonder is another "Wagtail"
plug. There are two categories of plugs that were represented time and time

again in patents but few show up. First, are the "Wagtails", and second, the
internal hook weedless jobs. If this plug actually looks like the patent, it
appears to have hooks that were exceedingly small. Also what would you do
if you lost the key or the spring broke on the motor. Would the props stop
spinning? Mr. Sherbrook was from Beulah, Michigan. The body material is
unknown.

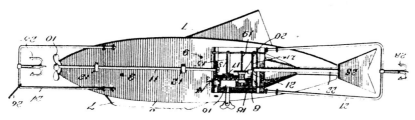

The Manitou Minnow

The Manitou Minnow was named for Manitou Lake in Indiana. It was
patented by Simon K. Bailey and George A. Elliot, both of nearby Rochester,
Indiana. The Manitou has a take down body. It came with a little wrench to
take it apart. Three color variations have been noted on this wonderful
3-3/4" 5-hooker - maroon and white, dark green and white, and light green and
white. The rarest ones are the light green and maroon. The Manitou Minnow has
showed up in numbers beyond expectation, although the quantity was not that
great. This is lucky for the collectors who have one in their case. The ones
that did show up were generally new in the original box with instructions and,
of course, the brass wrench. If you have a chance to pick up a Manitou, do it.
There are a lot more collectors than existing Manitous. There is a small chance
that some were not marketed. The patent, which incidentally looks just like
the plug for a change, might have been an infringement of Fred Rhodes' 1904
patent.

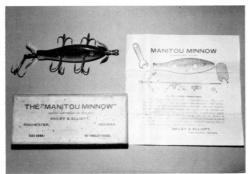

Irwin F. Kepler's Artificial Bait

Another weedless. The Kepler plug is possibly made of wood on the outside and has a mechanism, but it is more likely it was made with a metal body.
There is a nut on the side to adjust the gear. Ever see one of these?

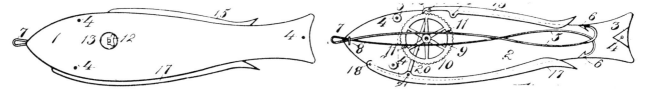

A. F. Bingenheimer - The Nemahbin Minnows

A.F. Bingenheimer is believed to have done business from around late
1905 until around the late teens. It could be both earlier and later dates

are appropriate - we simply can't prove it. It is possible the plugs were
in the early days only. Weedless hooks were usually featured on Bing plugs.
There either were some of Bing's plug that have non-weedless hooks or hooks
have been changed and weed guards broken off. These could have been changed
later. Mr. Bingenheimer was known for his elaborate weedless hooks. Major
companies, such as South Bend, offered plugs featuring the Bing's Weedless
Trebles.

An ad for the 1906 Weedless Nemahbin
Minnow resembles this plug, especially
if you added weedless trebles and put
the prop on the rear instead of the
nose.

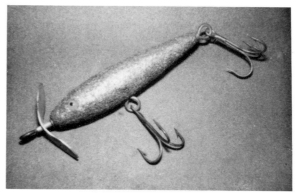

     The Bing's Weedless Nemahbin Minnow came in two other versions. The
first and more classic A.F. Bingenheimer plug has three single hooks attached
to the teardrop shaped body. The weedless wires clip under the 3-hook points.
This version came in gold, silver and metallic. The plugs to the left represent a non-weedless and standard weedless versions. The plug to the right
is metalized.

     Lake Nemahbin is a weedy but bassy lake in southern Wisconsin not too
far from Milwaukee.
     The most seen (all Bings are rare) version of the Weedless Nemahbin
Minnow has a hanging belly and tail hook. This plug is constructed in a
similar fashion to the 1905 William Shakespeare, Jr. minnows based on
Fred Rhodes 1904 patent. There is some thought that there was a connection
between the two companies. The Nemahbin on the left is in the earlier type
paint job. The one of the right is spray painted and is very similar to a
Shakespeare. There is a possibility of another Bing that is a Shakespeare-
like minnow smaller than the Bings to follow. These have notched props
similar to Shakespeare. In fact, the props throughout the Bing line are
reminiscent of Shakespeare.

The Ackerman Minnow

Patented January 16, 1906, the Ackerman is among the most elaborate and hard to find minnows. To our knowledge, very few have surfaced. There are less than four and all of them are 5-hookers. The patent is rather elaborate and long. It shows a 3-hooker and a 5-hooker made two different ways on the same theme. The wood is split horizontally and there is a metal wire sandwiched between that hold the hooks on. The two pieces are marine glued over the metal. There are caps fore and aft that clamp the plug together. The eyes are small pins through tiny clear glass beads with a circular black sheet behind it. The effect is good. We know of a redhead and a black with silver spots versions. The plug in the X-ray following has the wired inside feature. There is another version in the patent with a sheet of stamped out metal in the center instead of wires.

Jasper Leander Ackerman was from Monticello, Indiana, which was also home of the Hardy Minnow. We suspect these two men were acquainted.

Please note the length of the bolt that connects the rear hook to the front end of The Ackerman Underwater Minnow. There is a threaded tube up there. The Ackerman is 3-1/2" long, wood to wood. The bolt is at least 4" long from the clip on the rear hook to the thread.

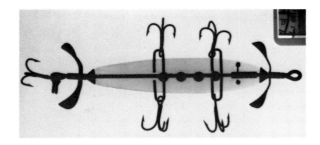

Edward L. Lull's Artificial Bait

Edward L. Lull of Elkhorn, Wisconsin invented a frog plug that had sort of a strange hook attachment where the hooks connect on the back of the belly. The idea is when a fish hits, the legs squeeze together and the hooks fly out. The patent mentions the fish swallowing the plug. It also mentions rubber legs.
Patented July 3, 1906.

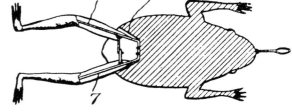

The Manistee Minnow

It is not known to us who, where or when on the Manistee. It is probably from Michigan. There is a Manistee River in the lower part of Michigan. The floater (top) is marked "The Manistee" on the side. We

suspect the plug underneath it is the 3-hook underwater version. This one
looks like it was found on the bottom of a lake or river. It had eyes
(they are long gone). The Manistee is rare and desirable. It would be
great to know more about it.

The Manistee Floater (top plug) is
3-1/2". The Manistee Underwater?
(bottom plug) is 2-3/4".

E. and B.D. Barnes

        This 1906 patent plug is 3-1/2" long and
appears to be made of wood. The one in the
photo is the only one we know of.

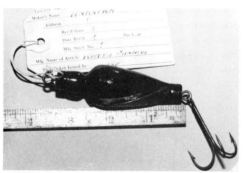

The Bonafide Aluminum Minnow

The two-piece Bonafide Aluminum
Minnow is a joy to behold. It
was patented January 15, 1907
by Hiram H. Passage of Plymouth,
Michigan who assigned half of it
to George E. VanDeCar of the
same town. The Bonafide is desirable and rare - a nice combination.

The Bowersox Minnow

        The Bowersox is a very important plug. It is the earliest patent
that incorporates features that relate strictly to a floating diving wood
plug with a metal lip. In this case two lips, one in back of the eyes and
the other about three-quarters of the way back. The design is typical
minnow type. The difference is that this one floats and dives and wiggles.

The Bowersox is very well made and a very hard one to find. It came in a
3-hook and 4-hook version. The three hooker follows. The four hooker has
two side hooks in front and one on the belly. The big one is around 4" and
the small 3". These measurements could be off but should be close. The
one we have seen was brown and yellow blended. We know of one of each in
existence. Patent dated February 5, 1907.

B.F. Burke's Rubber Plugs

Benjamin F. Burke of Chicago, Illinois assigned one half of his
April 9, 1907 patent to Matthew Corbett also of Chicago.
Burke's baits were made out of molded hollow rubber. They were designed to sink or float at will depending on how much water you let in. The
principle is the same as on Julio Buel's 1852 patent (see pages 41-43) only
the Burke plugs were made of rubber. The plug in the patent looks very much
like the one in the following (left) photo. It is a chubby 2"er. The plug
on the right is thought to be Burke's Bug Bait. There is another Burke
called Burke's Bass Bait #4 that is a floating-diver. See drawing. If this
one was made any time around the date of the patent it makes it a very early
Floater-Diver. Burke's Baits were around for quite a few years. These
appear to be the old ones. All Burke Baits are rather scarce, nice and
often overlooked.

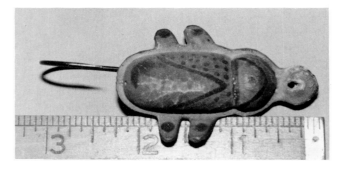

B.F. Burke also invented a weedless
rubber plug. The February 23, 1909
patented plug would be a nice one to
find.

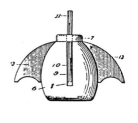

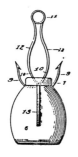

The "Ideal" Minnow

The "Ideal" Minnow is one of the true greats in plugdom. It is also quite a puzzle. There are basically two patents for the "Ideal" - two very close patents which were months apart. The first patent was issued to Edward C. Adams of Morristown, New Jersey on April 9, 1907 and the second patent was granted to William E. Davis of the same town on November 12, 1907. The patent drawings were almost identical the difference being that the Davis patent not only had removable hooks but hooks that did not become entangled with the beautiful, but almost excessive hardware. This was accomplished by Mr. Davis who added a "web flange - C'" (see patent drawing following) to keep the tail hook off the spinners. The Ideal was offered for sale by William E. Davis in 1908. It came in green back/white belly and has been reported in red body/white belly. The "Ideal" is 3-1/2". It is rare and choice.

There is some confusion between the "Ideal" and a plug advertised as the "Jersey Expert" in 1907. It is speculative, but possible, the "Jersey Expert" represents the earlier patent by Edward C. Adams. The "Ideal" as advertised had red lined fins (red one side). Another feature of the Davis patent is the ability of the plug to stay upright in the water. Both patents covered the removable hook features which worked on a spring device. The 1908 ad offers extra trebles - plug and hooks for $1.00. In 1909 the same "Ideal" was offered by Mr. Davis without extra hooks for 50¢. This seems quite reasonable for such a fine plug. The Davis "Ideal" is obviously and improvement over Mr. Adams' patent.

   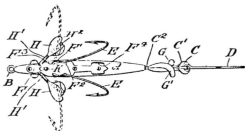

It is also possible that the Jersey Expert was named that because it complied with the 3 hook point New Jersey hook law.

The K & K Animated Minnow

"The Minnow that swims" came in various sizes and color configurations. The K&K also was available as a light surface bait for casting (built to swim about 4" under the surface) and a sinking bait for trolling. The #1 is a sinking 4-1/2"er available in golden shiner, silver shiner and black and silver. The #2 is a 3-1/2" sinker available in the same colors as #1 but offered in white and rainbow also. The #3 is a "light surface" 4-1/2" plug available in the same colors as #2. The #4 is the Wriggler, a solid, not jointed, K&K sinker, 4-1/2" long, available in black/silver, black/red and golden shiner. This is one that has not turned up in anny collection that we have heard of. The #5 is the small sinker (3") popularly called the "Minnoette" and made in all colors except white. #6 is the same size as #5 but is the light surface bait and offered in golden shiner, black/silver and all red. The #7 is a 3-1/2" light surface bait (same size as #2) and the same colors as #6. The #8 is a solid little beauty available in all white (for night fishing) and rainbow. There are very few examples known of the "Ghost". #9 is the musky K&K. This 5-1/2"er might be the toughest K&K of all. To the best of our knowledge none have turned up. The musky size came in the surface (fat) version only and made in gold and silver shiner finishes only.

The K&K Animated Minnow which sold out of Akron, Ohio, is believed to have been patented by John D. Kreisser of Cincinnati, Ohio on June 25, 1907. The K&Ks in the photo on the left (following) are, starting at the top, - #3 ("surface") in golden shiner, bottom plug is probably a #2 sinker in what is left of a rainbow finish. The hooks are replaced on this plug. Most K&Ks had removable double hooks similar to Jamison hooks. All K&Ks had lead molded into the nose. The hooks clip into a triangular metal insert under the chin and a wire peg on the sides. The plug on the right is the "Ghost".

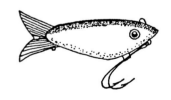

All K&Ks are hard to find and considered classic old minnows. They are expecially difficult to find in excellent condition. The paint jobs did not hold up. It was indeed such a problem that they sent some to James Heddon of Dowagiac, Michigan to paint for them. The two K&Ks in the Heddon box in the following photo are painted in Heddon's standard and popular rainbow and green crackleback finishes.

The K&K Wriggler

The original artist's conception of a K&K sure looks like a real minnow. How would you like to find one that looked like this!

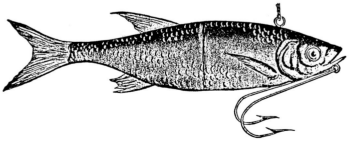

The Wilcox Wiggler and Redhead Floater
───────────────────────────────────

     The Wilcox Wiggler came in four versions that we know of. Two sepa-
rate patents covered the interesting features. The first patent covers the
first version. The patent was granted to Charles M. Wilcox of New Paris,
Ohio. One third was assigned to James Kirkpatrick of Anderson, Indiana and
another third to Charles Kirkpatrick of New Paris, Ohio.

     When a collector first encounters a Wilcox Wiggler he is astounded
by the construction and grace of the plug. Most collectors find the plug
puzzling. How is it put together? The Wiggler is indeed a thought provoking
plug.

     The 1907 patent is the type I Wilcox Wiggler. Once again, to our
knowledge, this version has not as yet been found. The construction is
complex. The articulated wood head on all Wigglers slips over a screw eye
that is interlocked with the rear two-thirds of the plug. The prop and
shaft slip over the rod and a loop is bent on the nose for the line-tie.
The side hooks are attached to an internal three-way threaded device. See
the patent drawing, following. Please let us know if you have a type I.
Get an X-ray if you can.

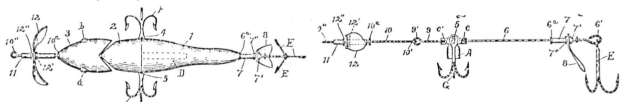

     The type II Wilcox (Patent date May 25, 1909) is an improvement of
type I. The construction is still very complex and difficult to figure out.
Probably the basic difference was what was a probable inherent weakness in
the 1907 (type I) patent. This was corrected by running the wire through to
a double threaded tube in front of the hook rig that was imbedded in behind
the place the gills would be if this was a real minnow.

     The type II seems to be the version most often found by collectors.
All Wilcoxes are rare+. They are one of the best and hardest to find miscellaneous plugs. The finishes on type II are another curiosity. The plug
has smooth ridges that are very realistically painted in blends of green,
grey, red and brown. The finish is so remarkable that it looks extremely
lifelike. The brown version almost looks like later frogskin plugs. The
Wilcox Wiggler is a truly unique plug. The side hooks on type II are connected to a wire that runs across the outside surface (see X-ray following).
Possibly the most rewarding feature of the Wilcox is the use of what the
patent calls a "single bladed spinner", or as plug collectors refer to it,
a single bladed prop. The erratic off-center action of the large (in comparison to the smaller front prop) prop makes the plug wiggle. It throws
off the horizontal balance. Combine this with a moving head and you really
have a plug. There is no doubt, the Wiggler would catch fish. We are
chicken to try it out. The glass eyes are of taxidermy quality - clear
opaque yellow with black centers. All Wilcox Wigglers are 3-1/2". The
May 25, 1909 Wilcox patent was totally assigned to The Wiggler Manufacturing
Comapny of Elwood, Indiana - an Indiana corporation.

     James Kirkpatrick, who was assigned one-third of the original 1907
patent was from Anderson, Indiana which is a fairly large town near Elwood,
Indiana. It is quite possible that some, if not most, Wilcox Wigglers were
made in Elwood, Indiana.

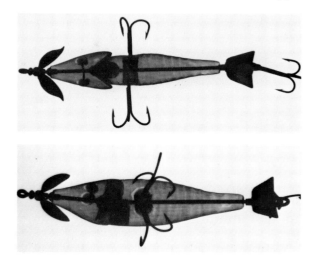

The type III Wiggler is either a less expensive model or a highly simplified version of the type I and II. The type III is still a high quality plug with most of the features of type II. The differences are two-fold. The paint job is two-tone on a smooth wood body and secondly the single hooks are open screw eye cup rigged as covered by the Heddon "Slope nose" patent of 1902. The cups are made of aluminum.

The type IV Wilcox Wiggler is like the type II except it appears to have plated brass cups as opposed to the aluminum cups of type III.

The Wilcox "Redhead Floater" is a 2-7/8" surface popping type plug. It is a 4-hooker (12 points). The rig is identical to the side rig on the type III Wilcox. These seem to be quite rare, but it is a possiblity that people weren't aware of what they were. There may be more surfacing.

The top plug is a type II, center plug is type III and the bottom is the Wilcox "Redhead Floater".

This great old 4-3/4", 5 hook underwater minnow (left, following) would wiggle on the front and spin, as usual, on the rear. The hook rigs (aluminum cups, removable hooks) are similar to the rig on the Redhead Floater and type III Wiggler. The paint job is similar but not exactly like plugs attributed to Myers and Spellman, Shelby, Michigan. There could be a connection. The front offset "spinner" idea shows up in another mystery plug that will be discussed in the following section on the Michigan Life-

like Minnow.   The plug on the right is incomplete but has a similar paint
job and other features.   It is a total guess but we think both plugs might
belong here.

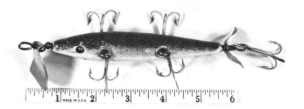

The Michigan Lifelike Minnow

The Michigan Lifelike was patented by Mr. Jacob Hansen of Muskegon,
Michigan. It was distributed by Mr. Adolph Arntz, a retail sporting goods
dealer from the same town. It is a patent for an articulated underwater
minnow that has a typical prop on the front end and an off centered three
blade spinner (prop) on the rear. The action is essentially the same as
the Wilcox Wiggler except the Lifelike is articulated - three joints on
the mid-rear end. A flat piece of spring steel is the trick here. The
hook hangers vary - generally they are like those on the plug on the left.
There is a known variation of this hook hanger theme where the slot the
hook fits in is straighter. It is similar but not the same. The other
hanger which is found on the 3-hook Lifelike is like the one on the 3-3/4"
5-hook underwater minnow on the right. It is a cap screwed in over a wire
insert that holds the hooks. These caps and the hooks are often missing on
this particular type hanger. It is fragile if the caps come off the hooks.
This plug is similar to the last 5-hooker above under Wilcox. The front
"spinners" are nearly the same.

The Michigan Lifelike 5-hooker is 3-3/4" and the 3-hooker is 2-3/4".
Nine colors were offered, the most frequent of which is a choice of light
or dark green speckled back/white belly. The others include natural wood,
aluminum (aluminum combinations) and brook trout! Wouldn't an excellent
Michigan Lifelike in brook trout finish be a neat plug?

Any variation of the production Michigan Lifelike is scarce to rare,
especially with all the paint still intact, the three hooker is even more
so. They came in cardboard boxes.

The all white underwater minnow on the right may or may not be a
Michigan Lifelike product. There is a consensus among collectors that it
is. This plug is quite scarce if not rare. There is one small 3-hook
version known.

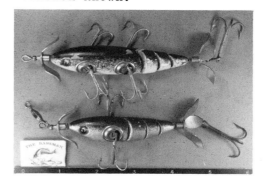

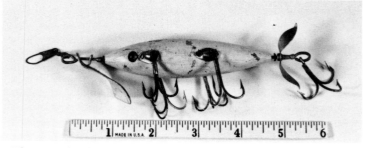

The Muskegon Spoon Jack Minnow

E.D. Myers - Shelby, Michigan

        The only patent we can find attributed to Mr. Myers of Shelby, Mich-
igan that pictures a plug does not, at first glance, resemble the plugs
generally attributed to Mr. Myers. The patent itself is quite interesting.
It is wired through end to end. At a point in approximately the center the
wire takes a hard right and becomes the hook hanger, then comes back up the
same way and goes on to the line tie. The patent picture is symmetrical
except there is a line tie on one end and a treble hook on the other. The
body was probably made of wood although according to the patent, it could
have been made of metal or "other material". The patent plug was designed
to spin in opposite directions at the same time. Quite a plug! This particular patent was granted to Edward Myers on May 18, 1915. This is ahead
of the chronology in this book. It is the author's opinion that the industry in or around Shelby, Michigan started long before 1915. How far back
isn't known. It would be nice to clear this matter up. We will do our
best to try and start.

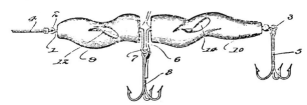

        It is obvious Mr. Myers knew how to bend wire. This is the major
clue in the patent that could link it to what collectors have been calling
Myers, Keller or Myers & Spellman. The plugs have been reported marked,
"Myers" or "Keller" on the top. These are generally surface minnows that
are side hooked 3-hookers. The plugs marked "Keller" were wired through
side by side and end to end. The one following (left) is a redhead and has
a reinforcing wire that wraps around the plug. It is not known if this is
original. The plugs marked Keller have been reported in redhead and blended
green. One other feature they have in common is a knob on the nose. The
plug on the right is the one generally considered to be the typical Myers
plug. The paint job is unique. It is hand brushed bluish-green back over
a white body. There is a single red gill mark.

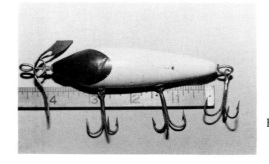

Hansen's "Pull-
Me-Slow"

        The plug on the left (following) is one of the few plugs printed
twice in this book. We feel this particular plug warrants this position.
It is not necessarily a Myers, Keller or Myers & Spellman. Nevertheless,
it could be all three or more. Please take a look at the hand paint job on
this plug in the color section of this book. The props are all similar on

these plugs. They seem to go through an evolution starting with this colorful plug. This particular plug has two features worth noting. First, the
"knob" on the nose is hollow metal, and second, the belly hooks are attached
in a manner similar to what we sill see later in Reynolds plugs and much
later in Hildebrandt and Clark (Indiana) plugs. There are many reasons to
group certain plugs together. The name Myers & Spellman seems to be a sort
of "catchall" for old unknown "Who Dunnit" plugs that have certain things in
common. More needs to be known here. Perhaps one of these will show up in
an original box with instructions.

     Another plug attributed to Myers is a redhead surface plug (see right
hand photo, following). The cup hook and prop are bothersome. Why Myers?

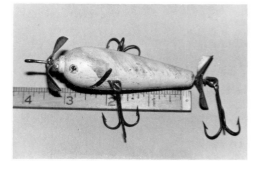

     Shelby, Michigan is a short, halfway between Muskegon (Michgan Life-
like) and Manistee (Manistee River, Manistee Minnow?) and very near the
eastern coast of Lake Michigan in the central lower part of Michigan.

     A not so final finish to the potential plugs of Mr. Edward D. Myers
of Shelby, Michigan is that they are over and above all still a mystery.
There is probably a connection between all the plug makers of this area over
a period of time.

Thanks to Ray Carver, Walt Blue, Clarence Zahn and Clyde Harbin on this still
puzzling puzzle.

Michigan "Who Dunnits"

     Before we leave this area in Michigan, let's take a look at the two
plugs following. They might not be from Michigan but something in them says
they were possibly around the same time as the Manistee (left plug), the
Michigan Lifelike and the early "Myers" plugs.

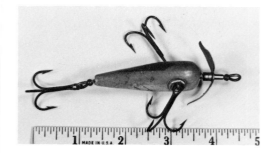

The Henzel Booster

     John G. Henzel's "Booster" is made of a muslin type material. The
object of this plug is to put food inside the bag and go fishing. The foods
recommended in the patent are "flour, rice, potato, egg and other food stuff".

Baking is recommended so it stays in the bag. The patent shows a frog. The plug itself does indeed resemble a baked potato rather than a frog. Most "Boosters" are probably long gone. They would deteriorate with time. John Henzel was from Chicago, Illinois and the patent is dated November 26, 1907.

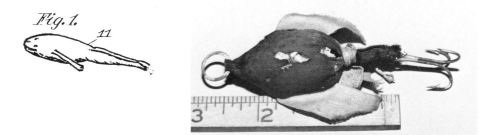

J.L. Clark's Expert - Rockford, Illinois

Sometime around 1907 the J.L. Clark Manufacturing Co. of Rockford, Illinois started to merchandise underwater Experts. The Clark Experts followed the original Woods Experts. It is not known if Mr. Clark purchased Mr. Woods' two hook patents and business or arranged for their use. The Clark Experts were followed around 1913-1914 by the more famous Fred Keeling Experts. Mr. Keeling lived in Rockford at this time.

Clark Experts are considered by collectors to be the most beautiful "true" Experts (Shaffer/Woods, Clark and Keeling). It is important to remember that the early Clark Experts might easily look like late Woods Experts. It is known that early Keeling Experts were virtually the same as Clarks. There is a collectors' consensus that Clark Experts all have four long sweeping gill marks. This seems to be generally true. However, Experts in Keeling boxes have also shown up with four gill marks. These can be safely called the Clark type Experts. See the color section for a wonderful example of Mr. Clark's round 5-hooker complete with type II Woods hooks. (See Woods page 75).

The J.L. Clark Manufacturing Co. has been in business from 1905 until now. There is a small display at the J.L. Clark Co. offices of Mr. Clark's diversified products through the years, including an Expert.

John L. Clark was born in 1845 in Burlington, Vermont. He moved to Rockford when he was 12. He served for almost two years in the Navy during the war (Civil!) He saw action in Mobile, Alabama under the command of Admiral Farragut. It appears Mr. Clark was in his 60s when he started manufacturing Experts. All "true" Experts came in maroon cardboard boxes. They are exquisite and like all true Experts difficult to find. Please refer to the Fred Keeling section (1913) for the continuing Expert story.

The Clark Experts came in the same genral size range as the Woods and Keelings. They seem to be flatter but some Keelings were also made this way. The 2-1/2" on the left is silver with red gills. Look close - it says "Expert" on the side. The plug on the right is white with red (gills), 5" musky Expert.   Henry Taylor is the man to thank for this information.

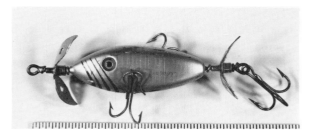

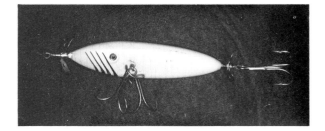

C.D. Caldwell Plug

      The Caldwell plug is one of the earliest Texas plugs. It was patented June 16, 1908. The patent copy is unreadable so we don't know what this plug was made of. It would be a shock if one of these was even ever made.

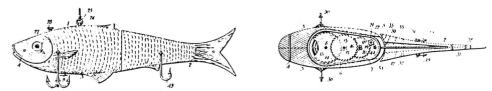

The Klein Plug

      Henry David Klein of Butternut, Wisconsin invented a plug that had the amusing feature of interchanging a wood body with a minnow. Ever see the Klein plug? It's possible you might just find the hardware. The wood body is removable. Patent dated March 10, 1908

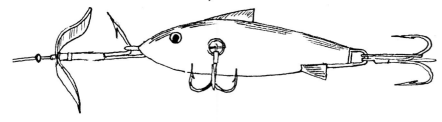

The J.B. Fischer Plug

      Another internal hook weedless plug. This one has two opposable single spring hooks - one goes backwards. It was patented December 15, 1908. This is all we know about the J.F. Fischer plug.

The Moonlight Bait Company - Paw Paw, Michigan

      The Moonlight Bait Company of Paw Paw, Michigan was formed on Christmas Eve, 1908. It was a co-partnership between Messrs. H. Emery Ball and Charles E. Varney, both of Paw Paw, Michigan, to be known as the "Moonlight Bait Co." The concept of the Moonlight Bait came before this time. Mr. H. Emery Ball had been designing, carving, painting, perfecting and giving to his buddies, a plug that really held the secret on how to catch fish at night. The Moonlight Bait Company will be covered in detail in a chapter devoted to Mr. Ball and his important products.

The Haynes Magnet

      There is no patent but there is a plug, circa 1908-1909. The black and white photo would be red and white in color. This plug is from Ohio. An early "Peckerhead".

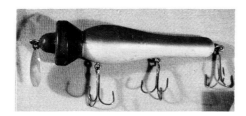

G.H. Slocum and Henry J. Hokamp Artificial Bait

This Chicago Based plug was patented November 10, 1908. It appears to be a metal sheet surrounding a body that could be wood. The wood part seems to be screwed in through the metal rim. This is a wierd one. The hook is also the line attachment?? That's a new twist. Maybe we can tell more when someone finds one.

Edward J. and Evelyn M. Lockhart

Here we are back in Michigan. The Lockharts were from Galesburg which is a town right smack in the middle of the plug industry. If you drove 35 miles from Galesburg you could be in Kalamazoo, Coldwater, Hastings or Paw Paw. A little further and you would be in Dowagiac.

The Lockhart plugs are very important and collectable. There are still some around, but as usual certain models seem to be harder to find than others. E.J. Lockhart's June 1, 1909 patent is for a plug that in 1912 was known as Lockhart's "Wooden Plug". "I love my live minnow - but oh! YOU WAGTAIL" was in an ad showing a 3-hooker which was later referred to as the Wagtail Witch. The size on these varies from 4" to 5", 4-1/2" being the norm. There is a 2-hook, 3-1/2" version of this plug originally called the "Water Witch" and later the "Wagtail Witch". The earlier Lockharts had simple screw eye hook hangers. This was replaced by a removable hook rig patented on November 21, 1911. The rig was such that all you needed was "you and your jackknife". It was sort of an "L" rig similar but not the same as the later Heddon "L" rig.

The principle features of the 1909 patent covered an all wood plug that would float when at rest, dive and wiggle and/or "waggle" upon retrieve. A large hole under the throat of the plug directed in a flow of water through a tapering hole that exited out the back near the rear, generally about 3/4 way down the back. Although this principle had been seen once before (Jay Rhodes), it had not been patented. It was later copied and altered by many manufacturers. We have here one of the very first true floating-divers.

Lockhart made a smaller plug based on this principle. It was variously known as the "Little Devil" and the "Pollywog".

The plug top left (following) is an old "Lockhart's Wood Plug". The one on the bottom a later 3-hook Wagtail Witch. Both of the Lockharts on the right are different in some way from known examples. The top plug is a 3"er, too big for a Pollywog (Little Devil) and too small for the 2-hook Water Witch. The plug on the bottom is a Jersey rig (3 hook point) version of the Pollywog. This is not to be confused with the Jersey Skeeter which will be discussed later. This rare plug probably has a name of its own.

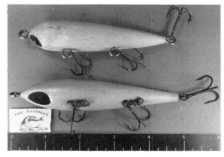

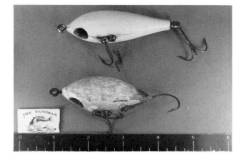

The 1911 patent also had an unusual feature. Instead of water flow-
ing through a single hole, water flowed through two holes on the side. These
"holes" were actually diagonal grooves in the surface of the plug covered with
a metal plate. As far as we know there has never been one found exactly like
the patent version.

The production version of the grooved plugs were the 4-1/2" Wobbler
Wizzard, also called the Wobbler Special (following, left) and a chubby 2-1/2"
Jersey rigged version called the Jersey Skeeter. Both grooved and holed Lockharts came in all white, all red, redhead and all yellow. The grooves and
holes were painted in contrasting colors, for example red hole/white body.

The Lockharts were still in business as recently as 1914 when they
received another patent. There was a third and different floating-diver
system. This one had a tapered metal tube under the throat instead of a hole
or groove. It also had a clever weedless attachment. We hope this plug
exists (left, following). This group of plugs in the following right photo
are all thought to be Lockharts. They came in the same tackle box as Lockharts, so to speak. Some are quite unique and experimental in nature. The
thin plugs in the vertical center have an addition to the regular Lockhart
"L" hook rig. These particular ones have wire staples on each side of the
hanger to keep the hooks from digging into the paint.
Thanks to Walt Blue and Clyde Harbin.

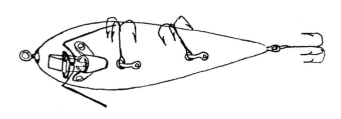 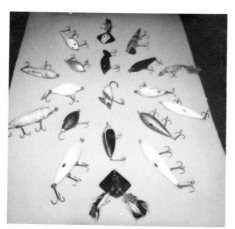

Three Lockhart plugs on the Jersey Skeeter
principle are the longer, probably 3",
Jersey rigged Water Wasp #1 (top), the
same plug but with a weedless attachment
(probably similar to the 1914 patent)
and the Water Wizzard (bottom) which is
similar to the Wobbler Wizzard except the
outside grooves start further back behind
the throat and it is around 4" long.

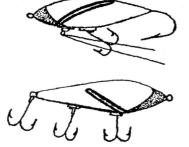

The Chautauqua

      The Chautauqua was distributed by John August Anderson of Jamestown, New York, a town on the southeast end of the beautiful Lake Chautauqua. The August 31, 1909 patent filed under the names Alfred Krantz and Gustaf Smith both of Jamestown was assigned half to Mr. Smith and half to Mr. Anderson who made and/or distributed it. The Chautauqua is a weedless plug. The spring wire hooks reverse into the body. Setting the hook releases these hooks. The finish is brass with red eyes and red wound hooks. The patent date is stamped on the tail. It is 3" (3-1/2" overall body size including tail). The inside of the body is filled with cork. The Chautauqua came in a blue cardboard box complete with instructions. The Chautauqua exists. A few have showed up but they are rare and desirable.

The Howe's Vacuum Bass Bait

      F.G. Howe invented the Vacuum Bass Bait on October 5, 1909. He was from North Manchester, Indiana. The Howe Vacuum is a true classic. It was very popular among fishermen and later became a regular part of the South Bend Bait Company's catalogued line of plugs. The best way to tell an original Howe's Vacuum from a South Bend is to take a close look at the hook rig. South Bend used a cup and open screw eye rig, the same as Jim Heddon's cup rig. The Howe rig features a hook that swivels, the eye goes through the cup and is flanged so it can twirl around.

      The Vacuum came in a tin box and was offered in the following colors: yellow, red, white, dragon fly, frog, rainbow. The old veteran in the photo following has a white body with red gills and was recommended for night fishing. "Bass feed much at night" so the catalog says. The Vacuum came in two sizes - 2-3/8", 3/4 ounce and 2", 1/2 ounce. You may still have a good chance of finding a Howe's Vacuum Bait, but not in very good condition as they were a popular plug and fished a lot.

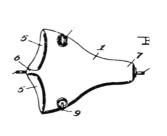

The Burthe Frog

      This cutaway drawing is of a mechanical frog patented November 30, 1909. The rear legs kicked as you pulled the frog in. This was activated by a coil spring. The covering mentioned in the patent was preferably rubber but could be something else. We'll know when we see one.

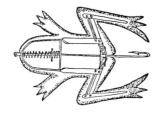

The Hanel "Concealed Fish Hook"

The body could be made of wood,
maybe not. This is another coil spring
operated weedless plug. Collectors
from Milwaukee should have turned one
of these up by now. If there is one to
be turned up we hope you will find it.
Patented January 4, 1910 - an early
Wisconsin patent.

Franklin A. Alger

Few plug makers ever made such a wide variety of well crafted, innovative, interesting plugs as Franklin A. Alger of Grand Rapids, Michigan.
His patent of May 3, 1910 shows a fish chasing a fish - a floating diver with
a metal lip. One of the very first, except perhaps the 1904 Fred Rhodes' patent, which touched on the subject. The Algers on the left shows a variation
of this theme. The circular piece of metal activates the wood body. This
particular plug is interesting in that it has a place where a lip was perhaps
tried. The lip in the patent wraps around and is screwed in. This one goes
in to a slot like so many plugs to follow. The hook rig is another sort of
"L" rig very similar to Jim Heddon's "L" rig. The plug on the right is another plug made by Mr. Alger. Just look at the quality!

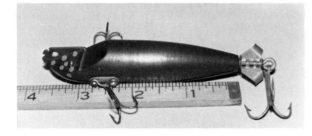

These plugs were all made by Mr. Franklin A. Alger of Grand Rapids,
Michigan. Very few of these plugs were ever produced in quantity. The plugs
on the bottom right of the photo became the Alger's Getsum which later found
its way into the Wilson line. The boxed plug in the center is called the
"Tantalizer" - extremely few of these have been found. The Getsum, in the
right (following) photo is a nice plug to have but is not extremely scarce.
See Wilson for more about the Getsum.
Thanks to Clarence Zahn who specializes in plugs made in Michigan.

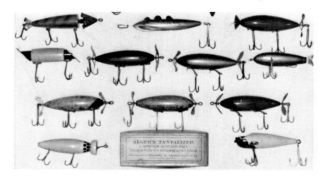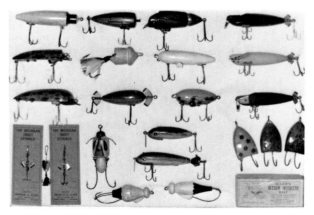

H.A. Williamson's "Animated Minnow"

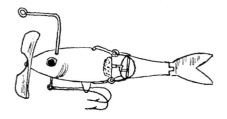

The name "Animated Minnow" is
the one on the patent. It is a decent guess this might have been the
name of this unseen St. Louis,
Missouri plug, which was patented
August 12, 1910. Another missing
"Wiggle Tail" plug.

J.E. Walters

John E. Walters from Niles, Ohio patented this beauty on August 30,
1910. This weedless plug has a single (or double) long shanked hook that
was set like a trap. Still another uncovered weedless plug. It looks like
it might have been made out of wood.

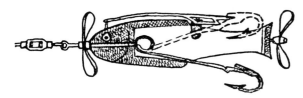

The Bohanan Artificial Minnow

Mr. Joe Bohanan of Farmington, Illinois patented the Bohanan Artificial Minnow on July 5, 1910. F.S. Vandersloot of the same town advertised
them nationally in mid-1911. The Bohanan is 3-1/4" and made of two pieces
of wood joined side by side by countersunk wood screws. The two halves
encapsulate a 4-hook, wired system. Feathers are clamped between the two
pieces of wood to act as dorsal, pectoral, pelvic, anal and caudal (tail)
fins. The eyes are opaque yellow with pupils. The mouth is carved and
the hand painted gill plate and gills are black and red. Mr. Bohanan had
some idea of how a fish was built! The photo to follow is the only Bohanan
we know of. It is silver with a blended black back. The feathers are mostly
long gone. There should be some of these out there.

Clyde Grove - Warren, Ohio

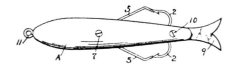

Just another "bifurcated"
(divided in half) weedless plug
that's never been found. Patented
July 10, 1909 by Clyde Grove.

The Charmer Minnow

        The underwater Charmer minnow was patented on October 11, 1910 by
Messrs. F.W. Breder and J.H. Loyd of Springfield, Missouri. Mr. Loyd assigned his portion of the patent to Marshall O. Brixey of the same town. The
underwater Charmer came in two sizes which were approximately 3-1/2" and
2-3/8" for the Midget Charmer. The barbershop striped tail spins while the
glass eyed front end stays put. Underwater Charmers are not exactly rare
but a collector should remember that desirability is sometimes more important
than rarity. Following, left, is the Charmer and the Midget Charmer.

        The 3-1/2" surface Charmer was patented and was reissued on December
12, 1912. On the reissued patent the drawing appears to show the surface
version. The Midget Charmer and Surface Charmer are the scarcest. This
red cedar plug sported a variety of paint jobs - orange, green, red, white
and gold heads with varied stripes on the tail (revolving section). Example
of these colors are gold with green or red or orange with red or green
stripes, etc. A very colorful charmer of a plug.

The G.H. Garrison Plug

        The George H. Garrison plug from Olympia, Washington, is made of
hollow wood. The prop on the tail turns a cam inside the body which makes
it wiggle back and forth in a very dramatic manner. The one in the photo
is dark red and has glass eyes. It is the only one known. The patent was
dated October 25, 1910

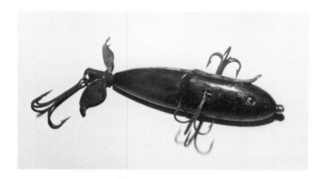

The Croaker Bass Bait Company

        Around 1910, Mr. L.A. Wilford of Jackson, Michigan came out with a
jointed bait. Truly one of the first jointed plugs. In fact the original
ad which mentioned "weeks" of experimentation in the year 1910, also mentioned how it worked better than plugs of the same general type. The

Croaker stayed on the surface, had better action than most and when "Mr. Bass" hit, you put most if not all nine hooks into it. That's it - a jointed sur- face hooks better than a straight one. As we shall soon see, there were many plugs of this type being developed in this area of the U.S.A. Jackson isn't far from Coldwater, etc.

The Croaker following (left top) is typical. It has large screw eye hangers and is red and white (a redhead). The plug below it is also believed to be a Croaker but a smaller, lighter and perhaps earlier version. This "Croaker?" is painted gold. A bass bait and trout bait were advertised. The trout bait could be the bottom one in the photo, but it is likely the trout bait was smaller. The Croaker is a big plug - the small Croaker is 4" long. Maybe they have big trout near Jackson.   Croakers are hard to find.

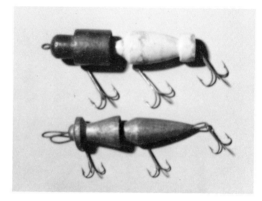

The Mushroom Bass Bait

The Mushroom Bass Bait was made in Jackson, Michigan around the time of the Croaker. It came in a 3-1/2" and 3-7/8" version. The paint job on the Mushroom Bass Bait is unique. It is hand painted as many plugs of the day were. The finish is effective - a quite froglike hand paint job consis- ting of heavy primer, and a rubbed, splattered decoration. The inside of the onvex wood cups is red, which is typical on this type of plug. All attachments are large brass simple screw eyes. The Mushroom Bass Baits that exist seem to be chewed up, having the brave remains of the excellent paint job. The Mushroom Bass Bait is hard to find even in not too good condition.

Made by
J.A. Holzapfel

The South Coast Minnow

H.C. Royer of Terminal Island near Los Angeles, California offered the wood South Coast Minnow in three sizes - 2-3/4", 3-1/4" and 4". He also offered flat fish shaped metal South Coast Minnows in four sizes - the same sizes as the wood plug and a tiny 1"er for trout. The South Coast Minnow is

one of the first single tail hooked plugs of this type. We will later see
Pfluegers Catalina and Heddon's Coast Minnow. There was another minnow of
this type made around the same time called the North Coast Minnow made by
W. Hoegee. These came in a 2-5/8" and 3" size. The photo is of a South
Coast Minnow. Once in awhile these show up but usually not in very good cond-
ition. They usually have four belly weights.

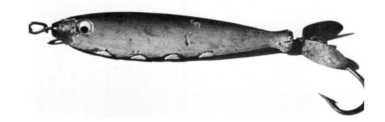

The "Peckerheads"

There are few plugs as fully represented by so many plug makers.
Moonlight's Bass Bait #1 is truly one of the earliest (circa 1906). Shakespeare
had two version called the Surface Wonder and the Night Caster. Pflueger called
theirs the Merit and Magnet. Heddon and Donaly offered variations of this
theme and perhaps the best known version is South Bend's well known Woodpecker.
These will all be discussed later in the book. There are many other versions
with unknown makers. We have seen the Croaker and Mushroom Bass Bait. There
are many others. Some collectors call these "Peckerheads". There are a few
examples in the specialized collection following.

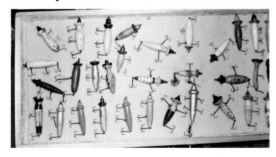
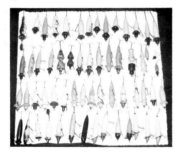

The "Moran Weedless Rubber Bulb Baits"

The Moran Weedless Hook and Butterfly Bait were both offered in four
sizes. Most of these Chicago based rubber plugs have probably already
deteriorated. The Butterfly must have been a nice plug although it might
be something like a parachute to cast.

The Creek Chub Bait Company - Garrett, Indiana

We have already met most of the people who were involved in the start of the large plug manufacturers. These major manufacturers will all be discussed in detail in their own chapters later in the book.

Creek Chub did not start heavily advertising and selling until around 1916. However, Mr. Heinzerling and his partners were making and experimenting with plugs as early as 1906. Much more about Creek Chub later.

The Chippewa

Wisconsin is proud of its own Chippewa. Few classic plugs are this classic. Just looking at a Chippewa makes you feel good, finding one in an old tackle box might even make your day. Generally Chippewas are not too difficult to find. Some sizes are worse than others. Perhaps the most common size is the 4" pike size. The toughies seem to be the 4-1/2" and 5" floater and the 3-1/2" sinker. Chippewas were the creation of Omer F. Immell of Blair, Wisconsin. The construction is unique. There is a wire that goes around the outside perimeter of the plug which serves to hold the spinner in the belly in place. It is soldered together at the line tie. These lateral serpentine type spinners are painted red on one side and generally stamped "Pat. Nov. 1, 1910" - one of the two patents awarded Mr. Immell. The other was May 2, 1911. The Chippewas that have turned up look more like the 1911 patent than the 1910. In fact the 1910 patent had a metal wag tail! This would be a Chippewa to find. Omer Immell was a renowned sportsman and writer. Mr. Immell published a book of poems copyrighted in 1935 called, "The Restoration of Trempealeau Bay" (a historically prolific game and fish area near the Mississippi River in west central Wisconsin that was, as usual, nearly ruined by commercialization. The river was rerouted. The fish and game were gone. "The sportsmen were 'licked'. All hope fled." Believe it or not a government dam promised to save the day. The last stanza of his poem (following) "The Voice of Trempealeau Marsh" say it all. Immell told the whole story in rhyme. He cared. He also made a great old plug.

Three earlier versions of the Chippewa have been reported. One has a horizontal cut in the tail to accept a split ring for the hook. Another example has a full wood body where most Chippewas have a metal frame insert in the belly that holds in the spinner. The third variation heard of but not seen, has no glass eyes at all. Colors were bright and durable. They included yellow, fancy sienna (crackleback), red/yellow, rainbow, green crackleback, green/white and green crackleback with green and red spots (see color section).

Chippewas came in the following sizes (from left to right hanging on bait basket) - all are called "Chippewas": the 5" Muscallonge Bait, the 4-1/2" floater, the 4" pike bait, the 3-1/2" bass bait (sold by C.J. Frost) and the 3" bass bait. The two plugs on the chair are the 5" Muscallonge floater and the Chippewa Skipper (C.J. Frost). The floaters, 4-1/2" and 5" have fatter backs and smaller spinners.

"O'er the rustle of the rushes,
    On the wind that whistles through,
An S-O-S call I am sending
    To broadcast my fate to you;
I'm a devastated area,
    Shorn of value by the dredge,
Give me back the Tremepealeau River
    A wild life refuge I will pledge"

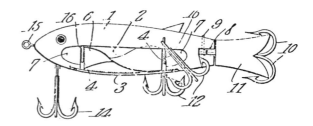

November 1, 1910
Patent

The Chippewa Skipper is a 4-1/2" surface plug that came with two
interchangeable metal lips and was offered in at least two colors - green
crackleback over white and white with red and green spots. The finishes on
both the "Chippewas" and the "Skipper" were high quality air brushed
professional paint jobs. In fact, both the Chippewas and the Skipper were
Paasche air brush painted, boxed and probably assembled together.

The Skipper and the 3-1/2" sinker bass model Chippewa were both distributed by the C.J. Frost Bait Company of Stevens Point, Wisconsin. The
Skipper was and still is an exclusive plug. The C.J. Frost Skipper is
unique. It is not known but suspected that Omer Immell designed it. There
have been no breakthroughs in this area.

One of the Skippers interchangeable lips makes the plug act like a
swimming mouse. The other makes it skip like a minnow or frog. Carrie Frost
founded one of the first fishing tackle businesses in Wisconsin. She was a
fly tyer and started in the late 1890s. The Skipper is rare.

There are a couple of "Who Dunnits" that have characteristics of
Mr. Immell's and C.J. Frost's products. They both are very interesting
plugs. The 3-5/8"er on the left is a floating-diver with hardware (shallow
cup, small screws in changeable nickle plated lip, etc.) similar to the
Skipper. The redhead on the right probably is not a product of either
Mr. Immell's or Carrie J. Frost's company. This 5" plug is one of our favorite all time plugs. The line tie is Heddon-like. The rear spinner is
mrked Pflueger and is indeed a Pflueger Black Bass Spinner that was in the
Enterprise line from the late 1890s until the early 1900s. The diving lip
is screwed on in a similar fashion to the plug on the left and the Skipper.
It is marked "F" - Frost? We will keep this plug here until we know it's
something else. It could even be a Pflueger - this is doubtful. The only
trouble with either of these plugs being one of Mr. Immell's or C.J. Frost's
products is that the only other known plug like the one on the left is a
redhead (the plug on the right is a redhead). We have never seen or heard

of either a "Chippewa" or "Skipper" in redhead. The one on the left also
has some characteristics of plugs by J. Reynolds of Chicago. More about
Mr. James Reynolds later.
Arlan Carter helped a great deal on the "Chippewas".

James Fuller/Austin Mills

This patent dated August 15, 1911
was granted to James Fuller and Austin
Mills of Moberly, Missouri. It was
probably a good idea. Why not put hooks
on a glass aquarium minnow type fish
decoy.

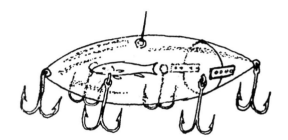

W.T. Jefferson's Frog and Minnow

W. T. Jefferson, who was from Evanston,
Illinois had a patent dated June 13, 1911.
His patented plugs would be hard to find today.
The "thin" material, "preferably rubber",
of the body of the frog or minnow slip over
a "wood or hard rubber" head. The object is to
conceal the hooks. Mr. Jefferson's plugs might
look something like this. Collectors should
look for jsut the head and skeleton metal body.
The bodies were fragile.

Frank Staples' Patent

Frank Staples, from San Francisco,
California had a patent dated July 3,
1911. That's all we know. The side
arms are important. The body material
is unknown.

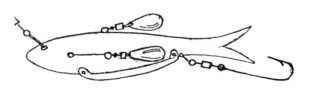

John Dineen's 1911 Spinning Minnow

Patented July 18, 1911, John Dineen's 1911 Spinning Minnow, 3-5/8",
was made out of a solid piece of copper or other metal. The "1911" has been
reported nickled and bent into the form of a fish. The "1911" joined at
the nose. It had punched eyes and was brass wired through, It had a
swivel and Bing type weedless feathered tail hook. The paint jobs are usually
chipped on these "1911s". They were nicely spray brushed but this is hard to

make durable. The John Dineen "1911" is unmarked. There should be more of these around than there are - maybe people are not recognizing what they are.

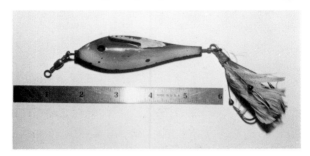

The Bass Hog

T.J. Boulton of Detroit, Michigan made the 4-1/4" Bass Hog. The Bass Hogs are white trimmed in red. A rather scarce plug.

The Case "Rotary Marvel"

The 3-1/4" Rotary Marvel has a metallized (metal plated) spinning head and is a surface plug. They are a bit tough to find, but still find-able. The hook hangers on the Rotary Marvel are Pflueger "Neverfail" hangers which were patented April 12, 1910. The Rotary Marvel came with red, yellow or white bodies and were sold by the Case Bait Company of Detroit, Michigan.

The Aeroplane Bait

The Aeroplane Bait was sold by H.G. Parker & Son of Battle Creek, Michigan. It was made to float or sink - don't ask how. We have never seen an Aeroplane, but it would be a great find.

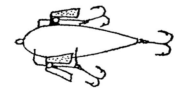

The Wiggle Tail Minnow

This Detroit plug was supposed to "act like a live minnow". Another Michigan plug that has not turned up.

The Henning Glass Minnow Tube

Chester E. Henning patented a glass minnow tube on September 11, 1911. Half of this patent was assigned to Allen J. Baldwin. Both men were from Benton, Ohio. These might be confused with the more noted Detroit Glass Minnow Tube.

Bob Bulkley Photo

H.E. Lowe Artificial Bait

Harry Lowe of Pittsburgh, Pennsylvania patented this "Artificial Bait" November 21, 1911. The concealed rear treble is coil spring operated. There are an almost unbelievable amount of spring operated plugs that were invented but never seen. Perhaps no one collects them. The plug was probably made of wood.

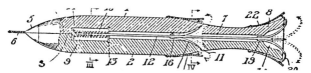

The Herrmann Plug

The O.H. Herrmann plug, patented November 28, 1911, appears to be one of the earliest electric light bulb plugs. Electric light plugs are another area of many inventions but few examples.

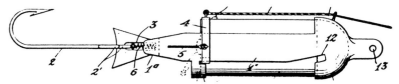

The J.W. Crane/R.L. Graves "Artificial Minnow" - December 5, 1911

This Memphis, Tennessee based Artificial Minnow was made for "catching, snagging or in any other manner decoying and catching larger fish." "Suitable cloth or rubber split lengthwise" made up the body. The patent speaks of preparation of this "variously colored minnow" in a manner where it will also smell like a fish!

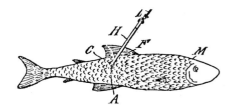

A.J. Dremel's Patent

This spring loaded Milwaukee, Wisconsin plug could still be out there. Patent dated February 13, 1912.

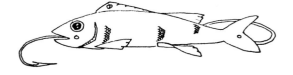

The Submarine Bait

This 3-3/4" hollow metal plug is part copper, part aluminum. It has a valve which allows water to enter. The Submarine is either a surface plug or underwater. It was the fisherman's choice. The Submarine was patented by Charles Blee and John Helmkamp of Fort Wayne, Indiana on March 18, 1912. It was sold by the Fort Wayne Bait & Reel Co. The Submarine is scarce-rare - a good plug to have.

John Nordlund's Patent

A spring loaded weedless plug from Eureka, California, Patent dated March 26, 1912

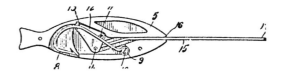

The Hendryx Plug

Not much can be said about this plug except that the tail spinner is stamped Hendryx and the plug exists. Someone else could have made it and used a Hendryx spinner. Until more is known, it is the Hendryx plug. Hendryx was known for spinners.

The "Meadow Frog"

This old hollow rubber frog looks like it has been hibernating for 75 years. The Meadow Frog was sold by Abercrombie & Fitch Co., New York City. It came in two sizes, the 2-1/2"er and the 3-1/2"er. The one in the photo would be 3-1/2" if it still had its feet. A lot of these were probably made but are long gone. They were possibly made by Pflueger.

C.W. Lane - Madrid, N.Y.

Two plugs have been attributed to Mr. Charles Lane. The first is called "Lane's Automatic Minnow" which was patented July 29, 1913. It is the plug in the artist's conception following. If you want to see Lane's Automatic in real life please go to the color section in this book. The Automatic has wiggling fins and tail. It is hand painted over metal. It sinks. How would you like to snag one of these on a log twenty feet down. Lane's Automatic speaks for itself - it's old, rare and beautiful.

C.W. Lane later marketed a wood plug with a fluted metal tail and a
diving lip. The same quality and individualism is seen in this wonderful
old minnow called the Lane's Wonder Wagtail Wobbler. This little guy is
2-3/4" long.

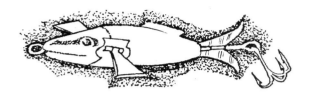

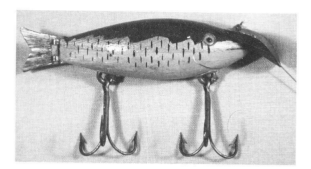

Clinton Wilt

Clinton Wilt patented the 3-1/4" Little Wonder on September 16, 1913.
It had a big brother called the "Champion" which was 3-1/4". Both are well
made. The idea is that the wood body spins one way and the props the other.
There is a sort of cradle mechanism going here. The metal work on Clinton
Wilts is more heavy duty than expected. Certain parts, the weight in the
case of the Little Wonder and the cradle in the Champion are very heavy
guage metal. The photo following (left, top) is the Champion, its little
brother is the Little Wonder. Both plugs are of the barberpole variety.
Clinton Wilt plugs came in 12 color combinations! The little wolf pack of
Little Wonders (following) are red stripes on gold, red on white and green
on white. They sport buck (deer) tails. No bass could withstand this
onslaught.

The Welles Patent Plug

Henry S. Welles of New York, New York received a patent on November
18, 1913 that proved to be not only important but the controversial plug
patent of all time. The patent itself didn't look like much of a plug.
The plug itself did. Very few Welles patent plugs are known. The few that
are are usually beat up and therefore unrecognized. The Welles patent really
started something. This matter will be covered later in the book. It involves major plug names such as Heddon's Tadpolly, Moonlight Zig Zag and the
Rush Tango. To make a long story short (which is more pertinent later),

this patent held up to the point that after a certain date all Rush Tangos
carried the Welles patent date rather than the original Rush Tango date.
The Welles patent plug following is silver and red with black printing -
it is 4" long.

The 1913 and 1914 patents clarify the idea of floating on the surface and diving upon retrieve - a very important concept.

 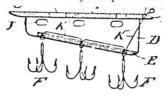 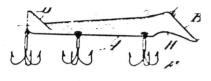

1913 Patent   1914 Patent

James Simms Artificial Minnow

An electric light minnow patent by James Simms from Matoaka, West
Virginia dated November 25, 1913. Find one! The body is made of glass.
Good luck!

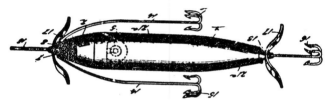

The Pontiac Minnow

The Pontiac Manufacturing Company of Pontiac, Michigan made a series
of 3 and 5-hook underwater minnows. The date of their manufacture has not
been pinpointed - probably sometime around 1909-1914, perhaps earlier. The
Pontiac 3-hook underwater minnow following (top) was 2-7/8" long. All Pontiac
products were well made. They came in red, white, yellow and green. A box
has showed up for a 5-hooker but no plug. 3-hookers are hard to find. The
3-hooker also came in a luminous paint job called the Radium Minnow. The
Pontiac and Radium had an unusual hook rig where the hook is screwed on over
a convex brass cup. The treble hook twirls around the hook eye. The third
version is called the Standard Minnow. It was less expensive but still of
very high quality. The hook hanger is different, having a wire "L" type
loop to accommodate the eye. The "L" goes to the outside of the convex brass
cup. The Standard is tougher to get than the 3-hook Pontiac.

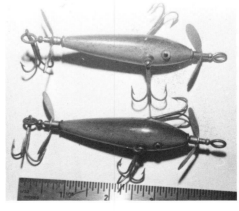

Six "Who Dunnits"

No comment.   St. George Plug
                                                     Michigan

Wilson Plugs/The Hastings Sporting Goods Works

Richard T. "Art" Wilson assigned one half of his May 6, 1913 patent and others to Aben E. Johnson of Hastings, Michigan. Mr. Johnson and Mr. Wilson were believed to have been partners in the Hastings Sporting Goods Works of Hastings, Michigan. The plug in the 1913 patent is the Wilson Fluted Wobbler. Art Wilson's first and most important plug. In an old ad, Mr. Richard T. "Art" Wilson relates the story of how he came up with this famous Wobbler. It seems Art Wilson was towing a row boat across a lake and noticed how it would swing from side to side. Art Wilson saw the potential in this type of motion and proceded to carve himself a plug. The first one had two grooves. It "came through the water like a dead stick". Art Wilson then carved two more flutes (four all together) and tossed it toward the lily pads. Wham! - a four pound bass. The rest is history. There are few plugs that caught more bass than the Wilson Wobbler. It came in many sizes and shapes from the tiny 1-3/4" fly rod size to the rather large Wobbler Frank Pasiewicz is holding up in the following photo. This huge Wobbler is either a store display or a shark plug.

 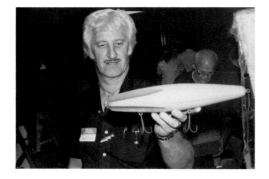

Other Wobbler variations are the musky - seen as a 6"er and reported as a 4-3/4"er. The musky Wobbler should not be confused with the large

6" "Bull Trout Plug" found out West. These are used for Dolly Vardens in
roily water and are usually "surface" rigged, that is the hook is in a
nickle plated surface rig similar to recent such hook hangers by Pflueger
and Heddon. Bull Trout plugs are not known to be Wilson products.

The need for a smaller Wobbler was apparent. It was a 3-1/2",
3-hook plug. The fat 2-hook version is called the "Super Wobbler". Super
Wobblers are around and sometimes come in a scale finish. The thin 2-hooker
with Bing's weedless hooks (see following bottom right) is the Fluted Weedless. There is a sinking Wobbler. This is a standard #1 type but is
weighted to sink. This is either a scarce variation or collectors don't
take the time to look and weigh their Wilson Wobblers. The 1-3/4" fly rod
version is hard to find (see previous photo). The Wobbler at the top
right of following photo is the standard common fish catching Wilson Wobbler.
The plug to its left could be one of the first handmade Wilsons. If it
isn't that O.K. too. It would have been nice if it was and someone could
prove it. It's probably a homemade copy - whatever.

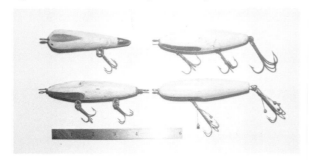

These two Wobbler variations both look
enough like Wilsons to be thought provoking.

R.T. Wilson's next patent (half assigned again to A.E. Johnson) was
granted January 13, 1914 and was for a plug generally known as the Wilson
Flange Wobbler, Wilson Winged Wobbler and more recently as the Good Luck
Wobbler. The name Good Luck Wobbler applied to both the #1F Fluted and the
Flange type. These versions had no cups just a screw eye hook hanger. Also
the aluminum flange itself is smaller. Probably another cost cutting method.

The Flange is one of the earliest metal lipped floater-divers to
succeed. It is a 4"er and came in frog as well as the typical red flanges/
white body combination. The Flange is hard to find with the original paint
on the flanges.

Mr. Wilson's next patent of March 27, 1917 (also half assigned to
Mr. Johnson) was for the Six-in-One Wobbler which was advertised as "A new
one for 1916". This 4"er has six positions on the plated metal lip for fishing at different depths. We have seen one of these in silver and red. A
great plug and one of the better Wilsons (following, right).

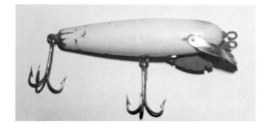

Another Wilson/Hastings product that deserves note is the metal lure called the Sizzler. Although it is not exactly a plug it is interesting to note the Sizzler is marked "Pat. Aug. 24-1904" by a man from St. Cloud, Minnesota. Mr. Wilson put it into his line sometime later. It came in two sizes - 2" and 3".

The other Wilson plugs were possibly never patented. The next Wilson plugs came in to the Hastings line around 1915. They are the Cupped Wobbler (top left plug in left photo following) a redhead 4"er. The cup is recessed into the head. The line tie is a long double looped wire. The Cupped is fairly scarce compared to most Fluted and Flanged Wobblers.

The Bass Seeker came in about the same time as the Cupped. It is a rather graceful plug - 3-3/4", 2-hook floater-diver (see following right).

The Algers Getsum (left following) came in two versions. Most Alger's Getsums had a rather elaborate metal plate to hold and protect the weedless hook arrangement. The 2-1/4" Getsum was patented May 9, 1916 by Mr. Alger and later sold by Hastings around this time. Mr. Franklin T. Alger was born in 1862 and passed away in 1940, (see Alger).

The plug on the right (following, left) is the Wilson Grass Widow, 2-1/4", and is similar to the Getsum. It has an oval shaped belly weight not seen in photo. Both Alger's Getsums and Grass Widows are among the harder Wilsons to find.

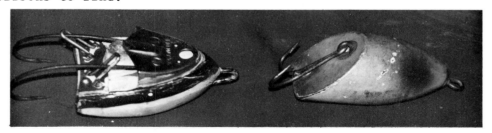

The Bassmerizer is probably the second hardest Wilson to find. The 3-3/4" Bassmerizer in the photo (following, left) is missing its tail lip. It is identical to the front lip but reversed. There is another Bassmerizer in the previous Wilson group photo - it is the top right plug, next to the Cupped Wobbler.

The plug on the right is the Staggerbug. It's the same blended redhead color as the Bassmerizer on the left. It is our feeling that perhaps more Staggerbugs are out there. There must have been some problem with this plug. Either it didn't work correctly (we refuse to try the one in the photo, it's chipped to the wood on the nose and if it gets wet the chips could get worse) or it was not marketed for some other reason. There is a possibility it was a patent infringement or something like that. Nevertheless, they are so rare - you are looking at it!

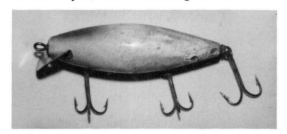

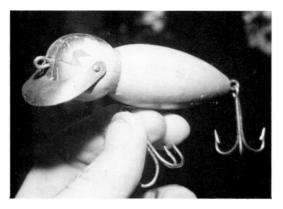

Art Wilson is pictured in old ads holding up the Wobbler using the "V" sign. The watch fob (to the right) is a wonderful plug collectors item. It is also a compass. On the back it says, "Hastings Sporting Goods Works, Hastings, Michigan".

There are not many reels in this book - check out the marking on this one. A reel with a plug on it - ALL RIGHT!
Frank Baron's help by sharing his research on Mr. Art Wilson's products is much appreciated.

Arthur Burkman

The two following patents are once again plugs that to the best of our knowledge have not as yet been found by collectors. Mr. Burkman's two plugs come as a mystery to most collectors. The plug of particular interest is the one on the left. This 1917 patent looks a great deal like the elusive Wilson Staggerbug. There is an area of possibility here. Also, the 1915 patent on the right is such that if you strained the imagi-

nation it has certain characteristics of a Manistee Minnow or a later
Dunks - that did the same thing but didn't have a prop. It can skip or
dive depending if the head was up or down. Much more needs to be known
about Mr. A. Burkman.

Arthur Burkman was from Traverse City, Michigan. A fishing town on
Traverse Bay not far north of Manistee. Finding Burkman plugs would be
historically significant.

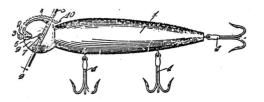
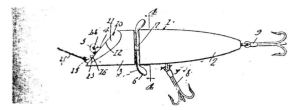

Jim Donaly Baits

James L. Donaly of Newark, New Jersey patented the "Redfin Minnow
Bait" on April 21, 1914. The Redfin Minnow came in hand painted colors of
two variations of red over white and a green back with white belly. Both
models had hand painted gill marks and red "fin marks". The bell hook on
the minnow is attached to the wired through line-tie and hook attachment.
They also had three thin metal "blades". Both aluminum and brass blades
have been seen - most are aluminum. One is on the nose, one by the anal
fin and the other by the tail (this combination works great). We field
tested a beater. It didn't float. It's a top water bait but doesn't float.
At least the one we tried was a slow sinker. (See following left). The
two plugs on the right are (top), the Catchumbig Bait, a 4" red and white
rarity, and the (bottom) Redfin Weedless Bait. Both the Redfin Minnow and
Catchumbig Bait were advertised as early as 1912. The Catchumbig Bait
was also called the Redfin Floater. Both plugs are Jersey rigged. The
Redfin Weedless, 3-1/2", is another red and white rarity patented October
16, 1917

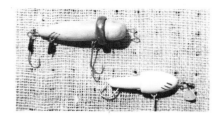

Jim Donaly must have liked the idea of fishing on the surface. His
next plug makes a lot of noise. The name Redfin Floater stuck! The new
version had a big marked aluminum prop. This version was around for a
long time. The Floater was resurrected in the early 1950s by McCagg of
Mount Kisco, New York who called it the Barney (that's modern history).
Donaly props are usually marked and the plugs aren't spray painted. The
three plugs following (left) are left to right, a mouse version of the
Redfin Floater (note aluminum blade tail, the fact that it's grey and the
side hook rig is extended), center plug is a classic example of the Floater,
and the plug on the right is a non-Jersey rigged version. The Floater came
in two sizes, the #1 was 2-7/8" and #2 was 2-1/4". The Redfin Floater in

this version came in a cardboard box. The name Redfin Floater was used
twice, first for the Catchumbig and more recently for the more popular
version following.

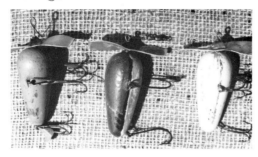

    Perhaps Jim Donalys staying on the top of the water led him to what
is perhaps the ultimate in surface plugs - the Wow, 3" (right) and Jersey
Wow, 3" (left). The Wows are familiar to many fishermen who ever had the
heart stopping experience of a musky or bass slapping a Heddon Crazy
Crawler out of the water or jumping clear over it doing flips, especially
at night. The 3-point Jersey Wow (backwards) version works better than
the Wow. The "Wow" was patented by James L. Donaly on July 17, 1928.
Heddon later arranged for patent rights for the Crazy Crawler.

    One of the greatest features of Donalys are the artistic hand paint
jobs. Jim Donaly's plugs were made, painted and assembled in his own home.
He had a shop in the basement with two work benches - one secured a metal
lathe and the other a wood lathe. Mr. Donaly was very interested in working
with aluminum. He even experimented with a furnace - molding aluminum is a
tricky process. About 40 to 50 finished plugs could be turned out a day.
There was night work involved. Upstairs on the kitchen table was the
painting and assembling department. Mrs. Donaly and their daughter used
camel hair brushes and used the paint can lids to hold the paint. Donalys
were made from, at least, 1912 'til the late 1930s. We do not know how old
Jim Donaly was when he passed away around the year 1935. Mrs. and Miss Donaly
continued to paint plugs for a few years after his death. All Donaly plugs
are very desirable. The Wows, Jersey Wows and prop version of the Floater
minnow seem to be found more than the Redfin Catchumbig, Weedless and the
Minnow. Donaly collectors are still looking for the diver.
Thanks to Phil Robbins, Bob Vermillion and especially Mr. John Scarlett who
provided us with the information about Jim Donaly. Mr. Scarlett assembled
plugs - especially Wows and Jersey Wows for Mrs. Donaly and her daughter in
the late 1930s.

Clarke W. Stewart of Olean, New York

This plug appears in the February 24, 1914 patent picture as an underwater type minnow with a choice of fish pictures laminated over a central (probably wood) core. If they aren't hitting on red tail chubs, switch to a shiner!. The layers of fish were expendable. It was recommended to have two cores in case you lost one and perhaps half a dozen if you were really going through them.

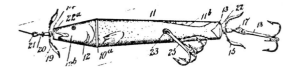

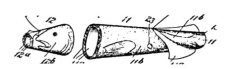

Glass Minnow Tubes, Etc. from Detroit, Michigan

The 3-3/4" Detroit Glass Minnow Tube is the plug following (left). They also made the Minnow Cage (right). The plug top left was made by Pfeiffer Live Bait Holder Company of Detroit, Michigan. Trout, bass and musky sizes were available. There is some belief that there is a connection between the Pfeiffer and the Detroit Glass Minnow. These Detroit plugs can be found but they are still very desirable to some collectors.

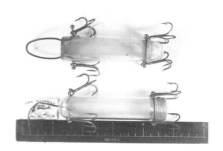

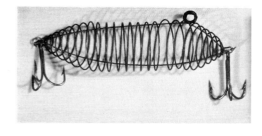

The Coldwater Bait Company, et al.

Plugs sold by the Coldwater Bait Company, Eureka Bait Company and W.E. Phinney were the products of Messrs. W.E. Phinney and Samuel O. Larrabee both of Coldwater, Michigan, a town not very far from Kalamazoo.

On June 9, 1914 Samuel O. Larrabee of Coldwater, Michigan received a patent for a floating/diving plug that worked on the principle of water entering under the chin and going out both sides at an angle. This made it wiggle. This particular plug was called the Eureka Wiggler and the Coldwater Wiggler. It came in 2-hook and 3-hook versions. The Eureka came in a very unusual "crackleback" finish. It would be interesting to know how they did this. Check the Eureka in the color section. There is a green/white version of this plug. See following left. The 4-1/4" Eureka also came in a smaller 2-hook version. The Eureka could be the older version of the two plugs. We don't know for sure. The Coldwater Wiggler (following right) also came in 2 and 3-hook versions. The colors of the Wiggler was usually all white with a red throat (hole) with three long thin red hand painted gill marks. Other colors were spray painted and

perhaps came along a little later. Coldwater plugs were being advertised
as recently as the early 1930s. Whether this was just remaining stock or
they were still in business is not known to the authors at this time.
These colors included fancy spotted (red and green spots over white), frog
and luminous.

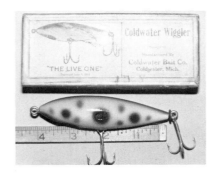

The Coldwater Ghost is a version of the Wiggler that is a bit of a
puzzle to collectors. There is some thought that they are constructed with
only one exit hole instead of two. The other idea is that this is the name
of the luminous version of the Wiggler. It was offered in 2 and 3-hook versions, both around 4". The one hole theory sounds alright. However, an ad
for the Ghost clearly states its wiggling action comes from water passing
through the holes. Can someone please clear this up? One feature to look
for on the Coldwater plugs is the sometimes presence of a large flanged cup
on the rear hook hanger. This doesn't seem to always be the case but it is
something to think about.

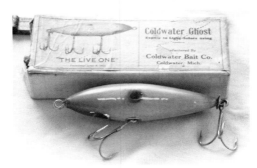

W.E. Phinney of Coldwater, Michigan received a patent for a plug that
could jump and skip when used on top and zig-zagged (a "wabbling motion")
when moved faster. All this was because of an adjustable line tie. Just
screw it in on the side. If you had one of these, you are probably the
first guy on your block that did so. The patent drawing clearly shows
cups which are present on all Coldwater Bait Company type products.

Willis E. Phinney received another patent on September 11, 1917 for
the Coldwater King. Another adjustable line-tie plug. This time it has a
lateral plate inletted into the center of the head. There are two versions.
The one most seen is the 7 line-tie version following. The other version
has 4 line-ties and is squared off in front (drawing).

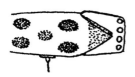

Willis Phinney and Samuel Larrabee got together on at least one plug, patented September 11, 1917. The Coldwater "Weedless" has two big special single hooks projecting from its belly. The weedless wire guards look like they would work. This is one of the better Coldwaters to find. All Coldwaters are good plugs to still find (following left).

The Phinney's Helldiver! Once again a multiple depth plug. This time you slide the lip in and out. There is a little screw under the chin which allows this. The Helldiver probably came in two sizes - 4-1/4" and 3". Early wood bodied plug sizes varied a lot, a variation of 1/4" is not unusual. The Phinney's Helldiver (Patent May 14, 1918) even came with glass eyes (see following, right). It also (usually) came in a no eyed version. The Helldiver is easily confused with the later Shakespeare Hydroplane, which is essentially the same plug except the Shakespeare version seems to be more simply constructed with a non-movable painted lip and a hook rig that simply screws in unlike all if not most Coldwater plugs which had cups. Clarence Zahn and Ray Carver deserve our gratitude for help on the "Coldwater" plugs.

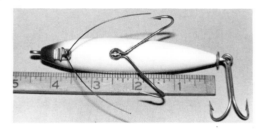

The Turner Casting Bait

The best information we have on this dual purpose Turner Casting Bait was that it was made by a Mr. Zachary T. (Dick) Turner who was a barber in Coldwater, Michigan. O.A. (Art) Turner was his son. The Turner Casting Bait came under two names. The other being the otherwise identical but luminous "Turner Night Caster". Both baits were reported to have been made out of broom handles. The round body on the few Turners that have been found does not rule this out. The Turner was a "Patent Applied For" Bait. No actual patent has been seen. There is a removable belly weight in the Turner. A wire clip holds the lead in place. It can be a surface or under-water bait. The colors offered were Potato Bug (orange/white) Frog Back, Night Bait (luminous), Crab (brown/white), Swallow (dark back/orange belly) Mouse, gold, aluminum, white, yellow, orange and finally cowdung which is a yellowish brown. There are some Turners around and many times they are missing the belly weight. The construction of the Turner is similar to the 1904 Rhodes Patent but not the same. It is wired through but the linked hooks are attached by a pin through the belly. It is not known if this was or even could have been a possible infringement. The Turner in the photo came in its original cardboard box. Unfortunately, the label was torn so we can't prove all the information above. There has been a goodly amount of speculation on this plug, most leading to an earlier Shakespeare/Rhodes connection. We can't rule this out. One of the big fat surface mystery minnows has turned up with a "Turner" type rig.
Thanks to Ray Carver, NFLCC Librarian.

Photos of the Turner Casting Bait are on the next page.

The Diamond Wiggler

The 3-3/4" Diamond Wiggler combined the ideas of grooves and holes. The Diamond Wiggler is a difficult plug to find. It was made by Bignall and Schaaf, Grand Rapids, Michigan.

The Stump Dodger

Albert Winnie of Traverse City, Michigan patented the Stump Dodger on July 7, 1914. He received an improvement on this patent October 24, 1916. The earlier patent features two line ties and two lips. Use the bottom line tie and the Stump Dodger is a top water plug. The top line attachment made it a floating-diver. If you find a 2 line-tie (simple screw eyes) it is probably the older version. The later 1916 patent had a more secure line-tie on the top only that attached to the top lip. This is the style most often seen. Stump Dodgers are usually marked on the back and sport a rainbow (green, red and yellowish) body. Several sizes have been seen including a fat 3"er, 3-3/4" and 4". The eyes are distinctive being a nail through a brass washer. Stump Dodgers have been overlooked by collectors. It is an older plug than generally thought. The 5" plug on the right might be a product of Mr. Winnie. It is a delightful "Who Dunnit" probably from Michigan. It is also very Shakespeare like.

The Stump Dodger came in two distinct hook hanger styles. One is a simple brass screw eye in belly, the other an "L" type rig where the eye screws in the wood on one end and has a loop to accommodate the tail hook. It is not known which one is the early hook hanger. This rig is similar to hook rigs used by Messrs. Alger, Lockhart and Heddon.

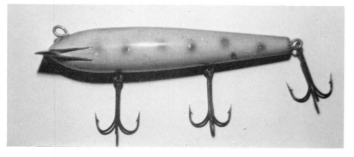

The Chicago Captor

The Chicago Captor was patented by Joseph Fischer of Chicago, Illinois on October 20, 1913. It was sold by The Fischer-Schuberth Company. The Captor following is the real Captor which is often confused with more recent plugs. The original Captors are very scarce. The Captor which is a quite weedless, floating bait came in three sizes - 4" bass, 5" pickerel and 5-1/2" muskolonge. Captors were black and white and probably also red and white.

The Apex Bullnose Plug

Another Chicago plug. The Apex Bullnose came in two sizes, 4" and the Apex Jr. 3". Both sizes came in redhead, redhead/yellow body and red body/ yellow head. The Apex "And Gosh How They Wiggle" Bullnose plug is hard to find but nobody seems to be looking very hard for one. The Apex came in a cardboard box.

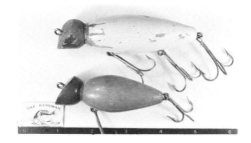

The Success Wobbler

By Midland Bait Company, Midland, Indiana, Also included in the line was the Fly Rod Wobbler and an option feathered hackle trailer.

The Millers Reversible

Just the name the Millers Reversible stirs up the old adrenalin in some collectors. This hard to find and interesting plug came in two basic forms. All type I Millers seen so far are approximately 4-1/2". The early model had a simple screw eye hook hanger and a rather thin back end. Most, if not all of this version were yellow with gold dots. (See left following). The later (circa 1916) model utilized Pflueger Neverfail hook hangers and had a fatter body (See right following). Colors known on type II were redhead, fancy spotted and yellow body with gold spots.

 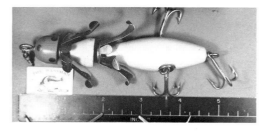

Nixon "Aristocrats"

The Aristocrats were underwater casting minnows extremely well made out of Persian Ivory. There is a tiny Aristocrat 1-5/8", a #2 - 3/4 ounce 3" side hooked 3-hooker (see photo), and a Coast Minnow (single rear hook) 3-1/4"er. All Nixons are rare and desirable. There is another Frank T. Nixon product reported by R.L. Streater that is a sort of Rush Tango like plug. Dick Streater further reports that Persian Ivory was a product called Ivoroid. Whatever it was it was advertised as a lot tougher than wood. The material really looks and feels like ivory.

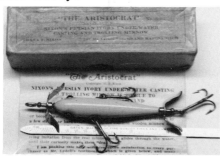

The Nifty Minne

The 4-1/2" Nifty Minne was made by Joseph Ness of Minneapolis, Minnesota. This wonderful plug is a favorite among collectors. It is a 5-hook minnow with a nonbreakable clear body. The props on both ends are clearly stamped "Nifty Minne". The front and rear end are connected by long threaded rods. You could put a minnow, grasshopper, frog, etc. inside. The Nifty Minne is very well made of nickle plated fittings. There is little doubt the Nifty Minne is Minnesota's finest plug.

The Rush Tango

Most plug collectors have heard of the Rush Tango. A lot of old timer fishermen have also. It was a good plug and caught fish. A lot were made over the years starting in 1914. There are few plugs in plug history that have been more controversial from a legal standpoint. LeRoy Yakeley of Syracuse, New York was assigned a patent on December 22, 1914 for the Rush Tango - a Design Patent. All Design Patents, including Patent #46,794, differ from the regular U.S. Patent in that all it features is a drawing of a plug - the Rush Tango. Mr. Yakeley assigned his Design Patent to Mr. Joseph K. Rush of Syracuse, N.Y. who was the president of the U.S. Specialty Company, also of Syracuse, N.Y. Mr. Rush proceded to manufacture the Rush Tango, and its variations in great quantity. The Rush Tango line consisted first and foremost of the Rush Tango itself, which was approximately 4-7/8" to 5". The paint jobs on Rush Tangos are unique. The early ones were heavily painted in enamel using a mottled effect consisting of either yellow or orangish red and green over a white or yellow body. Other colors seen in the Tangos are, all red, all white, redhead, redhead/yellow body and silver. The paint jobs became more elaborate as time went on and by the end of World War I, a special beautiful multi colored scale paint job appeared that was second to none - the Victory Finish, (following left, top). The Victory Finish is usually green back over yellow followed by red scales over silver with a light colored belly. It varied from a silver background to a gold or yellowish background. The top two plugs are probably the SOS #500 series - small fat 3"ers that stay on the surface when retrieved (Stay On Surface). The center plug is a standard Rush Tango in the characteristic mottled paint job. The small plug following, left, is the #300 Midget Tango, and the plug following, right, is a very unusual variation, in that it had two line-ties. Some of the earlier Tangos had a reinforced line-tie rather than the screw eye which was generally used. All Rush products have a cup hook rig, and all Tangos are belly hooked. It is doubtful if you will ever see a genuine Rush Tango with a tail hook. The Deluxe version of the Tango came with a metal reinforced lip in both a glass eyed and no eyed version. Both are scarce and rather recent, circa mid-1920s. The glass eyed version is downright rare, (see following right).

Other sizes offered in the Tango included the tiny Trout Tango - 1-3/4", following left. You can see the wonderful array of Trout Tangos, six plugs, in their own little box - a fine thing for a Rush Tango collector. The 5-7/8" Tarpon Tango on the right is equally unusual. The Rush Tango was also offered in 5-1/2" and 8" musky sizes. The 8"er would be a real find - big important plugs made especially for big important muskies. We have never seen this plug in real life. The 8"er was called the Field Special probably after

Marshall Field & Co. in Chicago, Illinois who was a sporting goods dealer.
There is also Rush Tango Juniors reported in 3-3/4" and 4" sizes.

   LeRoy Yakeley received two more Design Patents on August 10, 1915
(following, left) and July 11, 1916 (right). If would be a great find if
one of these plugs actually showed up. On June 13, 1922 Mr. W.C. Brown
of Syracuse, N.Y. invented a weedless device he assigned to Joseph K. Rush.
The plugs pictured in the U.S. Patent sure cover a lot of ground. The
patent shows a Bass Oreno, Heddon Crab Wiggler, a typical 5-hooker and a
Skinner type spinner and a Tango. (See following)

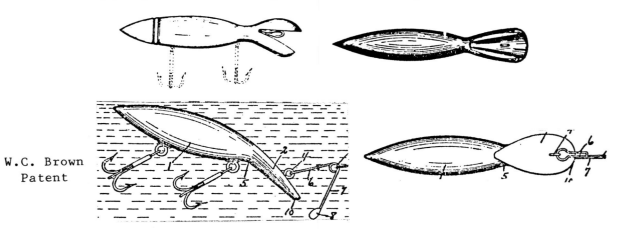

W.C. Brown
Patent

   The simplicity and diversity in the Rush Tango line is evident in the
other variations of this plug which Mr. Rush offered for sale. The Tiger
Tango, approximately 4", and its kin the Trout Tiger approximately 2" (half
size) are usually redhead or redhead/yellow body. The "Tiger" Tango (following
left) is typical and rather scarce. The trout version is worse. There is a
small 3-1/4" version of the Tiger called the Tango Lure which is quite scarce
and has a single belly hook. There are a few unusual Rush Tangos out there
that look like they were made for a specific purpose but not, as far as we
know, catalogued. The 5-1/2" slim beauty of a Rush Tango in the right photo
shows the potential of unusual and special fishing purpose Tangos. A musky
Tiger or Salmon Tango would not be terribly surprising.

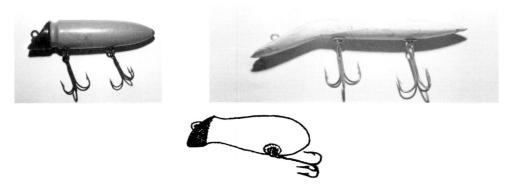

Mr. LeRoy Yakeley's first plugs looked
something like this plug. These were being
sold in small quantities to Syracuse, New
York sporting goods dealers in 1914.

It was the design on this plug and other products of Mr. Yakeley that
provided evidence in an extensive and expensive court case between LeRoy
Yakeley and Fillmore M. Smith. It seems Mr. Smith claimed earlier development of a "Rush Tango type" plug. The facts of this case showed that
Mr. Smith did, in fact, come up with the original idea. The transition of
Mr. Yakeley's plugs are on the left, following. The one in the photo,
Exhibit 1-C, is like the plug in the previous photo. Mr. Smith's plugs are
on the right. Mr. Yakeley gave evidence to substantiate his early use of
the Tango. It was a matter of a fish story with mixed up dates. The 1913
date given by Mr. Yakeley was disproven by a discrepancy in the weather on
the date in question. The date was more likely 1914. This along with the
court evidence following cinched it. The progression of Mr. Yakeley's plugs
suddenly jumped to the Tango type. Mr. Smith was working toward this end
all the time.

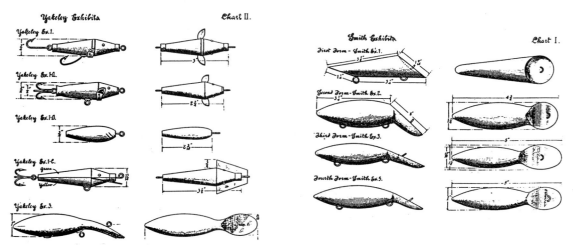

The patent dispute caused Mr. Yakeley to work out a licensing arrangement with Mr. H.S. Welles (see pages 119 and 120). The lawsuit was filed
March 22, 1915. Rush Tangos ads and boxes after 1915 carry the Welles patent
information.
    It seems Mr. Smith gave Mr. Yakeley some wood blanks for plugs to
paint. Mr. Yakeley was an experienced painter - he painted bicycles. Shortly
after this Mr. Yakeley was selling and patenting Mr. Smith's plug. Actually
Mr. Yakeley won the first round of this trial. Mr. Smith won on an appeal.
    The idea of a plug with a planed face that would float when at rest
and dive upon retrieve or other forward motion seems to have been another
case of independent invention among plug makers all over the U.S.A. at about
the same time.
    LeRoy Yakeley was also involved in another lawsuit with Emery Ball,
president of the Moonlight Bait Company of Paw Paw, Michigan over a patented
plug called the Moonlight Zig Zag. It appears Moonlight won and somehow
James Heddon's Sons ended up with rights to the Zig Zag for awhile. More

about this in the Heddon and Moonlight chapters.

Rush Tango products are fun and colorful to collect. The plugs have a chipping problem (big chips to wood) so it's difficult to find one in perfect shape. Remember, if it doesn't have a little cup in the belly for the hook rig it isn't a true Rush Tango.

Fillmore Smith of Syracuse, N.Y. assigned his patent for a Tango type plug to James Heddon's Sons of Dowagiac, Michigan on April 29, 1924.

Tango Imitations

As most plug collectors realize there are many Rush Tango look alikes. If it doesn't have a cup it is probably not a Rush Tango. It might be something made before or after Mr. Yakeley's or Mr. Rush's interest in the whole matter. Who knows? Some plugs are not stamped with who made them and when. This is indeed unfortunate. Perhaps the fish don't care but plug collectors do. The Tango types following illustrate this point. Following left could be an original Smith plug. It would be great if it was. Something says Reynolds (to follow). The finish and eyes are similar to the Reynolds' Tempter. The top right plug is thought to be the South Haven plug, 5". It is not known when this plug was made but it was supposed to have been made in South Haven, Michigan. It has a pin in the tail and a narrow (vertical) head. The cups are brass and almost too large for the plug. The South Haven plug might be something else. They sort of show up once in awhile in diverse forms. The plug we will refer to is painted all gold with a crude hand painted overlaying red.

The Tango type plug following might be just that. A very early version of a Rush Tango. It might also be something else. The patents are for Tango type plugs. George Strube was from Chicago. The action described in this patent is a "peculiar sinuous movement substantially in the form of S". With the line tie where it is it should do something wierd! The other patent is primarily for a line tie that accommodates removable hooks. If you have one of A.J. Keister's plugs, it is from Keota, Iowa and was patented July 16, 1918. One other Tango type plug is the more recent Tangos marketed by Horrocks-Ibbotson of New York. These are recognized by lack of a cup and sometimes by a distinct green narrow striped scale finish. This version does not fit into the chronology of this book.

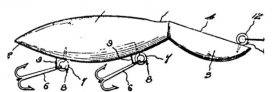
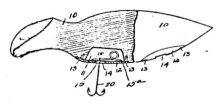

Fred C. Keeling

Sometime around early 1914 Fred C. Keeling of Rockford, Illinois
took over making Experts from the J.L. Clark Company of the same town.
The Keeling line started with practically the same variations of the
Woods and Clark Experts discussed earlier in this book. Keeling Experts
are quite similar and sometimes virtually indistinguishable from Woods
and Clarks. The holes in the Woods props seem to be a bit larger than
those on Clarks or Keelings. Clarks seem to be overall better painted,
the wood is a little thicker in the case of the round and taller in the
case of the shaped body Experts (flat). Clark has been attributed with
four gill marks as three on Keelings and Woods. All this is probably
somewhat true at best. For general purposes we will treat Clark and
early Keeling Experts together. There is no doubt they overlapped. If
this sounds confusing it's because it is. The early flat Keeling Experts
came in 2-1/2", 3" and two 5" musky versions of the 3-hooker. One version of the 5"er is a side hook Expert (see A) and one a belly hook
Expert (see B). The 5-hook flat Experts came in three sizes; the rare
4-1/4" Expert (C) and standard 3-1/2" (D). Expert "F" is the 5" round
Expert attributed more to Clark than Keeling but could be either.
Keelings round Experts were usually all copper or aluminum but did come
in other colors. The round Experts were offered in 2", 2-1/2", 3" and
3-1/2" sizes - 5" is unusual. Some of these Experts have been attributed to Clark. Nevertheless, the same exact Expert style has been
found factory new in Keeling boxes. Most Keeling Experts have holes in
the props. The only ones that don't are Experts made in the 1930s
toward the end of the Keeling line. These Experts were sometimes painted all one color, with no gill markings, have non-removable hooks and
are overall of less quality than we are used to in Mr. Keelings fine
products.

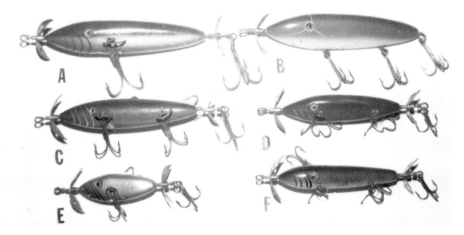

Among the most adventurous fisherman in innovative plug design is
Fred Keeling. He designed plugs beyond the Expert which he simply continued to make under the Shaffer/Woods patent. Mr. Keelings plugs were
specially adapted to unique fishing conditions. He apparently spent as
much of his spare vacation time fishing as possible. He concentrated on
two areas - summers were spent in his cabin in the Land O'Lakes region

of the Wisconsin/Michigan (Upper Penninsula) border on lakes with walleyes,
northern pike, small and large mouth bass and muskies. This is the head-
waters of the Wisconsin River - a major waterway connecting the north
country with the Mississippi River. Land O'Lakes winters are cold and
tough. We know, our home is about 45 minutes from the town of Land O'
Lakes. Fred Keeling spent his off time (winter) in Florida. He not
only was a pharmacist in Rockford, Illinois but dealt in sponges and
manufacturing fishing tackle, including Keeling rods. The Saint Johns
River in Florida is a very clear fresh water river that contains a native
population of whopper largemouth bass. The clarity and current of this
river made it quite a challenge to fool these big old buglemouths. The
slow action of the St. Johns Wiggle and the careful erratic motion of
the King Bee Wobbler (admittedly hard to fish) must have taken their toll.
The King Bee came in 2", 2-1/2", 3" and 3-1/2". The King Bee is a hard
Keeling to find (following, left). Another difficult to find Keeling is
the 3-3/4" St. Johns Wiggle (following, top left). It came with standard
non-removable trebles or a Jersey rig 3-hook attachment seen in this rare
version of a Keeling round Expert on the right.

        Fred Keeling's line of plugs offered in the mid-teens, including
Experts, were almost all glass eyed and painted either aluminum, copper
or white with red gills. The Experts had their own color schemes - red
over aluminum, etc. Some of Mr. Keeling's early plugs were quite innovative. They included two sinking plugs with diving lips for and aft and
called the Toms. The earliest Toms had hand soldered lips (the later ones
were stamped with "Pat. applied for" or the patent, unfound, date of 7/6/20).
The early Toms were 2" and 2-1/2" or Little Tom and Big Tom. The hook
hanger was quite innovative and included a version with a screw eye going
in to the lead belly weights. The King Bee (A), Tom Thumb (B) and 2"
round Expert (C) following, are all from the early series. The elusive
Red Wing has an "Expert" type front prop and soldered lips on the back to
make it wiggle (see following). The Red Wing is a 3"er. Try and find one.
We can't. The Red Wing belongs in the "early" Keeling line.

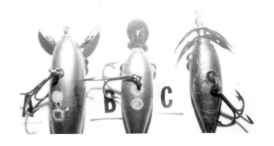
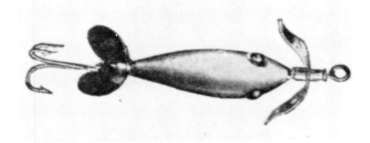

Toward the end of the teens Fred Keeling was offering a more complete line of Toms called Keeling's Tom Thumb Wigglers. These "Toms" differed from the early series. Fred Keeling had developed a one piece diving lip rig that is either marked "Pat Pending" or "Pat'd. 7/6/20". The Tom Thumb Wiggler in the later series comes in a wide variety of colors and sizes. A, B and C in the following photo are all 2" Baby Toms. A was handmade and has a soldered upper lip. This plug is reported to have come from Fred's tackle box. Fred was known to make and assemble plugs on the spot while experimenting with different ideas. He had a kit of parts, etc. just for this purpose. D is an unknown. It is probably a Keeling. The 2-1/2" size is the size of the mid to late series Little Toms (confusingly called the Big Toms in the early series). E is the later version of the Pike Tom. It has glass eyes and a perch type finish. This is typical of the third stage of Keeling products. A comb was probably used to mark this 2-3/4" Pike (walleye and northern) Tom when it was spray painted. F is a mid series Pike Tom (2-3/4"). G is an unusual flat version of the Pike Tom. H and I are Big Toms, 3". I is from the early series. We do not know what it was called. The early Big Tom was 2-1/2" and mid and later it was a 3"er. J is apparently a version of a 3-1/2" Tom of some sort. The cups on the side have screws in them. The only reason we can think of is to put on a set of trebles if you so desired. The screws screw into the horizontal weight that goes through the side of the plug. This particular plug comes in a smaller version - 2-1/2". K is a King Bee.

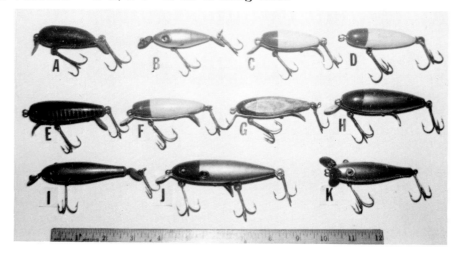

There is a plug called the Surface Tom, 3-1/4", H in the photo following. I in the same photo is the General Tom, 3-1/2". The General Tom has been seen with a flat tail. There is also a Long Tom - D and E, and a 3-7/8" Musky Tom (following photo, right). The plug on top in this photo is the 4-1/2" Flapper. The Keeling plugs A and B (following) are: A the 4-1/2" Pike-Kee-Wig, and B is the 3-1/2" Baby Pike-Kee-Wig. There is a spinnered version of the Pike-Kee-Wig with spinners on both ends. We feel this one might be the one called the U-Boat but we could easily be mistaken. The Kee-Wigs have a metal belly rig similar to the Tom Thumbs, with two different sized lips. These could be reversed to change the actions of the plug. C and F (following, left) are Keelings but we don't know their names. There are a lot of odd Keelings. We some-

times think Mr. Keeling must have made a plug for all possible fishing
occasions. G is the possible 3" Tip Top with the tail spinner. The Surf-
Kee-Wig has a tail flipper only. The Surf-Kee-Wig has a body similar to
the 3-1/2" Scout.

The 3-1/2" Scout (center, left) has a different lip than other
Keelings. The plug on the top has the same body. The bottom plug is one
of two versions of the scarce 2-1/2" Keeling Crab. It uses the same lip
as the Scout. The other version of the Crab (right) utilized the fluted
"Butterfly" lip. The lip is usually partially painted red.

The Keeling plugs (following) have been described except for C
whose name I don't know except a variation has recently shown up with
props on both ends. It was called a Keeling Surface Minnow (a Surface
Expert?). Plug C could also be a Tip Top. All the white cardboard box
it came in said was "Keeling Expert". D is the 4" Bear-cat. F is an unknown. These show up occasionally. G is the Flapper and H is the N450
model Flapper which was originally made with no wing and no props. There
is a third type Flapper with a prop on one end. Flappers sometimes came
in a beautiful red/lavender scale finish.

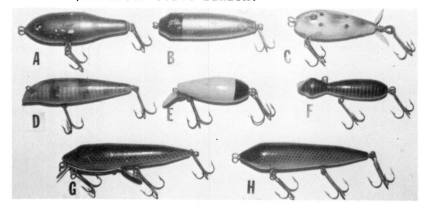

This "Show and Tell" collection clearly illustrates the depth in collecting Keelings. It is too bad this photo is not reproduced in color. Keelings are very colorful. From the early aluminum, copper and white, Fred Keeling went through a period of solid color combos such as redhead, red and white, and black and yellow. More recent Keelings (in the early 1920s) had fancy spray painted finishes and sometimes glass eyes. The paint variations are as varied and numerous as the plugs themselves. All of Keelings lure bodies were made by a small wood shop in Rockford. The hardware and spinners were also made on the outside. The Keelings were all painted by a lady and assembled in a building next to the Rock River where it still stands. Keelings are one of the most rewarding specialties in plug collecting. They are far from easy to find and quite frustrating in their seemingly endless variations. Two men brave enough to collect Keeling that helped immensely in this Keeling section are Henry Taylor and Jack Looney - thank you! Check out the Little Tom with the tail (second row, seventh plug).

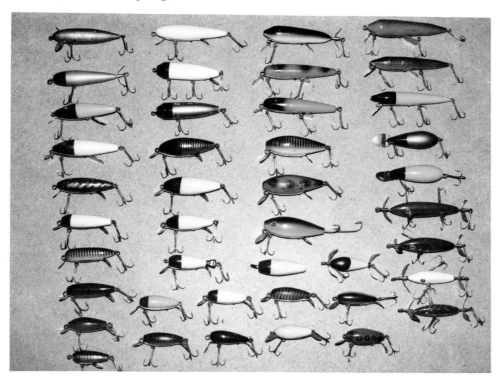

A couple of interesting footnotes to the Fred Keeling story. There has been research done as to who Tom was, but to no avail. We don't know who Tom was. Fred loved kids and spent time encouraging their fishing activities. He gave away a lot of plugs to youngsters. Fred Keeling was not in great general contact with his fellow plug maker competition until the 1930s when he offered his company to Heddon. Whatever happened here we don't know. All of Fred Keelings business was sold lock, stock and barrel to the Horrocks-Ibbotson Company of Utica, New York. Through the years Horrocks-Ibbotson was Fred Keeling's best customer. What do the Horrocks-Ibbotson Experts look like?

J.W. Reynolds Decoy Factory

        James Reynolds' plugs are all hard to find. Either they go un-
recognized or are truly rare. The March 30, 1915 patent is for a floater-diver that became known as the Swan Lake Wiggler. It had two double
removable hooks. Another similar plug is the 3-1/2" Spike Tail Motion
Bait following which sports a large removable single hook. This same
patent illustrates a version with changeable lips. Although the patent
was not assigned it is believed to have been the basis for the Pflueger
All-In-One Minnow.

 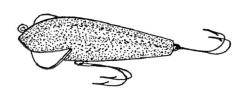

        Mr. Reynolds was issued three more patents. The April 1, 1916
patent was assigned to the South Bend Bait Company (following, left).
Interestingly, there is no South Bend plug to our knowledge that resembles this patent. The July 17, 1917 patent has not been seen (center).
The November 4, 1919 patent is another unknown Reynolds.

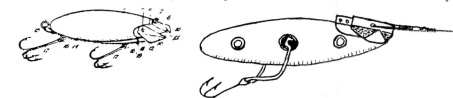 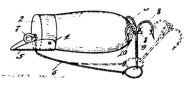

        The Reynolds Tempter is a well made, finely finished plug. The
4-1/4" specimen in the photo is black and white decorated with silver
flecks. It has large tack eyes and is cup rigged. The only other
Tempters we know of are all white.

The Bidwell Plug

        Clifford W. Bidwell was from Kalamazoo, Michigan. His weedless
top water plug is a good find. The patent date is July 27, 1915. This
3-1/2" plug probably has a name. We don't know it. The few Bidwells
we know of are redheads. The Bidwell is on the left. The "Who Dunnit"
on the right resembles this plug but is still a "Who Dunnit".
Pictures on following page .

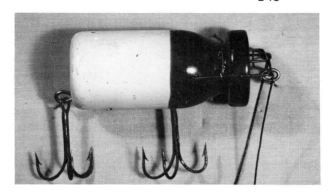

Payne's Woggle Bug

The Woggle Bug by the Payne Bait Company
of Chicago, Illinois came in two sizes. The
single hooks on this plug come out at right
angles upon strike. It was advertised at being
new and humane in 1915. Woggle Bugs are tough
to find - they are all redheads.

The Damsma Plug

Don't you Michigan collectors
realize that you should have found one
of these by now? Maybe you have. Let
us know when one turns up - it must be
a beauty. Mr. Damsma was from Kalamazoo and his patent was dated June 29,
1915.

William Zeigler

Mr. William Zeigler of Ambridge, Pennsylvania assigned half of his
plug patent to George Davis also of Ambridge. It was for a plug with a
mirror in it. The plug in the picture looks very little like the patent
drawing. The reason we put it here is that it is the only plug we have
seen with a mirror. It could be Zeigler's. The patent was dated April
25, 1916.

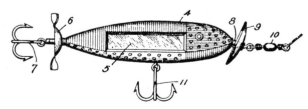

Edward J. Maus

Someone had better find one of
these. The Maus plug patented December 5, 1916 had interchangeable celluloid bodies. It should be a looker.
Watch out for this plug with just the
wood body. It could show up this way.

Schoonie's Skooter

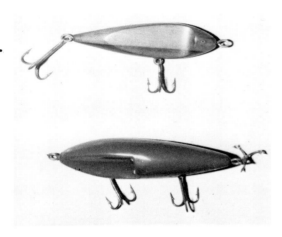

It glides, it floats and it scoots.
John Ray (Schoonie) Schoonmaker was another Kalamazoo, Michigan plug maker.
The Skooter is a classic wood plug. It
is not an easy one to find. The Skooter
came in two sizes and two colors - redhead and all red, 3-1/2" and 4". The
idea of the big flute on one side is re-
peated on the other side in reverse. It
was patented August 1, 1916. We bet it
does, in fact, scoot!

The Jim Dandy

The Jim Dandy "wiggles" and "wobbles". It was invented by Henry H.
Schillinger of Paw Paw, Michigan. Perhaps Mr. Schillinger's most famous
statement was, "I taught game fish how t' bite". The Jim Dandy came in
two sizes and in three colors - white, redhead and frog. H.H. Schillinger's
May 22, 1917 patent drawing shows a distinctive wire clip that goes around
the hook. This is indeed a feature to look for. Jim Dandys are around -
they are usually beat. I guess they really did catch fish. The bass size
is 2-1/4". The musky size is not a huge plug - it is approximately 3-1/2"
and is much harder to find than the bass version. The Jim Dandy was
offered and continued in the Shakespeare line for a short period of time.
The Shakespeare version has a small convex reversed cup and screw eye
belly hook rig. It came in Shakespeare colors.

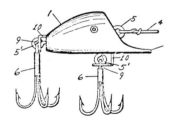

Dickens

John Dickens of Fort Wayne, Indiana filed his earliest patent,
for a plug which had a spring loaded reversible head, on January 29, 1916.
This was later replaced by the Liar. This could be the first Liar. It
looks a lot like a later Dunks (Carter) Dubble Header (not in time span
covered by this book).

John Dickens patented the "Liar" Convertible Minnow on April 8,
1919. This patent was backed up by a Design Patent on February 10, 1920.
The Liar can be either a surface bait or a "wabbler". The belly hook is
removable and can be put on either side of the Liar. Two sizes have been
seen - a 3" and a 3-3/4". Colors available in Liars are redhead, white,
red, yellow or black (see photo left). Dickens also offered a weedless

plug called the Weedless Wonder in the same colors. The Weedless Wonder
usually came tail hooked with a red feathered tail. It also came in a
belly hooked leather tail version (see following). The last plug is
believed to be a rather unknown Dickens "Chunk Plug". All Dickens are
rather difficult to find. However, no one seems to be too excited about
them.

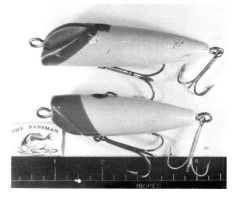

There is another John Dickens patent of September 25, 1923. The
patent picture looks very much like this plug. The hook rig is different
on this plug. Perhaps it's a Dickens, maybe not.

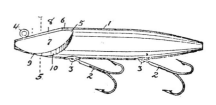
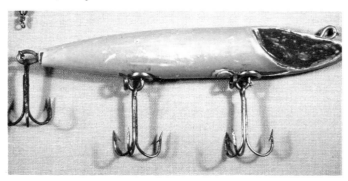

Tooley's Bunty Bait

There were at least two versions of Tooley's plugs - a 2-1/2"
surface fish tail spinnered plug
(top) and the 2" Bunty Darter
(bottom). Colors were redhead,
red body/white head and gold body/
redhead. A scarce-rare wood plug.
The top plug is rare. It is possibly the only known example. Please
note the large reversed cup hook
rig.

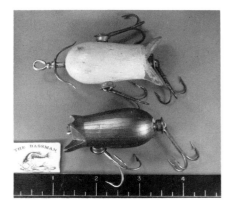

Al Foss

There is no one person as highly regarded as Al Foss. He was an
excellent fisherman, tournament caster and lure maker. Al Foss will not
be covered in this book because his lures aren't exactly plugs. Anyone
interested in Al Foss should contact Jim Frazier of Hollywood, Florida
who is working on a book about Mr. Foss.

Two Groove Head Plugs

There were two groove head type plugs patented by different men
that could be the following plug. It is probably more probable that
this plug is neither a W.H. Shuff, Kansas City, Missouri, patented
June 4, 1918 (top), plug or the O.R. Odell, Minneapolis, Minnesota
patented May 4, 1920 plug. Both plugs are worthwhile looking for.
The plug in the photo could also be a Dickens, but maybe not.

 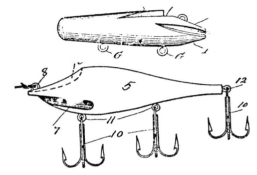

Louis Rhead

Louis Rhead's plugs and other lures are about as innovative as you
can get. Just take a peek back at the first page of the color section of
this book. Talk about something great to collect! There were two types
of frogs with two sizes in the general line. The New (1917) Little Jumping Frog (following photo) is seen to the top right of another Lou Rhead
wood frog on the bottom. The top plug is the "Floating Darting Minnow".
We also see a cricket, grasshopper, small minnow and what looks like a
helgrammite.

Louis Rhead's plugs were somewhere
between fly tying and plugs. A couple of
his neatest plugs were the Sculpin and
the Bullhead. You will know one when
you see one. They have tiny yellow and
black glass eyes. Detail in the hand
paint jobs were as artistic as they were
natural. Louis Rhead was a naturalist
that differentiated between such things
as red bellied frogs and pickerel frogs.
Our thanks to Marc Wisotsky for his help
in the almost impossible study of what
the prolific Mr. Rhead made and sold.
The main activity was from 1916 to the
early 1920s. Lou Rhead authored several
books. Some contain important historical
information. The illustrations are
great. Anyone seriously interested in
collecting Mr. Rhead's plugs or lures
should look for his books. Lou Rhead's
plugs are most appreciated by the few
people that collect them. How about
finding the 1917 "Waga-Waga", a carved
wood propellor.

Louis Rhead used many materials normally not used by plug makers
of his day - look for feathers, light woods, wire, very thin sheet metal
like tinsel - overall fly tyers art.

Henry Crandall

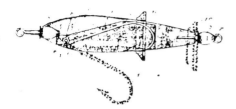

Still another Wisconsin weedless plug.
The patent was filed March 16, 1917 by Henry
Crandall of Racine. It looks like a decent
old plug.

The Reimers Frog

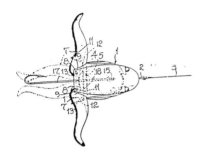

Here is a great looking mechanical frog.
The title of the September 11, 1917 patent is
neat - "Artificial Bass Bait or Frog". This
frog kicks. Some of the parts were probably
rubber (elastic), some metal and perhaps a
wood body.

J.W. Jay

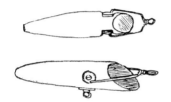

This multiple line-tie plug by James Jay of
Philadelphia, Pennsylvania was patented October 9,
1917. It features a variable line tie.

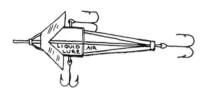

George Race

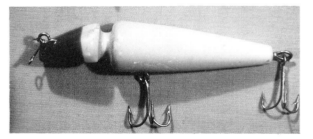

George A. Race of Cicero, Illinois patented
his plug December 4, 1917. The idea of the plug
is to hold a liquid lure fish bait, such as anise
oil or other bad smelling liquids, in a conical
metal portion of the head. It could be that this
had an absorbant casing. It this plug is out
there and has been fished, it's probably a mess.

The McCormic Mermaid

John McCormic of Kalamazoo, Michigan invented the Mermaid December
18, 1917. The body shape is unique and appears again in the Shakespeare
line in Shakespeare colors as the Mermaid and later as the Metal Lipped
Bass-A-Lure. The Mermaid has a hole in the nose with a recessed line-tie
similar to the one used on the Wilson Cupped Wobbler. It came in redhead,
red and black, all red, white or yellow. It is a 3-5/8" version. It
might have come in two sizes. Mermaids are scarce. Left (following) is
a Mermaid. The plug on the right is possibly a McCormic. It's a "Who
Dunnit". It could also be a Wilson, Shakespeare or Moonlight. Our best
guess is McCormic.

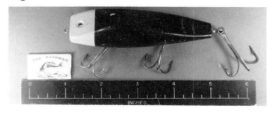

The King Wiggler

The hollow metal (brass) King Wiggler was jointly patented by Charles Farmer and Joseph Martin, both of Minneapolis, Minnesota. The 3-1/2" King Wiggler's motto was, "Should be in every tackle box". King Wigglers occasionally turn up. The King Wiggler was patented January 1, 1918.

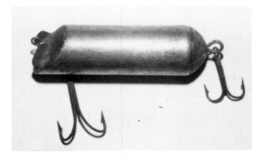

Lyman Mason

A chicago plug patented February 4, 1919. The body turns. Looks like a goodie.

Ruel Dingwell, et al

Mr. Dingwell was from Cambridge, Massachusetts and shared this February 25, 1919 patent with a Mr. Jones from Boston and H.S. Andreas of Rochester, New York. It has a lead body and spring attachment for the hook.

Medley's Wiggly Crawfish

The Medley's Wiggly Crawfish has one of the most colorful paint jobs of any plug ever. They are absolutely beautiful. One in excellent condition is hard to find - they chipped a lot. Harry Medley patented his crawfish on August 5, 1919 and assigned one-third to Harry Hamilton of Youngstown, Ohio. Mr. Medley was from California. The plugs themselves have been reported to have been made in California, but we don't know for sure. Two sizes were available - the 2-1/2" one treble belly hook model (left) and the 3" 2-hook model. The Crawfish has glass eyes and rubber feelers. Both H.L. Medley and H.A. Hamilton confirmed their patents on two separate dates. Mr. Medley's 1920 patent recognized the idea of making this plug look like a fish (that would swim backward). Mr. H. Hamilton's patent of June 15, 1920 is a Design Patent showing the elaborate paint job.

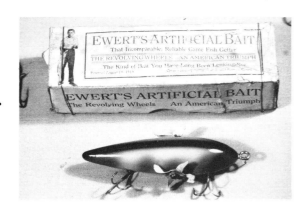

Ewert's Artificial Bait

A great plug from California. Walter Ewert patented this rare old side wheeler August 19, 1919.

Francis Rabbeth

Francis Rabbeth of Redlands, California had a patent dated September 9, 1919. This one looks like it might catch fish.

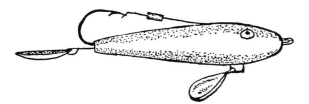

The Hookzem

At last a spring loaded weedless plug has been found. Mr. Henry Gottschalk patented this dangerous plug October 7, 1919. There aren't many of these around.

Leeper's Bass Bait

Henry T. Leeper of Fredonia, Kentucky patented this rather simply designed but near rare plug on November 14, 1919. Leeper's Bass Bait came in two sizes, a little 2-1/4"er and larger 3"er. There was a line-tie on both ends of the Leeper's Bass Bait so you could have a choice of actions. All white and red and white versions have been seen.

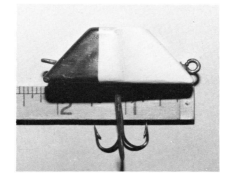

Samuel E. Doane

A New York City weedless plug which was probably made of metal and patented December 14, 1920.

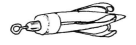

John Frame

John Frame patented this mechanical
wonder October 11, 1921. It is doubtful
if any of these are out there. We can
always hope and look.

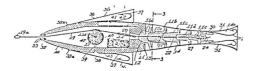

Winchester

Not many people think of fishing plugs when they think of Winchester.
Nevertheless Winchester offered three different plugs in several variations.
Winchesters are as well made as expected. The four digit numbers were stamped on the spinners of the 9200 series (9210-9217) 5-hooker and 9000 series
3-hooker Winchester minnows - left and center on top of Model 97 16-guage
Winchester Black Diamond (trap) model in following photo. On the right is
the 9200-9207 Multi Wobbler, a crab type plug which sports a changeable lip
for different actions. All three Winchester plugs came in eight colors including a patented decal scale finish patented on July 26, 1921 by Leavitt
Lane of New Haven, Connecticut and assigned to Winchester Repeating Arms Co.
(right photo). The decal finish Winchester colors 07 and 17 were good,
and certainly one of the first, attempts at a realistic finish. The last
two digits on the Winchester numbers refer to the color. Winchesters are
rather valuable - not only are they hard to find and nice plugs but they
are Winchesters!.

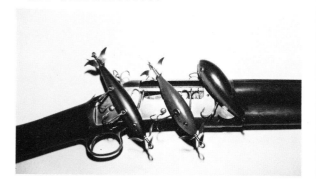

J.N. Piggott

This Design Patent (November 22,
1921) shows a plug that probably looks
something like this.

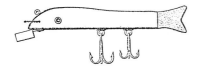

L.P. Kelley

The Kelley "Artificial Trolling Bait", as it was called in the February
1921 patent, could have been made of felt or rubber or perhaps something else.
The idea is that if a hook gets broken off on a rock or log, the plug is
retreivable and the hook replaced. This is a New Hampshire plug.

The Glowbody Minnow

Patented June 7, 1921 by William S. Warden of New York, New York, the
Glowbody was assigned to Baker, Murray & Imbrie of New York (better known to

collectors as Abbey & Imbrie which was an important New York retail sporting goods dealer for years). The Glowbody was "self-luminous". Most luminous plugs need to be exposed to light to work. The Glowbody glows all the time. Among materials recommended for the strip of luminous material incased in the glass body was a radium compound, mesothorium or zink sulfide. They all sound dangerous. Maybe it's best to house your Glowbody in a lead box. The 3-1/4" Glowbody is hard to find and well made.

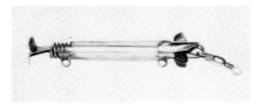

Hanson's Irresistible

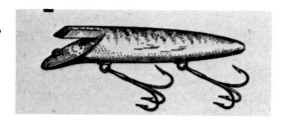

Anyone ever see a Hanson's Irresistible? It came in three colors - green, red and green and brown mottled back with a red mouth. This plug was from William B. Hanson & Company, Pittsburgh, Pennsylvania. This appears to be a rare one.

Carter's Bestever Baits

Thomas J. Carter of Indianapolis, Indiana was granted a Design Patent for what plug collectors know as a Carter's Plug. The distinct style of this plug (see Design Patent) was a fish catching wonder. The "Old Black Joe" is legendary around here. Design Patents are kind to plug collectors in that they look like the plug itself. The variations are what to look for in Carter's Bestever Baits. The earliest Carter Bestever came in three standard sizes, the large 3-5/8", medium 3-1/8" and midget 2-5/8". Remember all original Carter's wood plugs look basically alike. Variation on a theme. For example the 4-1/2"er following is Carter's Pike. The plug on the right is the 3" Carter's Craw. It goes backwards.

The early Carter colors were rather plain - redhead, black (Old Black Joe), all red, redhead/yellow, redhead/gold and redhead/aluminum. More Carters were added to the line available in different sizes and variations starting with the 1-3/4" Baby Carter, a small belly hooked trout and panfish plug. The standard sizes gradually became 2-3/4", 3" and 3-1/2". In addition there was a 4-1/2" Big Boy, a fat version of the sort of rare 4-1/2" pike. There was also an equally hard to find 5-1/2" musky. One of a couple of subtle variations was the Day-R-Night which was distinguished by a black head/white body and came in 2-3/4", 3" and 3-1/2" versions. They are 2-hookers with a tail instead of a belly hook. Another subtle variation was the Shore Minnow coming in 3" and 3-1/2" and distinguished by having the

rear hook on the tail and a three-tone color - black head and back over
silver with an all white belly. A couple of not so subtle variations that
are both among the most desirable J.T. Carter products are the 2-3/8"
single hook weedless patented February 8, 1927 (see patent drawing) and
the Surface Twin. Turn a Carter's Bestever on its side, put the cup hook
rig on the side and you have Carter's Surface Twin, a 3" and 3-1/2"
injured Carter's (see photo).

 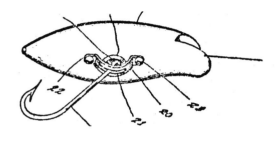

        J.T. Carter was doing business in Indianapolis, Indiana until the
late 1920s. The exact date when Mr. Carter's products were combined with
the works of the American Display Company of Dayton, Ohio is not known.
For a time Carter's plugs (around 1930) were called Dunk's-Carter's. The
Dunks period Carters are beyond the chronology of this book. The disting-
uising features of post 1930 Carters are the use of a scale finish, glass
eyes and a decal on the belly. (Carter also used a similar decal. They
are self identifying.) Dunks evidently ran the sporting goods portion of
the American Display Company. One plug that does fit into the time frame
in this book is the 2-3/4" Stubby's Hydroplane, a hollow aluminum plug
with a hole in it. Just fill it full of water and cast it far out.

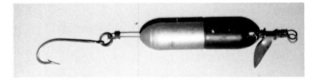

William Schmid

        This waggle tail plug was patented
May 30, 1922, from Bronson, Michigan. Any
out there?

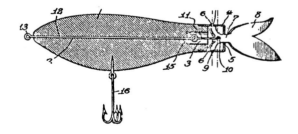

Frank Koepke

        A 4-1/2" Washington state hollow
brass, floating/diver plug. Not much is
known regarding Mr. Koepke's plug except
it was patented May 9, 1922. Some nice
plugs were made in Washington state -
this is one of them.

Five - 1920s Plugs

The exact date of these amusing and interesting plugs is unknown - those given are approximate.

The top plug following (left) is unknown and thought to be a Florida plug from the late 1920s. It has three holes in the cup. It's a well made plug. The winged single hooker below and left is the 1-3/4" Winter's Weedless Surface Bait distributed by N.C. Souther, Chicago, Illinois. These little beauties have celluloid wings and are hand painted. The plug that looks like a clothes pin is the Clothes Pin Minnow, Moline, Illinois. It also came in a smaller 3-1/2" size. The plug on the right in this photo is Cox's Tampa (Florida) Minnow, a 4"er that combines gooves with a metal lip. On the right (following photo) we have Kerwin's Bad Egg. Although this one is down to the wood, Kerwin's Bad Egg came in white, yellow, red and silver. This dynamite 2"er was made by Mr. M.F. Kerwin, O'Neill, Nebraska. All five plugs are tough to find.

The Griffith's Minnow

The Griffith's Minnow sports interchangeable brass fins for a cloudy day or copper for a bright day and silver for a very dark day. Four sizes were available - 1", 2", 2-1/2" and 3". Where are they?

The ABC Minnow

The ABC Minnow featured changable colors. You turn an eye and slip in another colored back. The ABC came in two versions with at least six different solid colored backs including white, black, silver red and green. The 4-1/4"er top (following, left) has eyes and a mouth. It is a surface jerk bait type design. The ABC below it is a 4" floater/diver. ABCs were patented by George W. Bolton of Detroit, Michigan on December 18, 1923.

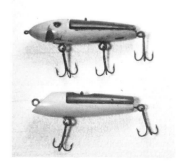

The Comstock Weedless Chunk

This is where chunk plugs got the name "chunk plug". Just throw it into the pads. Valparaiso, Indiana, where this plug originated, is just the place to do that. It is not far from South Bend, Dowagiac and Paw Paw - all chunk plug country. The Comstock Weedless Chunk is seen later as part of the Moonlight Bait Company's line. The Moonlight version often has painted eyes. The Comstocks do not. Also, there is a metallic keel on true Comstocks. See Moonlight

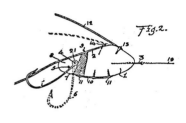

Fred Paulson

There were some great plugs made in Illinois - this is one of them. The 3-3/4" glass eyed redhead in the photo following resembles the patent to the point that it could be what it is (missing some parts). At least we are getting close. The patent indicates a giant windmill type prop ("wings or vanes" in patent). They could slso be locked out (feathered?) so it would also be some other kind of a plug such as a "diving bait, a wigginling bait, a skipping bait, and/or diving surface bait or a spinning bait". The "vanes" were put on sort of with set screws like an erector set.

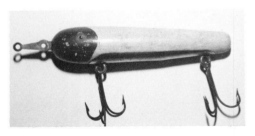

The Bite-Em Baits

Claude M. Rodgers and Arthur W. Wenger of Warsaw, Indiana patented the Bite-Em Lipped Wiggler. This sturdy plug with an adjustable diving lip came in a 4-1/2" 3-hooker and a 3-3/4" 2-hooker. The "Lipped" came in an array of colors. In fact, Bite-Ems are among the most colorful of all plugs. It's too bad the photos following are not in color. See color section for a selection of Bite-Ems. The two plugs below the 3-hooker Lipped Wiggler right, are (left) a 4-1/2" (also came in 3") Floater and (right) the 3" Pork - these are two of the more scarce Bite-Ems!

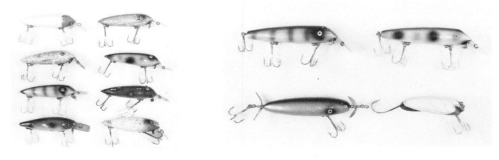

Perhaps the most famous of the Bite-Ems is the 3" Bite-Em Bait itself. The commercial version came in at least nine very colorful combinations. We feel fortunate to be able to present the two Bite-Em Baits on the right. They are handmade early developmental stages of the Bite-Em Bait. The standard Bite-Em Bait is probably the easiest Bite-Em to find. Bite-Em Baits were probably around before 1920.

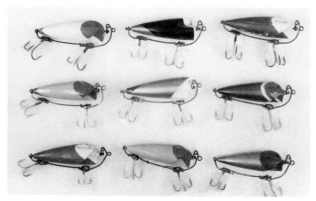 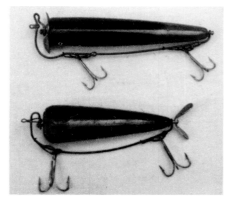

We do not know if this 1918 patent by R.F. O'Brien had anything to do with Bite-Em. The cradle that the Bite-Em spins in resembles Mr. O'Brien's plug. We'd like to know more about Mr. O'Brien.

The Bite-Ems on the top in the following left photo are 3" Water Moles. Second row left is a Bite-Em Bait, center is the standard 1-1/4" Bug and the Bite-Em Pork is on the right. Third row is a Floater (which has also been reported in a jointed version) and the 3-3/4" Bite-Em Wiggler. The Water Mole, Wiggler and Bug are moderately scarce Bite-Ems. Bottom row left is an unknown Bite-Em, center is the Lipped Wiggler and right is the tiny 1-1/2" Bite-Em Trout. The Trout, like so many (miniature) fly rod plugs isn't too easy to find. Many Bite-Em plugs are hook rigged with a sort of screw-in "L" type rig similar to the one on the unknown plug in the photo on the right. What is this unknown Bite-Em?

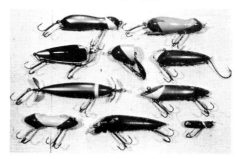 

Bite-Em Underwater Minnows are little known and extremely hard to find. The 3-3/4" 5-hooker on the right has a hook link type rig. The little 2-3/4" 3-hooker (belly) on the right has Bite-Em in a diamond stamped on the prop. It also has the "L" type rig. A rig very similar to those used by Algers, Heddon, Lockhart and on later Stump Dodgers.

Claude Rodgers went on to be affiliated in some way with the South Bend Bait Company. In fact, he designed and in 1929 patented the classic South Bend Plug Oreno. Arthur Wenger went on to be associated with Horrocks-Ibbotson. The Lipped Wiggler was later in the Horrocks-Ibbotson line. The plugs following (left) are the handmade original developmental Lipped Wiggler. The 2" Bite-Em on the right is a seldom seen Bug type Bite-Em. Bite-Ems are not easy. They are very attractive plugs and an important stage in plug development. Thanks to Jim Bourdon, Russ Mumford and Tom Steele.

The Glowurm

Most plug collectors are familiar with the Glowurm. Several years ago quite a few showed up all at once. We don't know how many. One thing the ad says that says it all is "It looks like a big worm" - a jointed worm. The Glowurm is long and been seen in yellow/green and red/white. The wood box it comes in is as neat as the plug inside. It's a big plug - around 4-1/4". The Glowurms that were found have probably been assimilated into collections. They are still around. It's a great old classic. Not a bad one to hang up while you can. The Glowurm was sold and made by Oliver & Gruber, Medical Lake, Washington.

Bert G. Goble

Bert Goble's plugs rate among the most attractive of all times. His earliest patent, March 18, 1924, only vaguely resembles the Goble Baits that have been found. The Goble Bait following is a 4"er with a fancy red over gold finish. What a beauty! There are a few around - very few. Apparently it came in more than one 4" size. Mr. Goble also patented a frog on April 19, 1929. A Goble Frog would be quite a find.

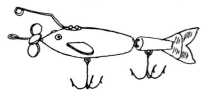
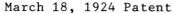

March 18, 1924 Patent

Goble (Continued)

Following (left) is a figure from the December 30, 1924 patent,
which was an iprovement over the March 18, 1924 patent. Also (right)
is a figure from the Mr. Goble's 1929 Frog patent.

The Vermilion Meadow Mouse

Frank K. Knill of Vermilion, Ohio made his plug
and other lures in his garage. The 3-1/2" Vermilion
Meadow Mouse is a great plug, hard to find and a
"looker" at the same time. F.K. Knill was granted several patents - 1922, 1924 and 1926. None for the plug
itself. Thanks to Bob Vermillion for information on
this man and his plug.

Alexander Cosey

This Cambridge, New York plug was patented October 7, 1924. The
patent drawing shows a highly embellished double jointer. There is no
real reason to think the plug in the following photo (right) is a Cosey.
This red, white and blue 4-1/4"er is cup rigged. The Cosey is unknown
except for the patent.

Erwin Weller

Wellers are Iowa's finest. They are around but usually show up in
rough shape. The paint jobs were attractive and provided in a variety of
colors - eight that are known of. The perch, piko and chub forms are
beautiful. The toughest Weller is the little known 4" pike size. This is
a straight pike type plug. Keep your eyes open for one. The standard
Weller is the Weller Classic. The plug looks like the one in the patent.
The reason we show the patent is that it's the only Classic we have seen
that still has its fabric tail. This is the most common Weller. The
Classic came in three sizes, the #1, 2-joint is 4-1/2", the #2 1-joint is
4" and the #3, a smaller 3-1/4"er. The sizes seem to vary a bit. The
smaller Classics are harder to find than the big job. The Classic (following, left) is the #3. The 3-1/4" Simplex Wiggler is the top plug. Note
the straight body. The Weller Mouse is a desirable Weller. It has a
feathered hook (following, right)

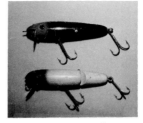

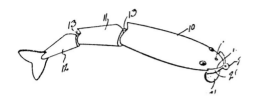

Note the two types of lips on the above Wellers. The style in the
patent is the early one. Another Weller that deserves more attention is the
little 2-1/2" Ozark Minnow - a solid plug with tack painted eyes. All other
Wellers have glass eyes. One final thing to look for in Wellers are odd
variations like the single hook #1 Classic. Remember the Pike Weller. The
Weller Classic was patented November 16, 1926 by Mr. Weller who was from
Sioux City, Iowa.

R. Danielson and Other Weedless Metal Plugs

How about that - finally one of these illusive metal weedless plugs
shows up. In fact a few have. We think the following plug is the August
16, 1927 Rubin Danielson, Chicago, Illinois patent. This plug is 4-1/4"
long and has a feature on the other side where you can push up the back
to reset the hooks. Don't ever try and take one of these apart unless
you want trouble.

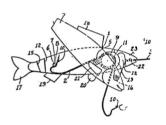
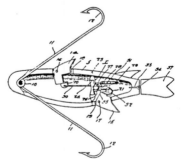

These weedless metal and wood plugs are really frustrating. Here
are three more before 1930. There is a whole bunch of these after 1930.
Check these out. Left to right - left: Fred Beidatsch, Milwaukee, Wiscon-
sin-July 18, 1927 (filing date), center: Lee Johns, Miami, Florida-August
31, 1927 (filing date) and right: Charles Stoll, Chicago, Illinois-September
2, 1927 (filing date). What can we say - keep looking!

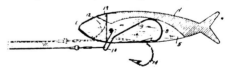

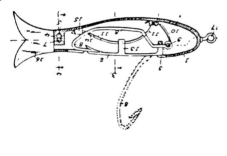

Outing

The Outing Manufacturing Company of Elkhart, Indiana offered a line
of hollow metal (brass) plugs of unexcelled quality. Clarence Dewey of
Elkhart patented what he called his Floater Getum on November 23, 1926.
The Floater Getum is approximately 4" and is perhaps the one least found.
The DuGetum is a floating frog and came in two sizes. See following photo

left. Among other more standard colors offered are two kinds of frogs and
a mouse. The two most beautiful Outing plugs are the 3-7/8" Bassy Getum
(top, following) and the 3-5/8" Piky Getum (following, right). The paint
jobs on these two plugs are exquisite and quite realistic. Paint chips
easily on metal plugs. Condition is important on Outings.

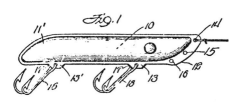

The two plugs on the left are special purpose weedless wigglers. The
top one is the Porky Getum, and the bottom plug is the Feather Getum. Both
plugs came in three different weights. Outings are getting more attention
these days. The collection, following, are all products of the Outing Manufacturing Company. The earliest patent was in 1926. By 1928 Outing had
sold out to Heddon who continued the reels but evidently cut out the plugs.

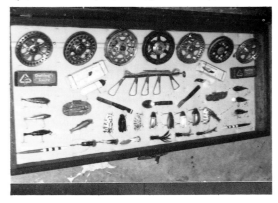

Moore's Yellow Plug

The Moore's Yellow Plug is an underwater plug. It gets down there!
In the 1924 season one hundred were sold. By March 1926 400 were sold.
Mr. H.C. Moore of Ypsilanti, Michigan personally witnessed 75 fishermen
all casting the Moore's Yellow Plug. The color is always yellow body/
black head, the size is 4-1/2" and the hook rig is closed screw eye (non
removable) with brass cups. There seems to be a few still around. This
plug would cast like a bullet.

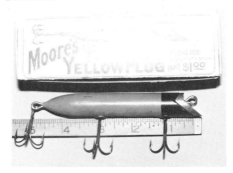

Pearl Plug

The Pearl Plug has turned up. It is extremely well made with a red-head and tail. The body is octagonal and covered with a pearl like substance which is held in with metal bands. The Pearl Plug is approximately a fat 3".

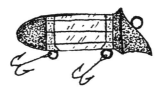

The WAB

The WAB (Weedless Automatic Bait) was another early plastic, weedless plug. The WAB was a popular plug - there are still some around. You could carry this one in your pocket. Squeeze it and the hooks pop out. The WAB is made of a combination of red and white plastic. This is how it works. WABS were sold by the Fenner Weedless Bait Company, Oxford, Wisconsin. The patent was dated February 2, 1926.

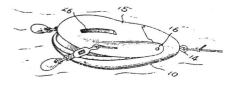
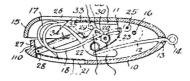
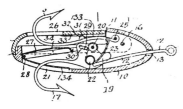

The Bass King

The Bass King and Bass King Jr. usually came in red and white. This was a well made, cup rigged Minnesota bait by the National Bait Company in Stillwater. There were two sizes - 3" and 3-1/2". These are still around.

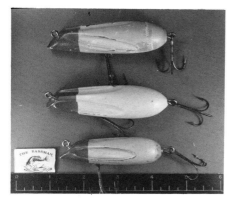

The Hildebrandt Wooden Bait

The Hildebrandt Wooden Bait was called the Go-Getter. Hildebrandt was known more for spinners and such things. This plug from Logansport, Indiana is interesting and looks sort of like a Creek Chub River Rustler - same type lip. Hildebrandt distributed this 2-3/4" removable hook plug around 1927. The color is usually white on the few specimens found so far.

Biff Bait Company

The Master Biff came in two sizes and two colors. The two sizes vary between 2-1/8" and 2-1/4", and right around 3". Early ads only talk about one size - a 2-1/2"er. The baby probably came along a little later. The colors are redhead and natural yellow perch body (hand painted black spots over a yellow body). Master Biffs make noise on the surface. The concave head and the two holes do the trick (following, left). The 1-1/2" Surface Single Wobbler (top) and the 3-1/2" Surface Double Wobbler (below) are unusual plugs. The entire wood bodies revolve around a weighted frame. Another noise maker.

The underwater version of the Biff was the Spiral Spinner which came in three sizes and worked on the same principle as the Surface Single and Double Wobblers only it used a flat coiled piece of metal. Mr. Bayer had a special hand powered machine for both the large and small Spirals.

The Biff Bait Company of Milwaukee, Wisconsin was offered for sale in mid to late 1926 to The Moonlight Bait Company of Paw Paw, Michigan. The offer was refused. The Biff Bait Company was represented by Mr. Albert R. Bayer, and started into business around early 1925. By late 1926 they had sold 30,000 plugs. That's a lot of plugs for someone who did not advertise extensively. Biffs were made on the outside. A "Master Plug" cost 18¢ and was sold for 90¢.

The Flex-O-Minnow

Streich's Flex-O-Minnow is a 3-1/2" lead-head rubber bodied weedless plug made in Joliet, Illinois.

The Wobahna

This could be a Wobahna, "The Laughing Plug". It is also possible it's not - just another guess. It is a great wood frog even if it isn't a Wobahna. The Wobahna was made in Racine, Wisconsin in the 1920s. These frogs show up occasionally.

Electric Light Bulb Plugs

We are going to go back in time to discuss electric light bulb plugs. One of the earliest is the James Simms' (West Virginia) patent of November 25, 1913. It probably looked something like the drawing on the left. The A. Sampey patent of 1915 shows a new direction in light bulb plugs (a 5-hooker). The plug on the right is possibly the Senate Lighted lure.

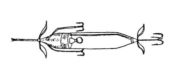 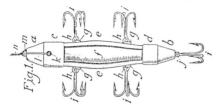 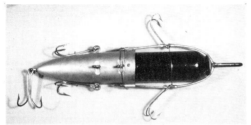

Dr. C.S. Wasweyler of Milwaukee, Wisconsin marketed two versions of the same wonderful plug. The version on the left was called Dr. C.S. Wasweyler's Marvelous Electric Glow Casting Minnow. This 1915 version might be a luminous plug rather than an electric light plug. The Glow Worm was advertised in 1916 as The Electric Luminous Submarine Bait. It probably looked like the drawing on the right.

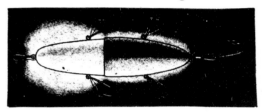 

The Lectro Lure by the Davis Lure Company of Peoria, Illinois sort of looks like the 1927 A.H. Wunderlin patent. There is also a 1925 Wunderlin patent (left). There are many more electric light plugs made after the time span represented in this book. One final electric bulb patent by J.A. Neff and dated March 20, 1928.

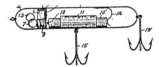 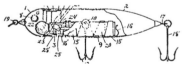

1925 Wunderlin
Patent

1927 Wunderlin
Patent

 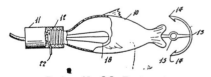

Lectro Lure
Davis Lure Co.

J.A. Neff Patent
March 20, 1928

The Brooks Shiner

The Brooks Shiner from Milwaukee,
Wisconsin should have been found by now.
It was made around the mid-1920s.

The Snakerbait and Friend

The Snakerbait was patented by Robert and Charles Clewell of Canton,
Ohio on November 13, 1928. The plug on the right (following) is truly an
old "Who Dunnit" Worm which has nothing to do with the Snakerbait.

The Mudpuppy

C.C. "Con" Roberts of Mosinee, Wisconsin started carving his original
Mudpuppy shortly before 1920. He filed for a patent on October 12, 1925.
He received it in 1928. There is no more famous musky plug around here than
the Mudpuppy. They are still being made. The Mudpuppy has been around longer than almost any wood plug still in production. The very early ones were
hand crafted. The two examples following (left) are the original product.
Early Mudpuppys were split down the middle rather than two-thirds of the way
down the body as they have been for some time. Early Mudpuppys came in 6-1/2",
and the 5-1/4" little Mudpuppy. (Following, right for early 6-1/2"ers.) All
the early models had the patented removable hook. You fight the fish not the
plug. Mr. Roberts later attached permanent hooks to a river model. By the
time you are done with a 36 pound musky on the Wisconsin River, your Mudpuppy
body might be two miles down stream.

We want to thank Doug Lenichek and Peter Haupt for their help. Doug
has spent a lot of time collecting, researching and fishing the Mudpuppy.

Fred Arbogast

The beginnings of Fred Arbogast's lures date from at least 1927. We
can only cover their brief beginning. The Tin Liz and Weedless Kickers are

made of cast metal. The ones to find are the three following - the Snake
(northern pike), the Walleye and the Crappie (pumpkinseed finish). The two
finned Sunfish is done in this color and is more common than the following.
A musky and bass have been rumored - wouldn't that be something. Most of
these have glass eyes - they are rather small. For example the Walleye has
a 2-1/2" body.

The "Spintail Kicker" or "Weedless Kicker", frog finish, left, and
the three Tin Lizes are more often found. They are worthwhile especially
the glass eyed versions and musky versions. The Tin Liz came in redside
chub, redhead and perch. Three sizes were offered - baby 2-1/4" 1/2 ounce,
standard 2-1/2" 1/2 ounce and large for big pike and musky 3-1/4" (a scarce
variation). There is also a Weedless Tin Liz, Twin Liz (two on a V wire)
and fly rod (thin metal) Tin Liz. The familiar sight on the right is an
early wood Jitterbug. There is a rumor about a glass eyed Jitterbug. Jitter-
bugs came along later and are still catching fish. The Jitterbug and other
creative products are still being made in the finest tradition of Fred
Arbogast of Akron, Ohio.

The Bonnett Plugs

Mr. Clarence Elmore Bonnett patented his plug on April 20, 1926. It
sort of looks like the very few Bonnetts we know of. There seem to be few
survivors. The stages of development illustrated below are good examples
of plugs made by Mr. Bonnett but perhaps never sold. The Bonnett we have
seen is well made but crudely painted and looks somewhat like the patent
following right. Thanks to Bill Jones for information on Bonnett plugs.

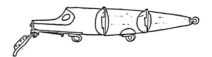

The Hagen Plug

Two sizes of the Hagen plug have been seen - approximately 1-1/2"
and 2". This well made redhead has painted eyes and spins around an axis.
The Hagen plug is from Manitowoc, Wisconsin. Pictures following page.

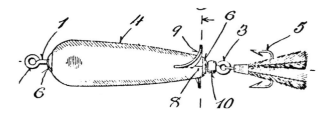

A Couple of Late 1920s Mice

The Kimmich Special (Mouse) is a neat deerhair bodied mouse not to be confused with the later and much more common Paw Paw Mouse.

The Mouse Bait Company of Fort Worth, Texas produced one of the great Texas plugs. One of the better wood mice to find.

Sobecki's "1929 Wiggler"

Anthony Sobecki of South Bend, Indiana received a patent on the 1929 Wiggler or Pollywog Wiggler as it was also known on April 1, 1930. This 4" redhead is distinctive in shape and difficult to find.

Bill's Pride

The patent for Bill's Pride was filed December 30, 1926. "Bill" was William C. Mills of Brooklyn, N.Y., a famous name. Bill's Pride is well made and came in all yellow or redhead. The Bill's Pride in the photo is 2-7/8". It was generally advertised in the 3" size - a solid version 2-3/4"er has been reported.

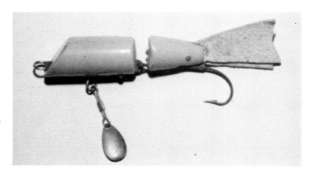

The Like Live Bait

The Like Live Bait was offered for sale by Mr. A.L. Lee of Jacksonville, Florida in 1929. You pull the line-tie and a spool with a rubber band is supposed to wag the tail. The 4-1/2" green, yellow and white Like Live in the photo is one of the few that has showed up.

It is curious that in the 1920s there were so many plugs patented that, to the best of our knowledge, have not been found. Perhaps it was due to the Great Depression of late 1929. This book essentially ends there. The following illustrations are all plugs from the 1920s.

1922 - Dennis P. Ryan, Toledo, Ohio - sandwiched metal with wood.

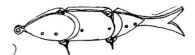

1922 - Walter Grounsell, Syracuse, N.Y. - chunk plug.

1923 - William Frament, Cohoes, N.Y. - hooks shoot out.

1923 - U. Smith, Fayette, Ohio - reversible head. Floater/diver or surface minnow.

1923 - W.E. Koch, New Rochelle, N.Y. - it zig zags.

1923 - P.E. Peterson, Boston, Massachusetts - Mr. Peterson passed away before his floating/diver was patented. The patent was assigned to the administrator of his estate - perhaps that's the reason none have turned up.

1924 - J.E. Ford, Green Bay, Wisconsin - this could be an interesting plug. It has holes drilled in it for different line ties.

1925 - Grover Cleveland Morriss, Austin, Texas - This minnow looks good. The plug body is described as made of any desired material.

1925 - C. Andersen, Watertown, South Dakota - a good looking double jointer.

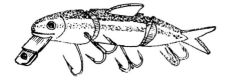

1926 - Sidney McLeod, Chicago, Illinois - a rubber plug.

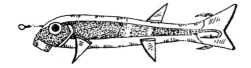

1926 - E.J. Babbitt, Holland, Michigan - an-
       other long lost weedless wonder. Has
       a pinned in body. Wood?

1926 - George Romaduke, Detroit, Michigan -
       this plug is made of "resiliant"
       material - perhaps rubber. It has two
       line ties, combination plug and fish
       decoy.

1927 - Charles Hughes and Bernard Kothe,
       Cincinnati, Ohio - the "propellor
       wheel" makes the tail wag.

1927 - C.M. Reed, Kabletown, West Virginia -
       a spring loaded plug.

1928 - John Otto, Chicago, Illinois - a lever
       action weedless type hook, you pull
       forward and the barbs shoot out.

1928 - Thomas L. Watts, Indianapolis, Indiana -
       patent is for a "variable direction
       control for trailing objects". It pro-
       vides and "up and down and side to side
       darting movements".

     The patent drawings below represent the diversity of late 1920's
patents. The last patent (following, right) is perhaps the funniest.
Mr. Smith pointed out the relative simplicity of his patent - only 62 parts.

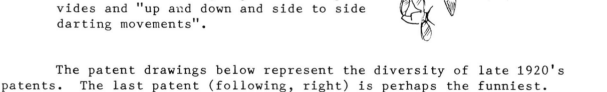

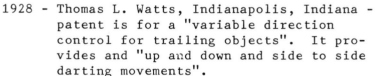

J.C. Caldwell - 1921

C.J. Brown - 1921

J.M. Kishpaugh - 1922

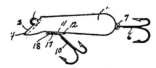

W.O. Jones - 1923

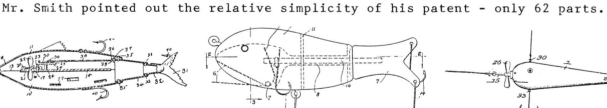

E. Prieur - 1928

G.E. Nelson - 1928

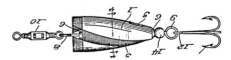

P.S. Heaslip - 1928

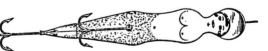

W.G. Kutz - 1929

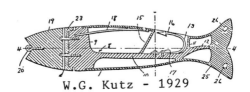

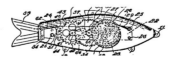

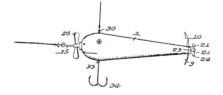

J.R. Smith - 1928

Lauby Baits

     Anton Lauby's plugs are very colorful (see color pages). Time wise Mr. Lauby barely makes it into the pre-1930 limit of plugs covered in this edition. The Lauby wooden "Wonder Spoons" shown in the following photo are two of the earliest Laubys known - believed to have been made in the late 1920s. They are hand painted - most Laubys are air brushed. The Lauby "Wonder Spoon" was later - 1935 patent. What a great idea - a wood spoon that floats. It was made in a wide range of sizes and colors.

     Another possible pre-1930 Lauby plug is the Lauby Minnow - later called The Minnie and made in three sizes. The early ones were probably hand painted. We cannot further discuss the Lauby Bait Company of Marshfield, Wisconsin. This belongs in the history of plugs in the great plug years of 1930-1941. Laubys are interesting plugs.

     Other interesting plugs, that may or may not have been made before 1930, follow. Little is known about most of these.

Little Pappy Joe

Jos. Doodle Bug
Marked - Homarth,
Indiana

Barr-Royers

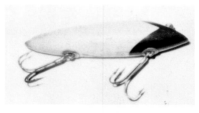

Ketchall Wobbler

Wright & McGill
Wiggling Minnow

Klip On Plugs

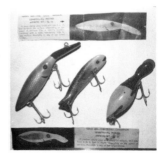

Possible Make Em Bite
Bait - Clark - Indiana

Clark - Indiana

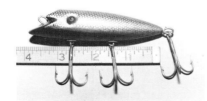

Winchester - Indiana

The following three are all thought to be Florida plugs from the late 1920s

Jim Pfeffer Sunfish

Floods Wooden Minnow
(see arrow for posi-
tion of line-tie)

Trumpetfish "Who Dunnit"
Has a turned up cup
belly rig.

More "Who Dunnits" thought to be from the late 1920s.

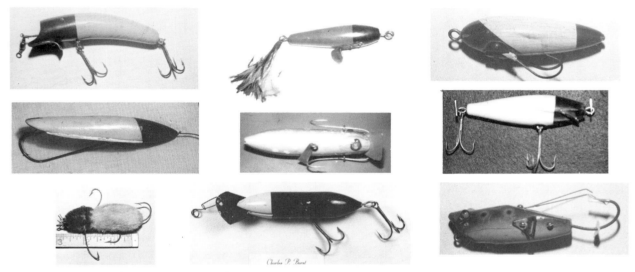

That's about it for miscellaneous old fishing plugs of the U.S.A.
There are probably a lot more out there that fit into this time slot. If
you are wondering where the Reel Lure, Drake's Sea Bat, Florida Flapper, etc.
are - they come along later. A couple of final notes to potential miscellaneous collectors. Don't get too excited over a little thin metal watch charm
that looks like this, unless it originally had hooks on it. It could be real
good or real nothing.

We hope you run across a plug like the following photo. Finally -
Good Luck! - keep looking. After all, why is Karl White smiling?

Chapter Four

PFLUEGER

Ernest F. Pflueger came to the U.S.A. from Germany. He lost his parents and was on his own at a very young age. Mr. Pflueger moved to Akron, Ohio around 1870 where he became interested in the business of decoration for horse harnesses and bridles. The one thing that fascinated him was the use of luminous paint for safety at night. Ernest decided to try luminous paint on lures. He started a fishing tackle empire.

The first two plugs marketed by Ernest F. Pflueger were the Luminous Flying Helgrammite and the Luminous Crystal Minnow - this was in 1885 or even earlier. Harry Comstock's and Jorgen Irgens' plugs were discussed on pages 51-53. Mr. Pflueger's versions were luminous as per his patent that covered luminosity dated February 12, 1883. The Luminous Crystal Minnow (left) was in the line at least in 1885. It came in two sizes. We have only seen the small 1-3/8" version (following, left). The Luminous Flying Helgrammite (right) was only advertised in the 1885 (or pre-1886) catalog in four versions.

The Royal Mallaeable Crystal body fly catalogued in 1886 was available in two sizes. It looks like a pike. If you find one without the feather, it's better than O.K. None are known.

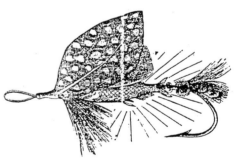

Rubber plugs in both luminous and non-luminous versions were offered in 1892. The "Hard Rubber Minnow" was offered in three sizes - 2", 2-1/2" and 3" - in several spinner versions. The top left Pflueger is a glass eyed hard rubber plug with a Minne-ha-ha spinner. The soft rubber 2-1/2"er below has a single spinner. Both came in many sizes and variations. The unusual spinners are the ones to look for.

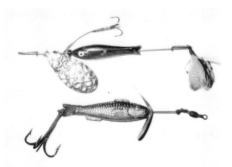

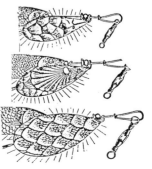

The 7" Muskallonge Trolling Minnow (following, left) which came out in
1892 came in luminous and non-luminous. A complete line of small fly rod
rubber lures was also offered (following, right). The Dragonfly has not been
seen in a catalog but all the catalogues have not been seen. The body is
made of wood.

The celebrated Pflueger's American Phantom Minnows (top, left) were
offered in the 1892 catalog in twelve sizes from the tiny 1-3/4"er to the
4-3/4"er. These came in seven colors. The cloth bodies were hand painted
on the early models and were lithographed (printed) after the turn of the
century. There was a version in the 1890s that was made of porpoise hide.
Most Pflueger Phantoms are marked Pflueger on the blade. An interesting
version of the Phantom is Pflueger's 3" Phantom Spinner (following, left)
The Phantoms were offered in both luminous and the less expensive non-
luminous versions. The Pearl Phantom was offered in three sizes and in luminous and non-luminous versions. The 3-1/2" example (following, center) is
unfortunately missing the line-tie. The Breakless Devon (following, right)
was offered painted or plated and came in five sizes - 2" to 3" in quarter
inch intervals. A keel is seen on some Devons. This lure looks very much
like the Wakeman. Both are usually marked on the blade.

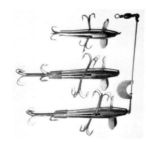

The May Bug Spoon is a joy to behold. It was made for skittering.
Skittering was a popular method of fishing from 1870 through the 1890s.
Can you imagine going out on a nice day in 1892 and skittering for pickerel
using the hot new May Bug Spoon or the out of production Flying Helgrammite?
It is a pleasant thought. Skittering is done with a long 13' to 15' stout
rod and a short heavy line. Although reels were used, they weren't necessary.
You go quietly along standing in the back of the boat which your guide or
buddy sculls (poles) or rows along. The idea is to put the lure in a hole in
the lily pads and jerk, slosh and skip it back and forth.

The earliest reference we can find to a Pflueger developed wood plug is
Pfluegers plug of 1896 which was made out of a cork body cut in half and attached to a center piece of stiff porpoise hide. This plug was later reproduced
by a Mr. Fenn who worked for Pflueger. This reproduction looked like the drawing. The plug on the right is another reproduction offered in evidence in the
William Shakespeare, Jr./Pflueger trial.

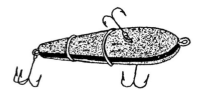 

Joseph E. Pflueger (plant superintendent) heard some fishing success
stories involving a plug made by a file maker from Kent, Ohio. He called
upon a friend, who worked at the file works in Kent, to go fishing with him
and see this plug in action. Joe Pflueger's friend was Mr. Trory. The file
makers name is unknown, but a guess would be, Mr. Pardee. The result of this
outing was the early Pardee, Kent, Friend, Manco minnows - all evolving into
part of the Enterprise line in 1900. The Pflueger version of this was called
the Trory Minnow (following, left). The props and finishes were improved
(plated). Early Trorys were wired through end to end and side by side. Screw
eyes were used later. By 1907 the Trory was history. It was hard and expensive to make and it didn't sell very well. Today the Trory is perhaps the
most highly prized Pflueger plug. One size was offered in luminous and non-
luminous.

There were two other plugs in the early Pflueger line. The wedge shaped
"Wizzard" came in 2-1/2", 3", 3-1/2" and 5". The 3-1/2" only was a 5 hooker,
the rest were 3-hookers. The Wizzard came in nine colors. The rare 5" musky
Wizzard is in the center (following, center). Sometimes the props were marked
Pflueger and sometimes "L & R" (left and right). This is always a sign of a
Pflueger. The "Competitor" was the inexpensive (round bodied) Pflueger of the
1905 period (following, right). The Competitor seems to be a tougher plug
to find than the Wizzard. Perhaps it isn't recognized. Look for the fancy
bead on the flopping prop. The Competitor came in three colors and four
sizes - 2-1/2", 3", 3-1/2" and 5".

Toward the end of the Wizzard/
Trory period (1905), a frog appeared in
the Pflueger line. The Kent Frog also
had its origin in Kent, Ohio. Two versions of this classic are known - one
has glass eyes (bottom), and the other
is fatter and has huge raised painted
wood eyes (top). Both are fortunately
somewhat available but particularly
hard to find in excellent shape.

The 3" satin cork (pressed ground cork) and soft rubber weedless (an improvement over earlier soft rubber baits) Conrad Frog was offered in 1897. There are some still around.

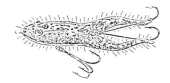

In 1907 Enterprise completely changed their obsolete line of wood minnows with an improved version to compete with Heddon's overpowering and William Shakespeare Jr.'s fast gorwing piece of the vast underwater minnow market. There are two distinct types of Monarchs. The earliest Monarchs were rigged in almost exactly the same manner as the Shakespeare (Rhodes Patent) minnow - so close in fact that this matter went to court. Shakespeare won. Pflueger disclaimed his patent in 1914. Fred Rhodes 1904 patent held. The shaped body Monarch remained in the Pflueger line after the trial with a new and different hook hanger generally referred to as "Never fail hangers" - patent October 24, 1911, a ring of wire that screws in, sometimes over a metal plate, sometimes not. There are two series. The early series are see-through hook linked. The bass sizes (left) were 3-5/8" 5-hooker and 2-3/4" 3 hooker. The surface versions were 2-3/4" and 4". The 2-3/4"er surface early version is following, left. Monarchs in both series, early and late, came in two hard to find musky versions. The large 3-5/8" (late series) following, center is rare. The 5" 5-hooker (late series) is shown right.

The Simplex belongs in the early Monarch time frame. It is almost identical to the Heddon Artistic Minnow. Color is the best way to tell the difference. The Simplex, following right, is green over silver - a neat little 1-3/4" Pflueger that is not overly scarce, yet.

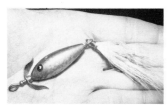

Neverfail Minnows were introduced in 1909 as a round bodies (relatively inexpensive) line. 3" 3 hookers and 3-5/8" 5 hookers were offered in twelve colors. Early Neverfails were see through constructed which later was replaced by "Neverfail hangers". 4 Brothers was another Pflueger trademark.

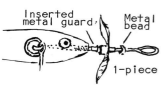

Twisted wire screw eye

May or may not have metal saucer

NEVERFAIL HOOK RIG

Inserted metal guard

Metal bead

1-piece

Typical later Pflueger prop - usually marked

NEVERFAIL
UNDER WATER
MINNOW
FOR ALL GAME FISH

The Pflueger Metalized Minnows are basically metal (nickel) plated
Monarchs in 3", 3 hook and 3-5/8", 5-hook versions. The 3" 3-hooker is known
in a belly hooked version (top right, following left). The plugs on the
bottom are Catalinas. The bottom right plug (left) was also called the
Catalina and later the Bear Cat. Both plugs are 4-1/2"ers and came in painted
versions as well as metalized. The painted "Bear Cats" have glass eyes as
does the earlier rare beauty shaped body Catalina following right.

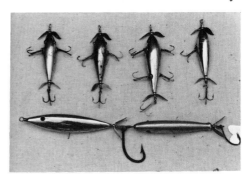

Pflueger's bottom of the line plug had a jobber's cost of 66-2/3¢ a
dozen. This was the Peerless. They made a bunch of them to compete with
Shakespeare's Little Pirate. Both 2-1/2" see-through and "neverfail" versions are known. There is a 2 hooker known with a neverfail hanger. The
name Peerless was another Pflueger trademark. They seem to have acted as a
sort of distributor. The letter "P" in a diamond is found on the unusual
high quality underwater minnow following center. The top two minnows have
screw eyes threaded into one another. The bottom minnow has screw eyes
through to the wood. Perhaps this was a stage of experimentation between the
controversial see-through and "neverfail" hangers. These are rare. Electric
Minnows came in two sizes and are equally rough to find. Electric Minnows
are clearly identified on the prop as per the 2-3/4"er on the right. The
top plug is the 4"er. See color section for a couple of beauties. There is
also a 3-5/8" 5-hook model.

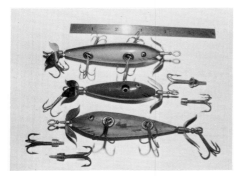
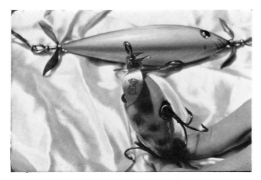

The 4 Brothers-Pflueger Surprise Minnow, following right, was patented
on March 16, 1925 by Messrs. F.L. Clarkson and O.P. Hummon. Two sizes are
known - 3" and 4". The little 2-hook 3"er is rare. The Surprise Minnow
came in seven creative colors. The 4" All-In-One (left) is a great find.
It had four separate lips. The eyes are faceted glass "diamonds".

The 4-1/4" Magnet (following) top left and Merit below, are Pflueger's
attempts at a "Peckerhead". They are identified by the "neverfail" hook
hanger. The 2-hooker is unusual. The Wizzard (second version) is a mouse
like plug patented by Charles Pflueger and Walter Adams on June 6, 1922. The
Wizzard came in six sizes from 1-1/2" to 3-1/2" and six colors. Early Wizz-
ards didn't have the little metal tail or eyes. Glass eyed versions are the
ones to look for.   See Wizzard following right.

Pflueger's metal lipped, floating/diving Pal-O-Mine was patented by
Joe Pflueger on June 25, 1927. The patent model (left) shows the unusual
fluted lip. The production model Pal-O-Mines had a smooth lip. It was available in a great variety of colors and variations over the yars. Pre-1929
Pal-O-Mines had glass eyes. Pressed eyes came later. The straight (pre-1929)
versions were 2-3/4", 3-1/4" and 4-1/2". Jointed versions came after 1930.
Pal-O-Mines are rather common. Look out for fancy colors.

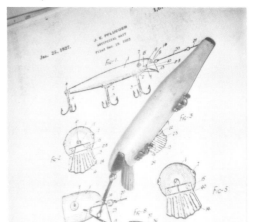
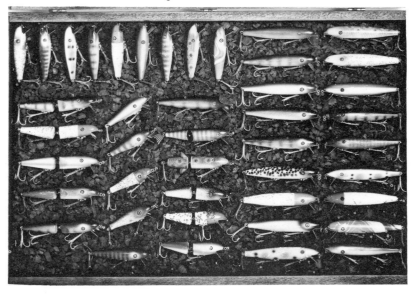

The O'Boy is sort of a chubby version of the Pal-O-Mine. It was
available in 2-3/4" and 3-1/2" sizes. O'Boys are scarce, (following, left).
Another hard to find late 1920s Pflueger is the Red Devil (following, right).
The example following is not typical. It utilizes the Snappie spinner blade
rather than the usual single tandem type.

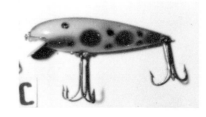
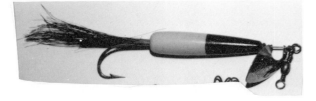

The following two Pfluegers, early pre-1929 Pakron (left) and name
unknown (right) are rare. It is possible the plugs on the right were experimental and not put into production. It is interesting to note that Joe
Pflueger was granted an extensive patent covering these plugs on September
10, 1929.

The Globe is as famous as any plug. It came on the market in the
mid-teens and stayed there. Early Globes are the ones of interest here.
The inexpensive wired through Portage Reflex (left, top) came in 2-3/4"
and 3-5/8". Portage is another Pflueger trademark. The earlier Globes
were neverfail wire rigged and available in 2-hook and 3-hook (side hooked)
versions. The 3-hooker is relatively hard to find. Three sizes came
along in the Globe line - 2-3/4", 3-5/8" and 5-1/4". There are basically
five colors. It took 37 separate steps to make the Globe. It only takes
one musky to destroy it. The center plug is a rare Pflueger squidding plug -
an underwater Globe? On the right are varieties and experimental Globes.

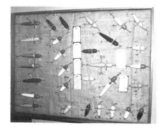

Mr. Ernest F. Pflueger really started something. The Enterprise
Manufacturing Co. actually started in 1864 as The American Fish Hook Co.,
New Haven, Connecticut. No plugs then - just high quality made in the U.S.A.
fish hooks. The Enterprise Manufacturing Co. was incorporated in 1886. For
a time there was a second Pflueger factory in Minnesota. What, if any, plugs
were produced there is not known to us. The Enterprise Manuacturing Co. was
a family business - Ernest A. Pflueger, president; Joe S. Pflueger, treasur-
er; Charles T. Pflueger, vice president and William S. Pflueger, sales manager - The Four Brothers. Generally, Pflueger plugs are not heavily collected,
but is a fertile field in which to collect. Special thanks to Joe Courcelle,
Trig Lund and John Anderson.

Ernest F. Pflueger goes
skittering.

Pflueger Prototypes

Chapter Five

Please see chapter Eleven
Hidden Heddon History
for further information.

HEDDON

It is hard to say when or what plug is Jim Heddon's earliest. The Heddon family history is such to show a background in fishing. Jim Heddon's father is reported to have carved at least one fish decoy at a very early date. Jim Heddon was a citizen of Dowagiac, Michigan. His early business was that of an expert in bee keeping and he authored works on the subject. He was also a fisherman when he had time. Jim Heddon's plugs are the result of a famous and legendary experience he had when he was waiting for a friend to go fishing at the mill pond near his hometown of Dowagiac. While waiting it seems Jim busied himself whittling a stick which he subsequently tossed in the water. A large bass took a swipe at it. The rest is history.

It is generally thought that Jim Heddon's first plug was his hand carved frog, a plug that was not only successful to his own fishing experiences but those of his fishing buddies as well. The Jim Heddon frog is a great rarity. It is extremely important to make sure a plug as valuable as the frog is authentic.

Jim Heddon went into the plug business around 1898 with his son, William. His frog had proven successful enough to warrant a further look into new and innovative ideas and designs. James Heddon was granted his first patent on April 1, 1902 for the plug affectionately known to collectors as the "Slopenose". It's birth name other than "Slopenose" and "Fish Bait", as it was called in the patent, was the "Dowagiac" Perfect Surface Casting Bait. By 1904 it was the "Dowagiac Expert". The 4-1/4" early version of the Slopenose features the removable hook which was a simple open screw eye. Just unscrew it and slip the hook off (following, top left). The Slopenose below has the very early "narrow brass cup" belly hook rig. This was followed by the wide brass cup which was soon nickle plated. The early Slopenose had a cup over the tail and they were painted blue nose, red metal collar and a white body. He stopped using the tail cups when he ran out of them. The number assigned to the Slopenose is #200. All #200s are not Slopenoses. Slopenoses are not easy to find. The 4-hooker (following, top right) is a very rare version listed in the 1904 catalog as the Dowagiac #2.

The Slopenose evolved into the #200 round nose version which represented just about every stage of the Heddon 200 line up until the end of this book. By 1929 the 200 was still in the line. In fact it had gone

through so many changes that 2, 3, 4 and 5-hook versions have been seen in
four stages of hook attachment development. The 4-hooker (following, left)
is "L" rig, frog body/blue head - a rare bird for sure. Probably a special
order. Blue head or redhead/white body and all red are other #200 colors.
The 5-hooker seen but not shown is "L" rig, blue and white. The two top
200s (following, right) are "L" rig, below, is the later bar rig in a
glass eyed version.

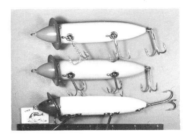

These plugs are Heddon experimental plugs utilizing the metal collar as
patented in 1902.

     James Heddon developed the underwater minnow during the period of time
when it counted. By 1905 he had a substantial part of the market. There is
some speculation involved in what follows. Jim Heddon's earliest underwater
minnow was first catalogued in 1904 as the "Dowagiac Underwater". The catalogued version had an enormous prop, round body and external hanging belly
weight (top left, following). The 3" in the center has a rudder like tail.
The metal caps and cups were gilded. The bottom plug is a transition between
the Dowagiac Underwater and #100. The two Dowagiac Underwaters on the right
are the 2-1/2" white bodied and 3" aluminum (paint) bodied.

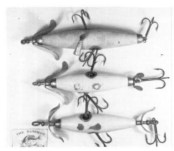
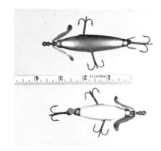

     The market for the underwater minnow was strong in the early 1900s.
By 1905 Heddon controlled a major share. The round bodied Dowagiac Underwater Expert evolved not only into the #100 but also the inexpensive 2-3/4"
#400 (1 prop) and #450 (2 props) Killers. The plug on the left shows this
transition. The Killers came in redhead and tail, all white, all yellow and
all red. The earliest versions (circa 1904) had the thin brass cup hook
hangers. Later came the regular brass cups and finally the nickle plated

brass. By 1907 the Killer was gone. Jim Heddon wasn't that much into making round bodied inexpensive plugs. Killers are "sleeper" Heddons. #450 Killer right.

 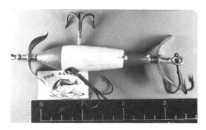

The Heddon #100 three treble minnow was first catalogued in 1905 along side the Killer and #150 5-hooker. Both the #100 and #150 are thought to have been sold or used in 1904. The earliest #100s had brass cups and props with no name stamped in. Note the shape of the body on the very early #100 (following, left). A very unusual and rare variation of the #100 is the metalized version (following, right). #100s varied in size around 2-5/8" to 2-3/4" (bodies on all wood plugs seem to vary up to 1/4" because of the manufacturing process). Heddon made a whole bunch of #100s. Another early version had the high forehead feature (following, left). The two #100s (following, bottom center) are early green crackleback. There is a story about the first crackleback plug. It seems Jim had an order to get out quickly. To facilitate the drying of the paint, Mrs. Heddon put some in the kitchen oven. The paint crackled. Mrs. Heddon thought they were ruined, but Jim delivered his new crackleback plugs to his customer who was well pleased. Many #100s were painted green crackleback. So many it is probably the most common color. Much of this crackleback painting went on in 1906-1907 when Jim's son, William and his fisherlady wife, moved to Chetek, Wisconsin to set up a new plant for making minnows and rods. By late 1906, they had booked orders for 200,000 - 60,000 more than they sold in 1905. There is a theory that the round bodied green crackleback with no name on the prop and two gill marks were made and painted in Wisconsin. The round bodied #100s were a lower cost version destined for the large retail dealer trade.

  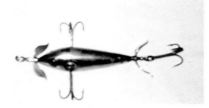

The #150 is the 3-3/4" , 5 treble hooker. It was in the line until rather recently. Many variations and colors are known. The #100s and #150s to look for are the early ones, brass cups, etc. and odd colors. Any scale pattern in these two plugs is worthwhile. The early #150 came in a wood box (following, left - note body design). A very unusual version is the belly hooker ("L" rig) to the right. This plug might have had a special number. The 2-hooker is rare.

Jim Heddon experimented with hook hangers and other ideas before he settled on the open screw-eye and cup hook rig. The following #100 and #150 variations are thought provoking - note the top two plugs. The Wag Tail below shows a Smith influence (see page 90). #100s and #150s are the most common Heddon minnows - look for odd colors, 2-piece or toilet seat hardware, old ones and condition.

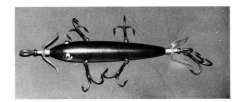

The #175 heavy casting minnow is a large, heavily weighted casting minnow. The body on the earliest #175s is slightly smaller than the standard 3-3/4". Almost the same body as #150s. This is a desirable and hard to find Heddon, especially in decent shape (following, top left shown with a #150 for comparison). Holes were drilled in the plugs by placing the body in a vise-device - each Heddon had its own device to be sure that holes were always drilled in the proper place (following, right).

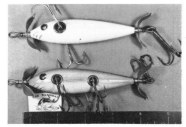
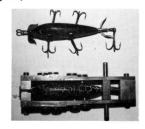

One of the big Heddon minnows was the #700 Musky Underwater Minnow first made in a 5-hook version. The earliest one (circa 1907), top, left, was larger than the more recent 5" version, below left. The 5-hooker was only around about three to four years - one of the best Heddons to run across. The 3-hook #700s are also hard to find even though they were made for a longer period of time, following, right.

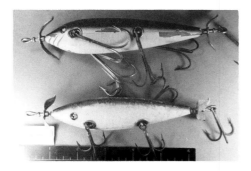

The "747" is 8" long. Three of
these have been reported - all rainbow.
The hand holding the "747" is a big
hand. There is also supposed to be a
large, approximately 8", #0 3-hooker,
hex - that would be one fine Heddon!

The Night Radiant Moonlight is one of the greatest and least understood
of all Heddon plugs. It is our feeling that it was an uncatalogued surface
plug put out to compete against the Moonlight #1 Bass Bait (circa 1906-08).
This is a guess. It's a rare one (following left). Another mysterious Heddon
plug of the same general type is the Heddon "Peckerhead" type plug (approximately 4-3/4"). The tail cap on the plug following, right, is an indication of
1905-07 manufacture. This plug has been seen in cup and L rig with a tail cap
and no tail cap. Both the following plugs are uncatalogued as far as we know.

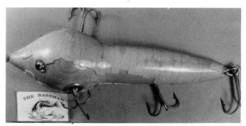

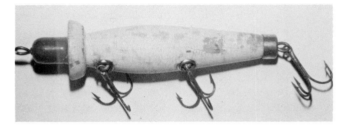

The 1-3/4" #50 Artistic Minnow (following, right) was in the line for
about 3 to 4 years. By far the most Artistics found are in yellow colored
body fancy mottled back (sienna crackleback) with gold plated props. The #50
was also listed in gold body. This is a tough color to find. Any Artistic
is scarce especially with the "weight buoy" - a round wood float painted lead
color - to be put 3" in front of the plug in order to keep the plug up and
cast further. Without the weight buoy the #50 weighed 1/2 ounce, with it the
weight was 3/4 ounce.

The #300 was a top water minnow that was sold through the years in an
amazing amount of variations. The earliest version (following, left) has
the typical high forehead and brass cups (circa 1904-05) and was belly rigged.
The second variation has the hook further forward. The variations go through
the four rigs - cup, L, 2-piece and toilet seat. A later version from the
1930s was called the Musky Surfacer and came in a surface rig. Sometimes
giant toilet seat and 2-piece were mixed up. There is a 2-hooker, 3-hooker,
4-hooker which is rare and a 6-hooker which is scarce. Although #300s were
around for a long time, they are only occasionally found.

Jim Heddon's second patent (July 23, 1907) was for the #500 Multiple
Minnow - a metal plug with glass eyes. The few examples that exist are
usually the standard 2-1/2" nickle plated. The #500 also came in gold plated
and in a musky size (following, left). The typical Heddon spinner or prop
was also featured in this complex patent.

The #800 and #900 Dowagiac Swimming Minnows (circa 1911) are among the most graceful of all plugs. They are both desirable. It is probable they made fewer 3-1/4" single (tail) treble #800s (following, right bottom) than 4-1/2" #900s (following, right top). Both plugs are usually found in yellow with red spots and black back. The #900 has been seen in a 3-hook (2-belly, 1-tail) rig rather than the usual double belly hook riding on a pin.

The 2-1/2" #400 Surface Minnow (left) was only around for a short time (circa 1909). It has been seen in blue head/white body, sienna crackle head/yellow body and rainbow. A good Heddon to have.

The little 1-3/4" #20 Baby Dowagiac, 3-hook underwater minnow (following right) was around in 1910 in the cup rig version. No "L", 2-piece, or toilet seat #20s have been seen. The #20 jumped from the cup to the much later surface rig. The #20 is a fairly desirable plug, especially in unusual colors.

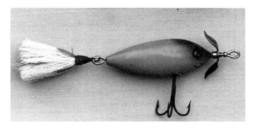

Variations of the underwater minnow theme were introduced. The #0 3-hooker and #00 5-hooker were hexagonal in cross section (5 sides). They came in cup, L, 2-piece and toilet seat rigs. #0 and #00s are scarce at best. They are a neat plug - look for L rig in the #0 or any in 2-piece or toilet seat - these seem to be the toughest (see following, left).

The Dummy Double came in two hook hanger styles - the "Football" above is scarce-rare. The L rig isn't far behind. They were usually in spotted finishes. The weedless Dummy Double (following, right) was called "Jim Heddon's Last Invention". It came out in 1913. Mr. Heddon passed away in 1911.

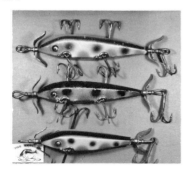
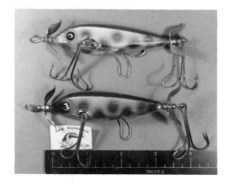

The #1300 Black Sucker came out in 1913 (possibly sold earlier) and stayed around for about 15 years. There are three variations in style. Two in hook rig (large cup and L) and three colors have been seen. Following left is the Black Sucker in natural scale. The most seen version is the unique Black Sucker finish - black back over a yellowish pink to white body, (right). See the color section for a look at the rare rainbow Black Sucker. A couple of rare uncatalogued Black Suckers follow. The one on the left is a 5-1/2"er with a belly cup rig. The Little Black Sucker (right) is large flat L-rigged and approximately 4" long.

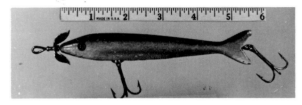

The 2-3/8" #10 and #11 Light Casting Minnows were in the line from 1913 until the mid-1920s. The only difference was in the colors. The #10 had yellow with red and brown decoration and the #11 had white with red and green decoration - referred to as "strawberry". The Light Casting Minnow is one to get, especially if you specialize in Heddon. A very rare variation is the side hook L-rig #10 in perch (following, right).

Perhaps the rarest of all Heddon plugs is the extremely illusive #1400 hex-shaped, single hook minnow. It was catalogued only in Catalog #11 (1913). The single hook underwater minnow is the Heddon to find.

The Coast Minnows came in four basic sizes - #1 was 4", #1 - 3", #3 - 2-3/4" and #4 - 5". They were made from 1913 to the mid-1920s and five colors were offered. All Coast Minnows are good plugs to find.

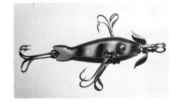

Jim Heddon's son, Charles, took over as president of the company upon the death of his father. Along with his brother, William, they changed the name on August 11, 1913 to James Heddon's Sons, Inc.

Charles Heddon received a patent on May 9, 1916 for the floating-diving #1700 Near Surface Wiggler. The #1700 came in one size only - 4-1/4", and has been seen in L-rig, 3-hook (belly and tail) only (top, left). Another patent was awarded Charles Heddon in 1917 for the #1600 Deep Diving Wiggler. Curiously this has been seen in cup-rig as well as L-rig. The #1600 Wiggler is also a 4-1/4"er and has been seen in 3-hook (side and tail) and 3-hook (belly and tail). The cup-rig is the rare one. The #1600s and #1700s are classic Heddons! There are quite a few still around. Photos following are left top #1700, below #1600. Right top belly up view of cup-rig #1600, center L-rig #1700, below #1600 L-rig. Both the #1600s and #1700s were in the line for around ten years.

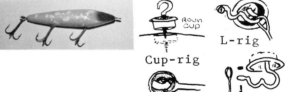

The year 1915 was the year of the Wiggler. It was also the year of the L-rig which replaced the cup-rig. The #1600 to the right is a rare early (cup) variation.

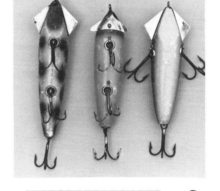

The 4-3/8" #3000 Spin Diver stands alone in Heddon. It is fairly rough to find and a real "looker". It's a fish tail combination between a minnow and a diver. They came in around 1918 and stayed about 8 years.

Heddon was apparently experimenting with a Globe/Decker type plug. A few have shown up - all different. This plug was probably never produced commercially.

The Crab Wiggler was patented on January 28, 1919 - a design patent by William A. Stolley who assigned it to James Heddon's Sons. Mr. Stolley worked for the Heddon Company and was instrumental in development of plugs of this period. There are four versions of the Crab Wiggler. The 3-3/4" #1800 Crab Wiggler (top left), 3-1/4" #1900 Baby Crab (third from top) and 2-1/2" #1950 Midget Crab (fourth from top). The fourth version is called the #7000, 2-1/2" Deep-O-Diver (bottom). The Crabs were all 2 belly hookers.

The Deep-O-Diver has one double belly hook. Two types of collars are known.
The Midget Crab (center, top) is the O collar, below is the U or horseshoe
collar. The U is thought to be the earliest. The Deep-O-Diver (bottom,
left) has a pointed upturned collar. The Midget Crab (left, second from
bottom) has a Deep-O-Diver collar - unusual. On the right is what is
thought to be the earliest Crab Wiggler. It used the #1600 body and is
cup-rigged. Crab Wigglers are common. The best ones are cup-rig versions
(top, left) and to somewhat less extent, the Midget and Deep-O-Divers.

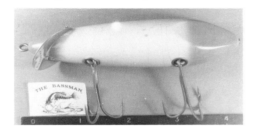

The Tadpolly is another Heddon that is generally relatively common.
There are two basic versions - the 4-5/8" #6000 (top two following, left)
and the 3-7/8" #5000 (bottom two, left). The rare Tadpolly Runt came along
later. A couple of strange Tadpollys are the "Prototype" Tadpolly (center)
and experimental Tadpollys (right). The center plug has been found in many
of the standard Heddon colors - frog, strawberry, redhead, rainbow, etc. This
cup rig plug was probably a production plug, not an actual prototype. It might
not have been catalogued because we haven't found the catalog or because of
possible infringements with Rush Tango, Smith, Welles, Moonlight, etc. There
are two type lips on Tadpollys - the heart shape and regular. The heart is
thought to be earlier. Most Tadpollys are L-rig, those that are not are
scarcer.

The 3-7/8" #2000 Wiggle King and the 4" #2500 Lucky 13 came out about the same time (circa 1918) and are very similar. The Wiggle King (left) has no upper lip to speak of. The Lucky 13 (center) is more curved. The plug on the right has the general shape of the #8500 Basser and is probably in a developmental stage. The Lucky 13 (right) came in the 4" #2500 and 3" #2400 Baby Lucky 13 version. The Wiggle King was only around for a short time and is generally scarcer than Lucky 13s. The best Lucky 13 is the cup-rigged Baby Lucky 13. Lucky 13s came in cup, L, 2-piece and surface rigs. 2-piece is unusual.

1920 brought many changes to James Heddon's Sons. The plant had gone from the kitchen to large new buildings. New innovations unheard of were being implemented. The Heddon Aviation Company, Inc. started on June 29, 1920. The "Flying Fish" was a "Jenny" and was used to deliver plugs. Perhaps this early aerial photo of the expanded Heddon factory was taken from the "Flying Fish".

Plugwise perhaps the greatest innovation of this era was a jointly shared patent by Henry S. Dills of Garrett, Indiana who assigned half to Heddon. Mr. Dills represents the Creek Chub Bait Company of Garrett, Indiana. This important patent was for the scale finish.

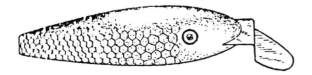 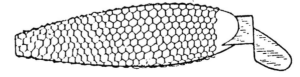

The 4-1/2" and 7-1/2" Vamps were covered by a design patent by W.A. Stolley on June 7, 1921. The earliest advertised Vamps were called Vampires. There are two versions of Vampire. If the hook rig "L" is tied

into the lip screw, it's a Vampire. In one case there is a wire line-tie
that goes under the lip similar to the pig tie (patented by Stolley May 3,
1921). It is not known which is earlier. There is at least one cup rig
Vamp (following left, top). A Vampire is below. The #7500 Vamp proceded
to have the front belly hook attached separately from the lip. After 1921
the Vampire was called the Vamp. The next Vamp was the #7400 Baby Vamp,
followed by the Jointed Vamp and huge 8" #7600 Musky Vamp. There was also
a couple fly rod Vamps (date unknown). For a comparison in size see following right photo - top 8" #7600 Vamp (look closely at the tiny uncatalogued
Vamp laying on top of the #7600); below right is a Vampire; left is a no
lip Baby Vamp thought to be a Harden version; the bottom item is the fly
rod Vamp with box.

There are probably as many varieties of Vamps as any Heddon plug. The
#7500s in the color section suggest the variation in color. A couple of very
unusual varieties are the round nose Vamp, left, the #7400 Harden Whiz, center,
and the large #7500 version, right. The Harden Vamps came along shortly after
the scope of this book, but we included them because they are neat.

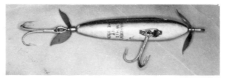

There were two more Musky Vamps
made before 1929. The 6" #7550 (top)
replaced the #7600 (below) in 1929.
The #7550 is a later special color
version called Allen Stripey.

The eyes were put in
individually by hand.

The #210 was the smaller logical
extension of the Slopenose. It was a
fatso, short 3-1/2" version. The #210
came into use in the L-rig period.
2-piece, toilet seat and surface hardware versions were available after 1929.

The 4-1/4" #6500 Zaragossa was a very important fish catcher. The
patent version (called the no chin version) is the rare one. Most have
round chins. All L-rig Zaragossas are worthwhile. Some of the rarest
varieties come after 1929 - the 2-1/2"er, Musky, Harden Special and Star
(not pictured). The no chin Zaragossa is shown on the right.

The Zaragossa on the left has been wound with silk. It's a beautiful job and an interesting idea. It is <u>not</u> typical - probably one of a kind.

The salt water minnows are scarce and varied in style. The earliest
3-1/2" #10-B and 2-3/4" #10-S Florida Specials had marked props in front and
were made around 1921. These were followed in 1924 by the 3" #500 salt water
special, no prop Little Joe and the 3-1/2" #600 Big Joe (following, left).
At the same time the 3-7/8" #800 Big Mary (center) and 2" #850 Little Mary
(right) appeared. The Big Mary and Florida Specials seem to be the least
found salt water minnows

 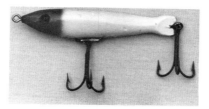 

The 4-1/4" #8500 Heddon Basser and Head-On Basser (following, left)
were introduced around 1921. There is very little difference between the
two except for the name on the lip and perhaps a slightly different angle
on the lip. Bassers are common in L-rig. The #8500 has been seen in an
interesting thin body cup version. One of the more difficult Bassers is the
heavy duty L-rig (musky) version (following, right).

 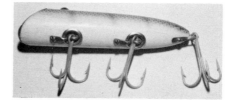

The patent for the Gamefisher shows glass eyes. At least one showed
up (left). The typical product Gamefishers were no eyed and came in two
sizes - the 3-3/4" #5400 Baby Gamefisher and the 4-5/8" two jointed,
3-piece Gamefisher (right, top). The Gamefisher itself in L-rig is a
rather common Heddon. The Baby was made for a shorter time and is a bit
harder to find. A couple of very rare Gamefishers are the ones on the
bottom row. The top left plug is thought to be a forerunner of the Game-

fisher. The center Baby Gamefisher is marked "Vampir". The Gamefisher on the right is stamped "Vampir" in raised letters and has a giant surface type rig??

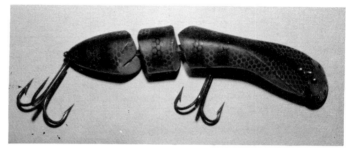

The 3" Walton Feathertail is an early 1920s plug that has a single upriding hook (left).

The #120 3" and #130 4-1/2" Torpedos (right) came along about the same time. Both the #40 Walton Feathertails and the Torpedos are somewhat difficult to find, especially the #120 Torpedos.

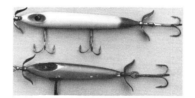

The pre-1930 Zig Wags were 2-hookers. The #8300 (following) is a special "Luny Frog" finish. There were many variations of this plug that are beyond the realm of this book. At least some Zig Wags were delivered by truck.

The #140 Flipper is one of the most difficult Heddons of this period (1927-1929) to find. The Flipper has been seen in 3-3/4" and 4" versions

(following, left). The SOS (Stays On Surface) Wounded Minnow came out in
1928 in three variations - the 3-1/2" #160 (following, center) 2-hooker,
the 4-3/4" #170 3-hooker (top center) and the heavier 4-3/4" #370 SOS Musky
which is rare (right) (sorry no hardware, it should have giant L-rig).
The SOSs, other than Musky, are reasonably available.

The Luny Frog was one of the earliest Heddons to be produced in plastic.
There are two basic sizes, the 4-1/2" #3500 and the 3-3/4" #3400 Little Luny.
The #3500 Luny came in green or meadow frog and the elusive red head (top, right).
The Little Luny is somewhat scarcer than its big brother, being made for less
time (bottom, right). The red stripe (closed leg) Luny (second from the bottom) is
so rare it's probably unique. The Luny went through various stages in development
illustrated by the experimental versions (following, left). If the Luny had been
produced in wood, it would probably look like the one on the top right. Lunys are
rather common but desirable plugs. One year the Luny was chosen by the NFLCC as
plug of the year.

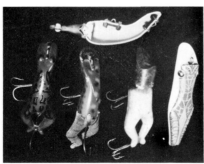
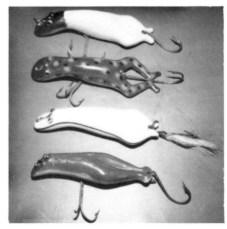

The 2-5/8" #110 River Runt was introduced in 1929 in a sinking wood
version (following, left). This was replaced in the 1930s with the famous
plastic River Runt Spook. Wood Runts are around. The 2-3/4" #4000 Meadow
Mouse was also introduced in 1929. The center top plug (missing tail) is in
cup rig and beneath it is the more common L-rig version. The cup rig appearing on this plug is a puzzle. There is another scarce early version of the
#4000 that has a transparent red nose. The #4000 was introduced in redhead,
brown and grey mouse. Another 1929 plug that is sort of rough to find is
the little fly rod 1-3/4" Tiny Tease (right)

    The 2-1/2" #220 Weedless Widow (following, center) was new in 1929.
It was designed and patented by a famous sportsman and tournament caster
William Stanley of Chicago, Illinois. The Weedless Widow was later supplied with a removable belly hook. The Weedless Widow is fairly common.
Other Heddon plugs were produced with "Stanley Props". They are uncatalogued
as far as we know. A couple of examples are on the right. There is also
a 3-hook (side) version of both the Torpedo and Flipper types illustrated.
These are not well known and seem difficult to find. The earliest Heddon
plug that Mr. Stanley had anything to do with was the #70 2-1/8" (circa
1924) Heddon Stanley Weedless pork rind lure (following, left). The #70
was made of plastic (Bakelite) and was Heddon's first plastic plug. They
are rather common. The one following, left has the scarce diving/wiggling
plane attachment.

  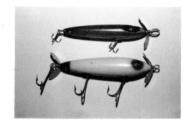

    The last two digits in the Heddon number refer to color. The following is
more or less chronological from the early 1900s until 1929. X after a number is
our indication of an unusual color to look for in most Heddons.

00 = fancy back (green crackleback), 01 = rainbow, 02 = white, 03 = aluminum-x, 04 = red, 05 = yellow,
06 = gold-x, 07 = fancy sienna-yellow-x except for the Artistic Minnow where it predominates. There
are other early Heddon colors that had no numbers or duplicate numbers - red collar, white body and
blue head (#200s only), the 00S white body with green and red spotted decoration (strawberry) and the
01S which is the same with a yellow body. The colors from here on are not necessarily chronological.
They are the 09 Series including scale patterns which came in with the Dills' patent and was featured
in the 1921 catalog. 09A = yellow perch, 09B = frog, 09C = crab, 09D = green scale, 09H = red scale,
09J - frog scale, 09K - goldfish scale-x, 09L - yellow perch. 02 became a blended redhead and tail.
All Heddon Minnows are desirable in the 09 scale patterns. 08 was white with flitters. The 09s continued and by 1929 there was the 09M = pike scale, 09P = shiner scale, 09R = mullet scale-x or pike
scale which is not x but nice, 09V = orange/black spots (sort of x), and 09X = blue scale-x. There
was a wild Heddon color called BF in 1929 (the Luny Frog color). Other plugs had special colors -
the Black Sucker color and the grey and brown Meadow Mouse (a Chipmunk was later made - look for one!)

    Collecting Heddon requires time, study and some luck. Heddons are very
popular. Good advice to a new Heddon collector is to get the books on Heddon
by Clyde Harbin and Wetzel and Harbin (see Bibliography). Learn to know the
Heddon prop. It varied little - long shanks both sides. The early props were
unmarked.   The L-rig (1915-1929)

                                               looks like this.

Look for Heddons in toilet seat and 2-piece rigs. They are dated beyong this
book but still O.K.

    Thanks to Clyde Harbin (The Bassman), Walt Blue, Jim Daniel, Bill Wetzel,
Ed Robison and Bruce Dyer. These are the men to talk to about Heddon.

Chapter Six

SHAKESPEARE

William Shakespeare, Jr. officially started in the plug business in 1900. He had been interested in fishing tackle since his 1896 patent for a reel. The wood Revolution was patented on February 5, 1901 by William Shakespeare, Jr. and William Locher giving a joint address in the text of the patent as C/O The Kalamazoo Shutter Company, Kalamazoo, Michigan. The production model of the 3-3/4" wood Revolution (following, left) is very rare and was only made for a short period of time. The wood Revolution was not in the 1902 catalog. The background of the development of this patent is vague at best. There are some clues in the form of plugs. The plug (right, following) is thought to be an early wood Revolution. This would put it before 1900! How far before, we don't know.

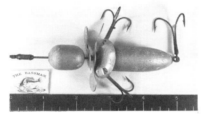 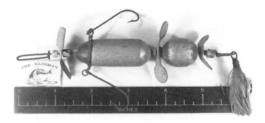

Collectors have experienced the rare occurrence of cork bodied Revolution type plugs. These are generally considered to be early Revolutions. The use of cork and aluminum requires special skills. The plug on the left is an example of the "Cork Revolution". The center plug could be a "Cork Worden Bucktail". Exactly the who and when of these is not known. The plugs on the right have an interesting history. They were found in association with other developmental products of Messrs. Jay and Fred Rhodes, also of Kalamazoo, Michigan. See pages 76-81 for more about the Rhodes men. The authors are not saying that the Revolution definitely had anything to do with Fred or Jay Rhodes. We neither can say it did not.

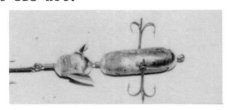  

The 1902 William Shakespeare, Jr. catalog featured the aluminum version of the Revolution bait, which was also patented by W.S. Shakespeare, Jr. and W. Locher on April 9, 1901. The Revolution was offered in three sizes - #1-3", #2-4" and #3-6" (musky). The #2 was by far the most popular and is the one found with the most frequency today. Any Revolution is a good plug - they aren't really that frequent. The musky size is the toughest to find. The Revolutions show up in an almost unbelievable amount of variations. The props are one major feature. The earliest were rounded end (Mickey Mouse) props stamped "Pat Appl'd For" followed by William Shakespeare, Jr. markings, and eventually, the Shakespeare props of all types included both notched variations - late Rhodes and later

Shakespeare. The other major variations included painted Revolutions - usually
the fish catching yellow with gold dots or redhead. A Revolution is difficult
to find in color. Paint chips easily on metal. A final major variation is
shown following with the flat back ("acorn") rear end and the earlier rounded
version (right). **The acorn (right) was a later version (circa 1907).**

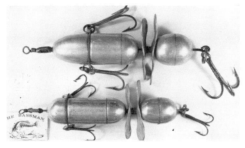
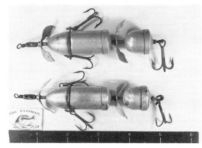

      One of the very earliest variations of the Revolution was the Shakespeare/
Worden Bucktail Spinner. We were introduced to Mr. Worden on page 76. We see
much more of him when we discuss the South Bend Bait Company. The Worden Bucktail is essentially the first half of the Revolution with a deer hair (bucktail)
tail. The Worden also came in variations similar to the Revolution. The earlier
ones were round back (left). The more recent were flat (right). Please note
the top plug (right) is a redhead. The Worden was made in one size only - the
#2 which had a 4" body. Wordens are **generally** harder to find than Revolutions.

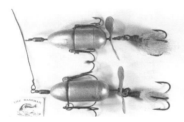

        Just when you think you have
seen all the Revolutions, you probably have not.

      The 1902 catalog offered two more plugs. The 2-3/4" Sure Lure Bait is a
weedless rubber plug. Mr. Shakespeare received a patent on the Sure Lure on
January 10, 1905, in his name only (left). The Evolution was made of soft
rubber and had a unique aluminum prop. It came in three sizes - #1-3", #2-4"
and #3-5". The 4" and 3" versions are seen following, right. The Evolution
stayed in the Shakespeare line for many years and with many prop styles. Any
Evolution is lucky to have made it this far. The early ones and the 5"ers are
the ones to **look for.**

Another item in the 1902 catalog was the rubber Tournament Casting Frog!
This frog was seen a couple of years later with a unique aluminum spinner, a set
of trebles and a rubber weed guard (center) The Frog was replaced by the Rhodes
Mechanical Frog in 1907 and was reintroduced in 1909 as the 3-1/4" Shakespeare
Weedless Frog #4. By this time it had the nickle plated notched props (right).

On October 16, 1905, William Shakespeare, Jr.
purchased the rights, including three patents and
equipment, to the products of The Kalamazoo Fishing
Tackle Manufacturers and/or Company for $6,000.00.
This was an excellent move by Mr. Shakespeare. It
solidly put him into the fast growing market for
underwater minnows and other plugs created by the
growing popularity of plug casting. One thing
Mr. Shakespeare always stressed was plug casting.

By 1907 William Shakespeare had consolidated his line with the newly
acquired Rhodes business. The Revolution and Worden stayed. The rubber Frog
was replaced by the rubber Rhodes "Perfect Frog" now called the "New Rhodes
Mechanical Swimming Frog". This was an expensive plug in those days - it was
$1.00. A top of the line Shakespeare 5-hook wooden minnow was only .60¢. The
Evolutions were listed as well as an extensive new competitive high quality line
of underwater minnows. There were three grades of minnows offered. The least
expensive was the Kazoo Wooden Minnow at .28¢. The Kazoo came in two color
blends - green back/white and the same in red. Kazoos have tiny glass eyes and
the hooks are screwed in. There was a 3" 2-hook (belly hook) (following, top
left), a 3" side hooker and a 4" 5-hooker. There was a commercial version of
the Kazoo that has brass disc eyes with a blued pin attachment. The Kazoo hooks
and line-ties are screwed in with a simple brass screw eye (top, left). The
top quality plug was the Shakespeare Wooden Minnow. The "see-through" hardware
(Rhodes' Patent) is featured on this plug. A variety of sizes and hook arrange-
ments were offered over a period of many years. The center plug, left is a
1907 version (high forehead just like Heddon) of the 3" #33, top of the line,
shaped body Shakespeare Submerged Wooden Minnow. It also came in the #03 1-3/4"
3-hooker, #23 2-1/2", #33 3", #43 3-5/8" and #53 4-1/2" all 3-hookers. The
5-hookers were the #44 3-5/8" and 5-1/4" musky size (right). (The #44 on the
right floats - it never had a belly weight???) The Rhodes Wooden Minnow was the
third plug offered (left, bottom plug) (circa 1905-1907). It came in 3" 3-hook
and 4" 5-hook, see-through rig, and was .42¢.

 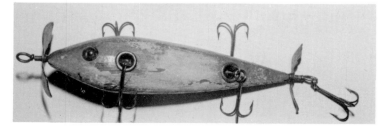

        William Shakespeare, Jr. filed for his own patent for an underwater minnow
on October 23, 1905. He received this patent July 21, 1908. The idea here was
a raised (inverted) cup which would keep the hook from scratching the plug. It
looks like this might not have worked too well. No matter - several weeks before
Mr. Shakespeare filed for this patent he purchased Fred Rhodes patent for a much
better hook hanger. The only known William Shakespeare, Jr. underwater minnows
follow. It is our guess the 3" 3-hook and 4" 5-hook William Shakespeare, Jr.
minnow was made between 1904 and 1906 and probably not catalogued because of
the intervention of the Rhodes acquisition. The distinctive small props show
up on other Shakespeares occasionally.

        The #23BWS (black, white & silver) "Shiner" left was made in 2-1/2", the
#43BWS in 3-3/4". The Shiners (following, right) were offered in 1909. Another
1909 plug is the 1-1/4" Whirlwind, a roundish wood minnow that came in red,
yellow or white. Both plugs are hard to find. The top Whirlwind is the older one.

        Shakespeare's addition to the "Peckerheads" was the 4" #42 Surface Wonder
(following, left) which was catalogued in 1920 and introduced in 1909, and the
2-hook 4" #680 Luminous Floating Bait (circa 1918).

 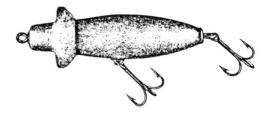

        The Punkin Seed is certainly one of the most graceful and sought after
of all Shakespeare plugs. The 2-3/4" #30 in the single treble hook version was
introduced in 1909 (following, left). The #31 2-3/4" 2-hooker (top, left) seems
to be even more difficult to find than the earlier. It is a floater - the earliest Shakespeare floater. One of Shakespeares most well known plugs is the Slim
Jim - a thin underwater minnow with a great name. Who was slim Jim? The 3" #33
single spinner and 3-3/4" were both 3-hookers introduced in 1909. Early versions
had thin vertical line paint jobs (following, center). There were some unusual
variations of the Slim Jim. The longer #53 and #54 were supposed to be 3-3/4".
The two plugs following, right are 4" and 4-1/4". The Slim Jim stayed in the

line past the 1929 cut-off of this book. By far the most common Slim Jims are
the later pressed eye versions. The two Slim Jims (following, right) are unusual.

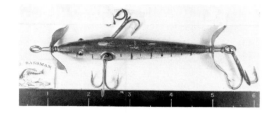

The "Shakespeare" Floating Wooden Minnow came in two sizes - the 3" single
belly hooked #31 and the 3-5/8" 3-hooker (2 belly) following, left. For some
reason the Shakespeare Floating Minnows are much harder to find than most underwater minnows. When you take a close look at the Shakespeare surface minnow
following, center, you will notice the top plug has the little soldered convex
ring on the belly hook similar to the Ultra Minnow as described on page 68.
Sometimes, but not always, props are one of the best methods of identifying
minnows of either the underwater or surface sort. Please note the short shank
props on the Shakespeare Floaters (center). Another Shakespeare floating bait
is the #41 Favorite Floating Minnow (right) that probably came along in the late
teens and is not seen too much.

The Mermaid plugs were originally the McCormick Mermaid (see page 47).
The Shakespeare version came in two sizes - the 3-5/8" #583 3-hooker and the 3-1/4"
Little Mermaid. Look for a lack of cup rig and Shakespeare paint jobs on Shakespeare Mermaids (following, left). The Bass A Lure was a logical progression in
style. The Mermaid started a long history of floating/diving plugs. The early
model (following, center) (1922) shows the same body configuration as the Mermaid
with the addition of a lip. Shakespeare was one of the first to use a realistic
scale pattern on its plugs. They used a rubber plate printing method similar
to flexography. Shakespeare's finishes of this nature are strikingly beautiful,
as per the Bass A Lure (following, right).

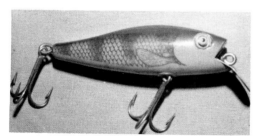

Shakespeare's "metal plated" plugs were available in a large selection -
left following photo: top row, left to right - #578 Swimming Mouse, #447 copper,
center row, left to right - #03 gold, #44 nickle, bottom row, left to right -
#00, #33. Quite a choice. The mouse (top, left) was and is one of Shakespeares
most popular and common plugs. The early versions had small glass eyes and a

longer thinner body. A metalized mouse would have been unheard of except for
left, top. Other metalized Shakespeares are desirable and not easy to find. The
4-3/4" Pikie Kazoo #637 was introduced around 1924. It was a straight bodied
3-hooker. The jointed version, right, is unusual. Many variations in this plug
follow.

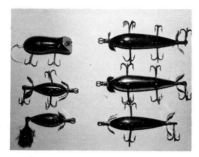 

    The 3-5/8" #638 Kazoo Chub Minnow (following, left) was in the Shakespeare
line in 1923. The #638 is one to look for. It wasn't around long. The 3-7/8"
#590 Bass Kazoo came in a seldom seen glass eyed version (top, right). Seven
colors were offered in the Bass Kazoo. The #590 is hard to find in excellent
condition - it must have caught fish. Both plugs circa 1923.

 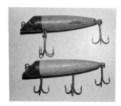

    The Hydroplane was made in two sizes - the 4-1/2" 3-hooker came in at least
eight colors. The 3-3/4" baby version was made early and is much scarcer. The
Hydroplane (left) was originally the Coldwater Helldiver, see pages 127-129. The
transition between Coldwater and Shakespeare probably took place in the late teens.
The hook rig is either a simple screw eye or a screw eye through a small convex
inverted cup. This cup is an extremely important identification feature for
Shakespeare. The 3-1/8" #4YS Shakespeare Floating Spinner (following, right)
was a wired through Revolution/Decker type wood plug. It was later made in another size - 3".

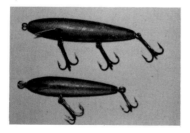 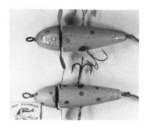

    Around 1909 William Shakespeare, Jr. changed his distribution policy and
cut out his jobbers - he went direct. By the late teens the Shakespeare catalog
contained most of the important competitive plugs on the market in addition to
the rapidly increasing Shakespeare line - Jamisons, Schoonies Skooter, Moonlights
including the Fish Spear, Rush Tango, Lockharts, Wilsons, South Bend and a decent
portion of Heddon. In fact Jim Heddon admitted that Shakespeare was at one time
one of his top three customers! The earliest 3" Rhodes round bodied Torpedo looks
a lot like the Heddon Killer. It had redhead and tail and was see-through with
flat hangers (Patent August 17, 1915). Around 1924 the Torpedo went through a distinct change. This version was a round brass tack eyed convex cup version called

the #33RWT and was 3" with a red back or green back over white. The Little
Pirate was Shakespeare's least expensive plug. This plug was offered in 1909.
The use of simple screw eye side hook hangers is a way to identify this rather
common plug (top, center). The Pflueger Peerless was its chief competitor. The
early Peerless had a small cup see-through hardware shown below center for comparison. The side hooks are missing. The #3GWF Rhodes Mechanical Swimming Frog
(right) (rubber) **was catalogued** at least from 1907 to 1920.

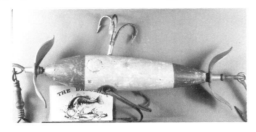  

The 1-3/4" #00FS Shakespeare "Fancy Back" Minnow (top, left) competed with
the Heddon Artistic and the Pflueger Simplex. The #00 was later offered in the
green scale that was the early natural Shakespeare color - circa 1921 (following -
left). Another little minnow was the 1-3/4" belly hooked underwater minnow #03.
A rarity in Shakespeare plugs is the 6" Albany plug. The one shown center,
following has the flat see-through hangers invented by William Shakespeare, Jr.
on August 17, 1915. The 5-1/2" belly hooker on the right might be a later version
of the Albany.

 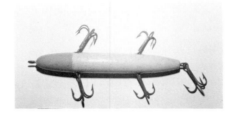 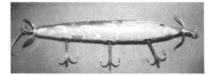

The Jim Dandy Wobbler is a 2-1/4" Shakespeare version of the Wise Jim Dandy.
The name Jim Dandy stayed on in the Shakespeare line with a line of interesting
inexpensive plugs offered in the early 1930s. The Shakespeare version of the Jim
Dandy is recognized by Shakespeare colors and the typical small "convex cup" hook
rig (left). A couple more unusual plugs occasionally turn up that are attributed to Shakespeare. We don't know their names or when. The top plug is 3-1/4"
and the bottom is 3-1/2".

 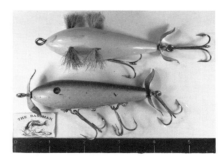

Two salt water sinking minnows were offered by Shakespeare. They are both
3" and about as difficult to find as any Shakespeare - and that's saying a mouth-
ful. The only difference is the subtle one in the shape of the body. The #722
Saltwater Special and #721 Saltwater Minnow were offered in white or white with
gold speckles (following, left). The larger size T. Robb plugs are sort of plugs.

There were various versions.   T. Robb was a noted fisherman and designed these hand tied beauties for fishing in the pads and weeds.   There are few artifacts of the plug world as colorful as T. Robbs.   The Kazoo Trolling Bug is a good example.   Look for these.

In the late 1920s Shakespeare brought out some of its finest most collectable plugs.   The 5-1/2" #6640 Tarpalunge (top, left) was designed to take 100 pounds of dead weight.   The 4" #6666 Strike-It is scarcer than the Tantalizer (center) and came in two sizes and two styles.   The earlier one above is 4". The "ball" tail hanger on the Tantalizer (following, center) indicates it was made in the very late 1920s.   The Plopper or 7-11 (right, top) as it was later called, apparently came in an **extremely rare** 2" baby size (right, following).

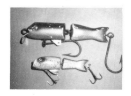

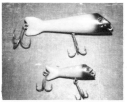

The 2-3/4" #6534 Sea Witch Midget (left) is a rather common Shakespeare. The glass eyed version is by far the best one.   A couple of other little beauties possibly brought out as early as late 1929 are the curved bodied 3" #6529 Barnacle Bill (on the rare side) and the 3-3/8" #637-1/2 Baby Pikie Kazoo (right).   The #637-1/2 is hard to find but nothing like the beautiful Barnacle Bill.

The 2-5/8" #6555 Waukazoo Surface Spinner is shown here in its production version (left).   One of the most beautiful and sought after of all Shakespeares is the 4-1/4" #6535 Darting Shrimp (center).   The 4" #6637 Kazoo Wobbler (right) was joined by the Striped Bass Wobbler #6636.

Shakespeare colors are too confusing to list.   Look for anything above a red head.   They made some great colors - pickerel, for example.   Following are all Shakespeare props starting with the earliest, left to right, from 1900 to 1929 when type 7 props were stamped.   Note short shank (arrow) on type 7 props. This chapter would not have been possible without the help of Walt Blue, Jim Cantwell, Arlan Carter and Clyde Harbin.

#1   #2   #3   #4   #5   #6   #7

Chapter Seven

MOONLIGHT

"There is nothing new under the sun but strange things are seen at night". This motto was printed on the letterhead of the Moonlight Bait Co. of Paw Paw, Michigan.

In 1906 a group of friends and neighbors formed a fishing club called the Moonlight Bass Club. These men had one thing in common - their love of fishing. They were holders of a sort of secret. These fellows had little time during the day to fish. It didn't much matter because daylight fishing for bass is not always the most successful time to catch a big one. The guys who formed the Moonlight Bass Club learned that big bass come out at night. Their method of catching bass at night varied. Early in the game one of their members named Horace E. Ball started using wood plugs that he had designed. Fellow members were supplied with these creations and they caught enough bass that in 1908, only two years after founding the club, Mr. Ball formed a partnership with another local man named Charles E. Varney. They named their company the Moonlight Bait Company and proceeded to make and market their first bait, the classic Moonlight Floating Bait #1.

Horace Ball, who came to Paw Paw in the fall of 1894, was, by 1906, custodian of the county courthouse in Paw Paw, Michigan. The first Moonlight baits were made by H.E. Ball himself. The earliest production Moonlight baits were turned out on a lathe by a local wood worker. They were finished, assembled and painted by Horace Ball in the courthouse basement. The progression of Moonlight plugs follows a general pattern. They had a numbers system starting with #1 and letters followed the number indicating variations. The Moonlight Floating Bait was offered in four versions. The #1 which was the original luminous version was introduced at least as early as 1906 and came in two basic sizes. The approximate 3-3/4" #1 is a 2-hooker (belly and tail). The #1M is an approximate 4-1/4" offset 3-hooker. This #1M (following, left) is the version most found. There is also a #2 which is a #1 with two Bing (Milwaukee, see page 91) weedless hooks. This is a scarce variation which came along later than the #1M. The #3 Trout Bob or "Bob", as it was called in its infancy in 1911, (top, center) for some reason is a terror to find. The quite unusual 2-1/4" #3 (following, center) is the only one in town. The Fish Nipple is the approximate 2-3/4" (depending on how much the rubber body shrunk) #4 and represents the earliest Moonlight patent granted to Messrs. Arthur R. Miller and Horace (Emery) Ball on January 10, 1911. #4s are scarce.

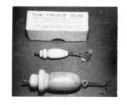

Lure #5 was called the Paw Paw Fish Spear. The approximate 4" 2-hooker sports two line-ties so it could be a sort of jerk bait (nose tie) or a floating diver (top of head tie). The redhead/yellow bodied example left came in a yellow cardboard box. The Fish Spear or "Spearpoint", as it was locally, was not ever made in great numbers. The #5 is hard to find.

The Zig Zag was plug #6 in the Moonlight line. There were two major variations. The 4" #6 is a 3-hooker (left, following). The 2-1/2" #6M was a
2-hooker (belly and tail - two double hooks each). The 2-hooker (following, right)
in both photos is longer and a later cup-rig version. The #6s on the right, in
the belly-up photos, shows the typical slightly convex brass washer typical of
early Moonlight plugs. Look for this feature. The 2-1/2"er is tougher to find
than the 4"er. The cup variation is unusual. The #6 actually got its start as
early as 1911 when Emery Ball first made and field tested it. He had trouble at
first getting it to zig zag instead of turning over. The secret was a lower line-
tie. The #6 was a success. Mr. Ford R. Wilber (the third and more permanent
party in the Moonlight Bait Co.) shared a patent for the Zig Zag granted February
3, 1914. This patent went to court concerning the Rush Tango. The Moonlight
patent ultimately held up. More about this a little later (1923). An interesting
footnote on the #6 is that the idea came originally from the wood model that acted
as a mold for the preceding rubber Fish Nipple. Mr. Ball was experimentally fishing
at a local pond when he cut the head off the wood mold at a slant, put a line and
hooks on and saw it sort of zig and zag.

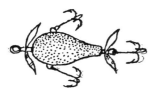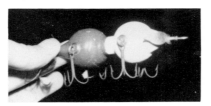

There are three Moonlight plugs that came out around 1912-1914. All three
are rare. The 1913 Special on the left has never been found as far as we know.
The Dreadnought (center) is a rare 4" beast of a plug. The 2" Paw Paw Underwater
Minnow (right) was only made for a short time.

Plug #7 is the 3" Bug (left). There are very few Bugs in collections.
The Bug was soon replaced by the 4" #9 Ladybug patented on June 26, 1917. The
Ladybug had obviously been made before that. Examples like the top left plug
are found with simple screw eyes - the earliest Moonlight hook hanger. The Bug
is more difficult to find than the Ladybug, but not by much. Some Ladybugs had
string legs. The #9 Ladybug (following, right) was one of the earliest Ball plugs
to be air brushed. The colors on the early series Moonlight plugs were simple -
luminous, luminous/redhead, all white, redhead, redhead/yellow, all red, etc.
Certain odd colors were for certain plugs. The Bug came in black. Spotted,
striped and rainbow finish were seen toward the mid-teens on some Moonlights when
Mr. Ball finally started to use an airbrush. This ends the early stage of the
Moonlight Bait Company: 1906-1923. Many changes follow.

In 1923 there was a dramatic change in the Moonlight line. This change
was mainly due to the merging of the Silver Creek Novelty Works of Dowagiac,
Michigan with the Moonlight Bait Co. of Paw Paw, Michigan, the survivor being
the Moonlight Bait & Novelty Works of Paw Paw, Michigan. This move was made as
a result of an agreement between James Heddon's Sons, Inc. of Dowagiac, Michigan
and the Moonlight Bait & Novelty Works of Paw Paw, Michigan. The agreement
between Moonlight and James Heddon's Sons is most interesting. It is also rather
puzzling. Part of the contract stipulated that Moonlight could manufacture the
following plugs as long as they were made in Paw Paw, Michigan - the Zig Zag,
Fish Nipple and Ladybug. It seems that by 1924 Moonlight was once again able to
make its own plugs. This arrangement also included Heddon's granting permission
to make a Wilber/Ball patented boat seat. The agreement also stipulated a .03¢
per plug royalty on the Zig Zag patent. Regardless of what happened in 1923, we
see the Silver Creek line of plugs merging with the Moonlight - a great combination.

Silver Creek offered the little 1-3/4"
Silver Creek Wiggler fly rod plug very early in
its history. The Wiggler has an interesting
design and is either overlooked or a rare plug.
The Wiggler belongs in a Moonlight collection.

The earliest Polly-Wogs (circa 1921) had notched lips and many were sold dir-
ectly from Dowagiac (left). Most were probably sold through distributors such as
Schoenfeld-Gutter Company, Inc., World Building, New York City, who catalogued the
Silver Creek line under their own name "Sea Gull". The large Polly-Wog was 4"
(top, right) and the small was a great little 2-1/2"er (below, right).

The plug that made some plug collectors plug collectors is the Pikeroon.
The Pikeroon is not only an extremely graceful and beautiful plug but it came in
some interesting and highly collectable variations. The 4-1/4" 2-hook #1000 series
Baby Pikeroons are perhaps the ones most seen (left). The 5-1/4" "Large" 3-hook
(2 belly, 1 tail) #900 Pikeroon came in glass eyed and painted eye versions (center). There seem to be fewer #900s than #1000s. A hard to find Pikeroon is the
4-1/4" #2500 series single hook Pikeroon (right).

The 4-1/2" #2000 Jointed Pikeroon (top, left) is a bit harder to find than
the straight #1000. The huge (approximately 6") #3100 Musky Special (below, left)
looks like old "Itself" hit it a few times. #3100s are nearly rare. There are
at least three variations in hardware at the joint on #2000s. Top one is thought
to be the earliest. Different scale patterns show up on the Pikeroons in addition to the glowing array of colors (see color section). The difference in scale

patterns is due to the stretching of fine netting which was used to mask the scales (right).

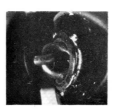

The following four Pikeroon type plugs are on the rare side. The 4" #1200 5-hooker (left) and the 3" #1100 series 3-hooker (next to it) were floaters. It was recommended using a 1/4 ounce Dipsy Sinker six inches in front of the nose to make #1200s and #1100s go under. The drawing second from right is the 1-3/4" #1400 which we've never seen. What a beauty this must be! On the right is the little #1000 Feather Minnow with feathers missing.

An original Silver Creek catalog shows the 1-1/2" #600 "Bug" bait (left) and the 1-5/8" #650 Fly Bait (center). The Sea Gull catalog offered the following plugs in the group photo, right. A = 1-3/4" #500 Trout Bait ("Trout Eat Us"), B = 2-1/2" #400 series (Small) Bass Bait, C = 3" #300 Bass Bait (Large) ("Bass Eat Us"), D = #330 Trolling Bait. These have a lateral groove in the head. Some did not. Note painted eyes on A, B and C. Note blended redhead paint job on D and E which is the 4" #200 Trolling Bait. All plugs in this photo have small screw eyes.

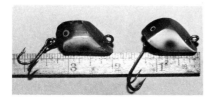

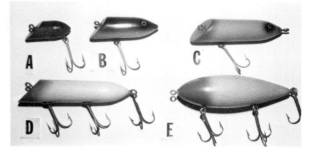

The #2100 Little Wonder had some relatives. This type plug was in the Moonlight line through 1929 in several sizes. The actual Little Wonder (following left photo, right bottom) is joined by its bigger brothers. The large 5" musky size (top, left photo) is not seen very often - few of these plugs seem to turn up. The 4-3/4" Moonlight (center row, left photo) appear to be real Moonlights! Another version of this type plug is the 3-1/2"er (center photo) which is probably an earlier Moonlight version of the #3350. The 2-1/2" #800 1929 version of the Ladybug Wiggler came in five bug colors. The one below right is colored like a Ladybug. The little guy next to it is a possible fly rod version.

 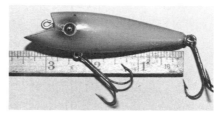 

Around 1926 Moonlight was working on still newer and more innovative ideas. The only plug remaining in the line was the original #1 (others came back later). The 99% Weedless #600 came in two sizes - 2" and 2-1/2". The 99% Weedless differed from its Comstock predecessor. Look for painted eyes and metal work on the belly (see page 154). The small one is rougher to find than the big one (following, left). The approximately 3" #3000 2-hook (belly and tail) surface bait is a high quality glass eyed plug (center). The #3000 must have had a big brother. The 3-hook surface plug on the right is obviously a Moonlight. It is in a box marked The "Beecher" Bait.

The following Moonlight plugs on the left are: top left = the 4" #2900 Torpedo type bait, bottom left = 4" #2600 Brilliant Bass Seeker. The silver flash feature of this plug was patented on August 23, 1927 by Messrs. Clyde C. Sinclair and Floyd A. Phelps. Mr. Sinclair went on to formally start the famous (and later) Paw Paw Bait Company of Paw Paw, Michigan. The Paw Paw Bait Company was incorporated on July 9, 1935 with Mr. Sinclair as president. The top right plug is the 3-1/2" #2700 Bass Seeker Jr. Some Bass Seekers had standard paint jobs. The Wilson Wobbler below, right is the Moonlight version (brass surface cups). On the right is the 3-1/2" #1900 (Jointed Bass Seeker). All these plugs can be found but probably with a little difficulty.

Moonlight made several plugs especially for retailer Abbey & Imbrie of New York who advertised them under their own name. Below left (left to right) are the 4-1/2" #3200 Whirling Chub, the 3-1/2" #3700 Flash Head Wobbler and the 4" "Whippet" similar to the #2900 Moonlight. The plug on the right is the 4" Crippled Minnow #3400. Note the glass eyes. This plug was later introduced into the Paw Paw line as the Great Injured Minnow.

Moonlight apparently made some round 3 and 5-hook underwater minnows. Look closely at your "Heddons" for Moonlight paint jobs (left). Note the Moonlight prop, similar to Heddons, is usually unmarked. The plug center is a possible Moonlight. The glass eyed plug on the right is an Injured Minnow type attributed to Moonlight. It has an interesting configuration. This one has been seen with a prop marked Abbey & Imbrie. It is also quite Heddon-like.

This plug is the 2-1/2" #50 Mouse which was seen later in the Paw Paw line.

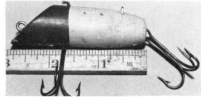

This plug has been attributed to Moonlight. We can't prove this and tend to disagree. It is a 2-3/4" chunk plug built to accommodate a pork strip on top. It's quite possible it is a Moonlight - that's why it's here.

The Paw Paw Bait Company deserves more than just a word here. Of all the companies that blossomed after 1929, Paw Paw is perhaps the least appreciated. Many Moonlight plugs went into the Paw Paw line. Remember Moonlights have no eyes early, painted eyes circa 1926 and glass eyes circa 1923. Paw Paw generally have painted tack eyes. We have never seen a glass eyed Paw Paw. Period! Late series (1923-1929) Moonlight colors are best experienced by looking at the Pikeroons in the color section. Moonlight are as hard to collect as any specialty - especially the early series. We may never see a complete collection in a lifetime. Please don't let this discourage you. Brave men collect Moonlights. Remember - "Strange things are seen at night".

Thanks are especially due to Trig Lund, Walt Blue, Bill Jones, Bill Stoetzel and Kit Wittekind.

Chapter Eight

SOUTH BEND

South Bend plugs probably started before the turn of the century as the idea and product of Mr. F. G. Worden of South Bend, Indiana. Exactly how far before the turn of the century we don't know. It could have been as early as 1894. Mr. Worden's nickname in the industry was "Bucktail". He incorporated the idea of adding deer hair to artificial lures, including plugs. By the turn of the century, plugs were not only being fished with, but patents were becoming more necessary. The Worden plugs have a very sturdy design. Some bear the patent date of December 29, 1903 which was for a trolling spoon or spinner. This patent was issued to a Paul Junod of Celina, Ohio. The Junod spinner is the Worden spinner. There must have been some connection or agreement between Messrs. Worden and Junod, and eventually South Bend. Mr. Worden supplied his bucktail idea to William Shakespeare, Jr. who came out in 1902 with the Shakespeare "Worden" Bucktail Bait made of hollow aluminum (see page 193).

The identifiable Worden plugs include four of the five plugs on the left. The only exception is the second plug from the left which is a Shakespeare Kazoo Minnow painted exactly like a Worden. The center and right hand plugs have yellow and black glass eyes, the others do not. The least expensive version was the all white flop prop version (left) and the no eyed (Worden's Combination) bait, second from right. Almost all Wordens are round as are the South Bends to follow. The only version not seen here are the possible 3 and 5-hook flop prop all white plugs. Most Wordens are green back/white belly with a red air brushed gill mark. The center plug is a close-up of the Worden 3-3/4" 2-hook model. Note the Junod patent prop. This plug is orange - very unusual. The plugs on the right are speculative. They could be early Wordens (pre-1903). Following, below right is a strange version of the Junod prop. It has holes in it. Will wonders ever cease? Ever see one of these on a plug?

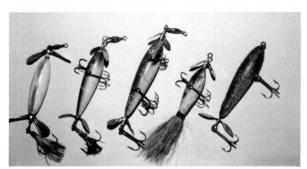

Mr. "Bucktail" Worden started what was eventually called the South Bend Bait Company in a two-story house in South Bend, Indiana.

By 1914, and possibly earlier, they were making and distributing plugs
and other fishing tackle in a three-story factory complete with loading docks.
The South Bend Bait Company sold a formidable number of plugs. The earliest
South Bend plugs were underwater minnows. There was a transition between Worden
and South Bend which was primarily in prop design, painting and general style.
The earliest, and by far the rarest, South Bend minnows have a single notched
prop similar to the one Shakespeare used (left). The underwater minnows (center)
represent some of the models offered in the early teens. Top left is the 4-1/4"
#913 3-hook (side) Panetella Minnow. The Panetella also came in 4-1/4" #915
5-hooker and a very scarce 3-hook (2 belly, 1 tail) 4-1/4"er. Early Panetellas
have an overpainted brass tail cap. The little 2-3/4" plug (bottom, right) is the
only one like this we have seen. Apparently it is a cheap underwater minnow to
compete with Shakespeare's Little Pirate and Pflueger's Peerless. Note the use
of the same prop as on the #565 (not pictured because it's metal) Weedless Spinner
Hook (see enlargement on far right). Second row (left) is the 2-1/2"
#901 Midget Underwater Minnow which came out in the late teens and is one to
look for. Second row (right) is the 3" #904 3-hook Minnow in "Hex" paint job,
circa 1914. The idea here was to compete with the popular Heddon #s0 and 00
which were 5-sided. Hexagaonal = 6 sides, Pentagonal - 5 sides - why not the
"Pent"?? The "Hex" paint job creates an illusion. The "Hex" is round like
almost all South Bend minnows. Third row (left) is another #904 in yellow
background. It came white and red with spots also, a very attractive plug.
Third row (right) is the "Worden" Combination Minnow with South Bend props.
Bottom row is two 3" #903 South Bend Standard Underwater Minnows. The 5-hook
version is the #905. It also came as the #906 ("Hex") which is tougher to
find than the #904s.

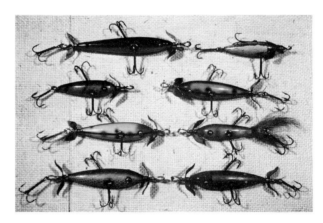

Several of the underwater minnows were fitted with bucktail trebles.
These Min-Bucks are much harder to find than standard versions. Once again, we
find the musky minnows are generally scarcer than their smaller counterparts.
The big 5-1/4" 3-hook Muskie Minnow (following, left) is rare. The 5-hook version is very scarce particularly in the #955 Min-Buck version. Another tough
South Bend is the 3-5/8" Muskie Casting Minnow. The version on the top left is
believed to have been made by South Bend especially for Hibbard, Spencer &
Bartlett Company of Chicago. This version has been seen with props stamped
with their trademark "OVB" - "Our Very Best".

Two of the earliest South Bend plugs that got going in the very early
teens were the two Woodpeckers - the 4-1/2" #923 and the #924, a luminous Woodpecker.   The 3" #925 Midget Woodpecker came in an unusual weedless version (top,
left) that sports Bing's weedless hooks.   Woodpeckers are around, there are fewer
Midgets.   The Woodpeckers below should be in color - you would see that all South
Bends are indeed not redheads.   The plugs on the right are the beautiful South
Bend Floating Minnows - #s 920, 921 and 922 which came with Bing weedless hooks
(top) and the standard #920F (below).   Both plugs, on the rare side, are fine
examples and show the beauty of early and highly collectable South Bends.

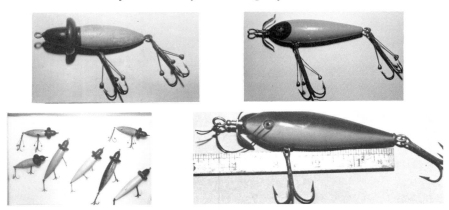

This 3-1/2"er is a "Coast Minnow"
type plug thought to have been made by
South Bend in the early teens.   At one
time this plug was thought to be a
Heddon by some people.   We do not share
that opinion.

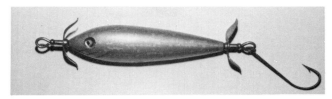

There were many sudden and important changes in the South Bend line in the
mid-teens.   The Surf Oreno originally came in two sizes - the Midget Surf Oreno
#960 (bottom, left) and the 3-3/4" #963 Surf Oreno, itself.   The earliest South
Bend Surf Orenos were like the #960 in the photo, top left.   The #962 3" Midget
Surf Oreno (bottom, left) has the "harness" that was an attempt to better secure
the long screw eyes.   The harness version came in around 1927 to accomodate the
stressful needs of the plug and the softer wood supply.   Surf Orenos are around
but they are usually beat.   Don't try and talk a fisherman out of one.   Around
here they are standard in most tackle boxes.   Nothing is as good as an original
Surf Oreno for muskies.   The Surf Oreno comes up in about a 25 to 1 ratio with
Heddon's scarce #300 equivalent.   Surf Orenos were made for a long time.   Some
of the most interesting variations are beyond the dates covered in this book.
Painted eyes are seen on the 1-1/2" #961 Fly rod Surf Oreno.   The 5-1/2" Musky
Surf Oreno had an elongated body.   The plug on the right is not a Musky Surf
Oreno but a #966 Lunge Oreno (post 1929).   The Musky Surf Oreno has standard
South Bend (blunt) props on both ends.   Starting in the early 1920s South Bend
props were stamped "South Bend".

 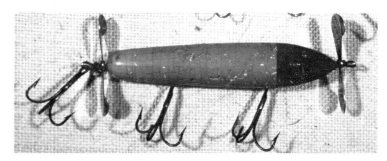

There are not many fishermen or plug collectors that have not heard of,
fished with or found a lot of Bass Orenos. They are around to this day because
they are fish catchers. Mr. J.S. Olds patented the Bass Oreno on December 19,
1916. There are a whole bunch of Bass Orenos and Bass Oreno variations. The
earliest Bass Oreno we have seen that really seems O.K. is a 6" 3-hook musky
version with non-plated brass cups, a brass tail cap similar to the one on the
1912 Panetellas, and in a typical green and white Worden color (left). The
earliest Bass Orenos had no eyes. The finish was expertly done not only in
redhead but in yellow body with green and red spots, red, rainbow, frog and
redhead/aluminum body. The earliest South Bend 3-1/2" #973 Bass Orenos had a
closed screw eye in a brass cup. Shortly after this the screw eye opened up
and allowed the simple removal of the treble hook - simply unscrew it and take
it off. The Bass Oreno line goes like this - from the earliest on. The 3-1/2"
#973 Bass Oreno and 2-3/4" #972 Babe Oreno which were available at least as early
as 1915. There was also a 3-1/2" #973W (Bing's weedless trebles). Salt water
Bass Orenos (3-1/2", #977) are not easy to find. They are 2-hookers (belly and
tail). The #977 center is all metal. It is believed to be the all metal pattern
used to make #977s. If that is what this is then someone added hooks and went
fishing with it - it's not the standard #977. The 4-1/2" #976 Musk-Oreno was
also from the mid-teens. The 6-1/2" #978 Troll-Oreno (left) came out in the early
1920s. The #978 is a 3-hooker. The tiny 1-1/8" Fly-Oreno came out in the early
1920s as did the 1-3/4" Trout-Oreno (right). They made a lot of Fly-Orenos and
Trout- Orenos as they did the Bass Orenos.

Three single hooked large Bass Oreno types came out in the mid-1920s.
These are look-alikes except for size and were designed for specific salt water
fishing - the 4-1/2" #985 Coast-Oreno, the 6-1/2" #986 King Oreno (below left)
and the 8", 2 single belly hooked Tarp Oreno. These three plugs are rough to
find. The earliest Teaser (no hooks) were used to attract salt water fish. The
earliest version was the 8" #980 Oreno Teaser (center, left) plug. The 11" #981
Zane Grey Teaser is from the late 1920s (center, right). The other two Teasers
in the photo are after 1929. I guess they put hooks on Teasers - Shark Oreno?
(right) Bass Orenos in general are extremely common. Nevertheless, it is important to remember that some people collect all Bass Orenos, every color in just
one size. Check out the color section on Bass Orenos. Lots of colors, some are
hard to find and some are absolutely not. All Bass Orenos up until 1929 were
either no eyed or glass eyed.

The 4-1/4" #975 Pike Oreno was patented by Frank Austin Cass and assigned
to South Bend on April 17, 1923. There is some thought that the earliest Pike
Orenos had no metal lip (left, top). The earliest metal lipped versions had no

eyes and no markings on the lip. The bottom, left #975 has a marked lip. The
3" #974 Midget Pike Oreno was only made for a few years. It is a good one to
find. Notice the removable single hooks. These were introduced around 1916
when Mr. Ivar Hennings was General Manager of the South Bend Bait Company.

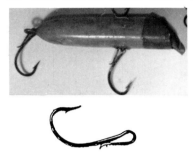

It would appear that the South Bend Bait Company had rights to Professor
Howe's Vacuum Bait in the early 1920s (see page 107). The earlier Vacuum Baits
like the earlier Bass Orenos were no eyed. Later versions are glass eyed. One
of the great all time South Bend finishes is the "dragonfly" left. There are
two size Vacuum Baits - the large #1 - 2-3/8" and the small #21 2"er (center).
The 3-3/4" #940 Teas-Oreno came out in 1929 in a glass eyed version (below, right).
Note the 5" or so uncatalogued "giant" in the center. This musky plug came in
the same tacklebox as an 8" Heddon "747". It seems major companies could be
talked into making special plugs. Regular #940s are around. The glass eyed
versions in fancy colors are the best. The Baby and Midget came in after 1929.

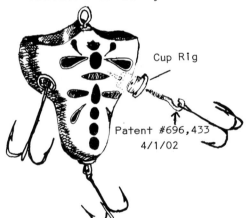

Cup Rig

Patent #696,433
4/1/02

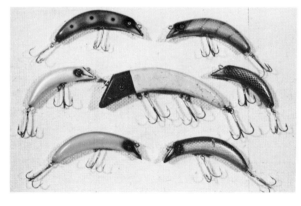

The early pre-1930 #929 3-3/4" Plunk Oreno came in a glass eyed version.
The later Plunk Oreno looks nothing like this one. The #929 is not common by
any means.   The 3" #935 Whirl Oreno came in another size after 1930. It was
patented January 8, 1929 by Louis A. Chapleau and assigned to the South Bend
Bait Company. Whirl Orenos are more desirable than scarce (center). The 2-3/4"
#982 Sinking Midget and the 3-1/2" Gulf-Orenos came out in the mid-20s. Both are
rather scarce South Bends (right).

The Fish-Oreno is the underwater version of the #973 Bass Oreno patented
by J. Pagin on October 30, 1925. The Fish-Oreno sinks because it has a plated
metal head that's heavy enough to take a relatively large piece of wood down.
The earliest Fish-Orenos were glass eyed and painted in most of the important
South Bend paint jobs. The set below left includes some fancy colors. See
Bass Orenos in color section for a selection of South Bend colors. Fish-Orenos
are around - a nice one is nice. The #967 Wiz-Oreno is a 2-3/4", mid-1920s,
Babe Oreno body with a strange alteration (see below, right). The school of
glass eyed Whiz-Orenos, right, are in seven different colors - now that's collect-
ing!. #967s aren't easy to find in any color.

The #965 Crippled Minnow is a neat glass eyed plug. It's hard to find
and hard to recognize. That's a combination. Another one that sometimes
frustrates South Bend collectors is the 4" #999 (center). The 5" #991 triangular Squid Oreno and the 5" #989 round Tun-Oreno are all metal terrors of the
deep. They sink, now! (right).

South Bend colors are not easy to figure out. Originally they used the
entire color name written out as follows:

Solid White	Green Back, White Belly	Red Cracked back, White Belly
Solid Red	Green Back, Yellow Belly	Red Cracked Back, Yellow Belly
Solid Aluminum	Green Cracked Back, White Belly	Sienna Cracked Back, Yellow Belly
Red Head and Tail, White Body	Green Cracked Back, Yellow Belly	Slate Back, White Belly
Red Head, Aluminum Body	Red Back, White Belly	Rainbow
Red Head, White Body	Red Back, Yellow Belly	Yellow Perch

It was difficult to spell out the entire color name so South Bend abbrevi-
ated. The letters that follow the three digit numbers stand for the above colors -
example: GCBW is green crackleback/white belly, YP is yellow perch and so on.
South Bend props after the Junod (Worden) prop were sort of blunt ended. They
were unmarked until the late teens when the name South Bend was stamped in.

Not too many people have collected South Bends up until now. Lately we
have noticed a sudden new interest in this fine company. If you are at all interested in collecting South Bend, get Jim Bourdon's fine book. Special thanks to
Jim for his help on South Bend and the rest of this book. We especially appreciate Jim's sharing of information and wonderful insights throughout the research
herein. Thanks also to Phil Byrne, Earl Glasshagel and Steve Ongert. A footnote
to South Bend. Many of the rarest and most sought after South Bends are after
1929.

Chapter Nine

CREEK CHUB

The original Creek Chub plugs were handmade. The plugs on the left are reported to be made by Carl Heinzerling of Garrett, Indiana around 1906. It is possible the date could be slightly earlier or later. Nevertheless, these plugs represent the oldest Creek Chubs we have seen. The plug on the right is similar.

 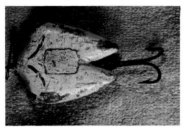

Another man, Mr. Henry Dills, received the first patent for a Creek Chub plug. Mr. Dills did not assign Design Patent #54,071, November 4, 1919, for the Open Mouth Shiner to anyone. Mr. Dills' Patent #1,352,054, September 7, 1920 (not a design patent) shows the use of the metal lip on a plug that was Creek Chub's first advertised plug - the #100. Mr. Dills next patent was for the Pikie Minnow. This Design Patent was granted on June 21, 1921 and there we have the early Creek Chub line. One interesting footnote on patents is that the patent date of 9-27-20 stamped on many Pikie lips does not jive with either of these two patents. The plugs following could be early works of Mr. Dills. The plug on the left has a metal lip fitted to the head, not inserted. The plugs on the right have all the earmarks of very early commercial Creek Chubs. We could be wrong here but it will not hurt you to keep your eyes peeled for one of these.

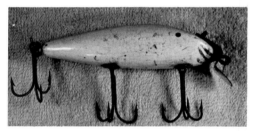 

Creek Chub was kind in their numbering system. Generally speaking, they started with the first catalogued Creek Chub plug in 1916, possibly earlier, which was the 3-1/2" #100 Creek Chub Wiggler (left, bottom). The second plug is the 2-3/4" #200 Baby Chub Wiggler (left, top). These are very early versions. The 2-3/4" #300 is the Crawdad, a popular classic old plug. It originally came in natural crab and the all white, pink-eyed #302 albino. The Crawdad came in two sizes, the regular 2-3/4" #300 and the 2-1/4" #400 Baby Crawdad. The #300, center, is not the earliest one but appears in a seldom seen color - white head, black body. Crawdads had rubber band legs pinned in the belly. The Crawdads, right, shows they made different versions - not all these were made before 1929.

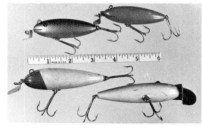  

Creek Chubs' #500 was the 3-1/4" Open Mouth Shiner. The early #500s came in a grey box (left). #600 is the 5" Husky Musky. The #600 right is one of the earliest **versions**.

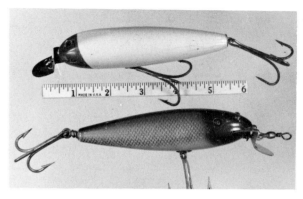

The 4-1/2" #700 is the Pikie Minnow. It is not known when the earliest Pikies were out - probably before 1920. The Pikie went on to be probably the most popular all-time plug. Collecting the variations can be practically unending. See color section for colors. These are all #700s. The early series Creek Chub plugs (#s 100-700) originally came in a cardboard box with the picture of the plug on the cover. Every box was a slightly different color. We will discuss Pikies further in the second series. The earliest Creek Chub plugs in the early series had a screw eye belly hook rig through a small flat brass washer. The plugs with lips had no markings and the paint jobs were excellent but crude compared to what came later. The earliest paint jobs on Pikies, #100s and #200s did not have scales and had hand brushed red gill marks. Some had glass eyes. Redheads and most solid colors had no eyes. The second variation was a small shallow cup. Any plugs with typical nickle plated cups are later. Early Creek Chubs had two line-ties which provided three separate actions on the #s 100, 200, 600 and 700. You could unscrew the line tie on top of the nose and turn the lip over and the standard floating diver could be used "for surface splatter". Take the lip out, use the top line tie and you have a plug recommended as a "near surface wobbler".

This #700 is a very early Pikie, but not the earliest. The earliest commercial Pikie was probably a glass eyed, no scale in pikie color.

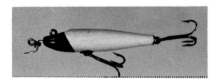

The 2-3/4" #800 Deluxe Wagtail Chub was the first plug after the early series - #s 100-700. The cardboard box is now the familiar green, red and white Creek Chub box.

The 3-1/4" #900 Baby Pikie is described as the "thoroughbred from the famous Pikie Minnow #700". The #900 Baby Pikie is the first in a series of Pikies to follow. Below, left top is an early glass eyed #900, and below is a no eyed #900. The 2-3/4" #2200 is the Midget Pikie (not pictured). The jointed version of the 4-1/2" #700 is the #2600 Jointed Pikie (center, top). The two plugs below are early #700s - the bottom #700 has hand painted gills.

The Husky Pikie is the 6" #2300 on the right. The early ones (pre-1930) have the hooks firmly screwed into the tail rather than wired through like the later ones. The single "Jersey Rig" hook was advertised by Creek Chub as available on request, as were special paint jobs. Creek Chub would also repaint a plug on request.

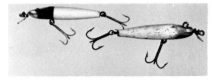

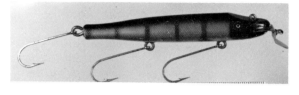

The 2-1/2" #1400s don't grow on trees, but they sometimes end up in them. There is perhaps no Creek Chub plug as creative as the Big Creek Bug Wiggler. The #1400s are hand decorated by brush. The #1400 on the left is red, white and black. The other color available is just as bug-like - gold with brown wings outlined in black! The #1400 is the largest of two other relatives - the 7/8" #1000 Trout Bug and the 1-1/4" #1100 Trout and Bass Bug. The three Bugs are all in the 1925 catalog and came in black as the third color. Bugs have string tails. Polly Wiggle is the name of the #1700 which was a chunk plug. Two sizes were apparently made. The 1-3/4" was advertised. There aren't an awful lot of #1700s around either.

The Flat Side Chub is the 3-3/4" 3-hook (side and tail) #1500. The Baby Flat Side 2-3/4" 2-hook (side and tail) #1600 came out in the mid-20s. The "Injured Minnow" as it was later called is a great plug - it floats on its flat side with the hooks down. Some ex-bass around here knew about the #1500. The plug (following, left) is not a Flat Side Chub, but has the same flat body. If it had the belly hooks on the side it would be. The plug right is fatter. It is not an Injured Minnow - count the hooks and look for belly weights. These two plugs (left and center) actually are #1800 Underwater Spinner Minnows. This rare and desirable plug is one of the top Creek Chubs to find. It has a little brother - the 2-3/4" #1900 Creek and River Fishing Lure - a 3-hook underwater minnow with a hook on each side and one on the tail. If you look at all #1500s and #1600s, you run across you may find a #1800 or #1900. Look for those hooks on the other side! Don't despair if you find an Injured Minnow - just go fishing with it, but if you find a Flat Side Chub (thin body like on the left) hang it up. These two rare Creek Chubs are probably unfished. Remember, the #s 1500 and 1600 float on their side and #s 1800 and 1900 sink belly down.

Creek Chub was big on making wood fly rod plugs. These are all hard to find. The #F10 is one to look for. The body is 1-5/8" (4-1/2" overall) (left). The #F50 Fly Rod Crawdad (center) and the #F90 Crippled Minnow (right, top). There is a fine line between fly rod plugs and everything else in the world including Poppers. These are plugs as are the two Fly Rod Pikies (right, bottom) - 1-1/4" #1200 for trout and the 1-5/8" #1300 for bass.

Few plugs have caught so many fish as the 3-3/4" #2000 Darter which was introduced in the late 1920s. The Darter was made in many variations later but the #2000 is the one. In this family it accounted for a 6 pound small mouth, first keeper musky, largest possible lost musky and many attacks by northern pike and large mouth bass. Fish with a Darter, don't collect them, is good advice. The cardboard Creek Chub box with the #2000 was the standard packaging in this era. The model number is marked on the end.

The 4" #2100 Fintail Shiner came in two separate variations. The earliest #2100s had painted cloth fins and tail (below, left) that have not lasted well down through the years. The later version had metal fins and tail. Finding a good, intact, early one isn't easy. The (Baby) 3"er (below, left) is downright rare. How would you like to catch a World's Record bass. The 3-1/2" #2400 Wiggle Fish (top, right) has been reported to be the plug that did the job. The 2-1/2" #2500 Baby Wiggle Fish has a single belly hook and is more difficult to find than its big brother. The bottom plug, right is an interesting #2500.

Henry Dills patented a rubber legged frog on October 19, 1926. Look for the wood body without the legs. This could be a "sleeper".

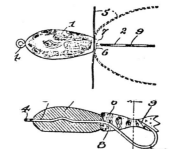

Two desirable and classic pre-1930 Creek Chubs are the 2" #2800 Weed Bug (left), patented on October 18, 1927 by Sam F. davenport of Auburn, Indiana and assigned to Creek Chub Bait Co., and the Gar Underwater Minnow. Try and find a Gar in a tackle shop. #2900 is a 5-1/4"er. Two colors were listed but there are three colors (following, right) Look for any Gar!

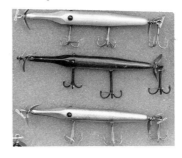

The Lucky Mouse apparently was advertised as early as 1929. The Albino (white mouse) 2-1/2" #3600 (top, left) is the better mouse to find of the two alternative colors which were black and grey. There was also a Fly Rod Mouse #F200 (below, left) that is quite scarce. The 3" #3200 Plunker also came out around 1929. The version on the right is the Plunker to have if you must have a Plunker. It is the early (pre-1936) "arch back" version in the red, white and black "bug finish". Most Plunkers are rather common. Be careful on "arch back" Plunkers. Some came after 1930 in an inexpensive version called Sure Strike. Look for cup in tail for a Creek Chub "arch back". Other Plunkers came later.

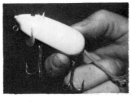

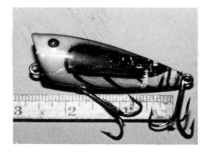

The Creek Chub colors were the last one or two digits in the number just like Heddon. They are presented here in a semi-chronological order starting with the 00 "natural" colors. For example a #100 is painted "natural Creek Chub", #700 = natural Pikie, #s 300 and 400 = natural Crab, #1400 = natural Bug, #1700 = natural Pollywog and #2000 = natural Frog. Beyond this the colors are as follows:

No. 1 Natural Yellow Perch	No. 10 White with Blue Head-x
Example: 701, 201, 2101	No. 11 Black with White Head-x
No. 2 White with Red Head	No. 12 All Red-x
No. 3 Natural Silver Shiner	No. 13 All Black-x
No. 4 Natural Golden Shiner	No. 14 Yellow Spotted
No. 5 Red Side Minnow	No. 15 Tan-x
No. 6 Natural Gold Fish-x	No. 16 Steel Blue (River Peeler)-x
No. 7 Natural Mullet	No. 17 Luminous-x
No. 8 Rainbow	No. 19 Natural Frog
No. 9 Green Back-?	No. 20 Green Gar

The thing to do is study which colors are rare on what plugs. This takes time. Some of the generally better colors are followed by an X. Remember certain Creek Chubs are rarer in certain colors. A Crawdad in #20 or a #20 in Crawdad are good examples - probably never happened. Creek Chub would accommodate a customer. We once saw a local guide's tacklebox which was a boat locker full of ever combination and wierd color you could think of in Pikies. Any color he wanted he got from Creek Chub.

Creek Chub props have a little hump back and are not soldered or forced on a tube. Pre 1930 Creek Chubs usually have glass eyes. Some solid color versions have no eyes and the #2000 Darter has painted eyes (the exception).

The Creek Chub Bait Company of Garrett, Indiana started off in small quarters. Approximately 600 square feet of floor space had to accommodate the first factory. By the end of the scope of this book (late 1929) they required 10,500 square feet and a three-story building. Approximately 50 Creek Chub employees were pictured in a group photo taken about this time. It took a lot of people to make a lot of plugs by Creek Chub. In 1929 Creek Chub advertised that "the Pikie has proven itself to hundreds of thousands of fishermen, etc." That's a lot of Pikies. It's a good thing Creek Chub had a lot of room. In 1929, when everything else fell in the depression fishing picked up. So did the plug business. This book just misses some wonderful Creek Chubs. After 1929 things changed and all sorts of Creek Chubs were developed - that's for another time. We leave them there - a wonderful bunch of people making high quality fish catching plugs called Creek Chubs. Creek Chub has shown great strength. They also made a lot of plugs - fewer of some. Color variations are extremely important. Many of the rarest Creek Chubs were made since 1929. More than fifty million Pikie Minnows alone have been made since then.

Bill Jones, Joe Georgetta and Rich Treml's efforts on Creek Chub are much appreciated.

Chapter Ten

SHOW AND TELL

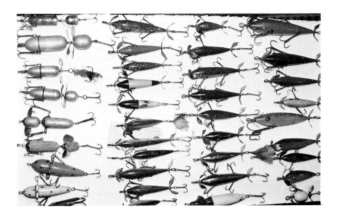
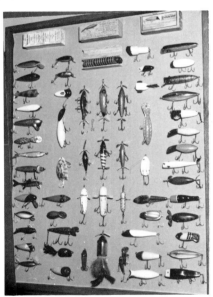
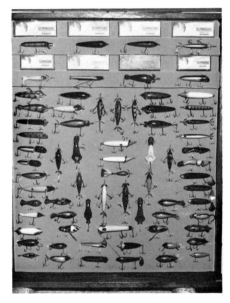

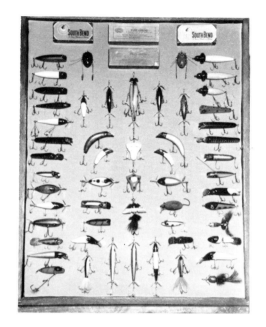

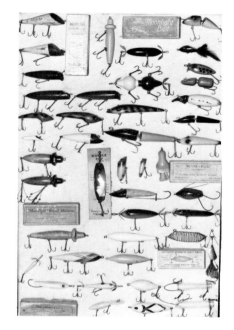

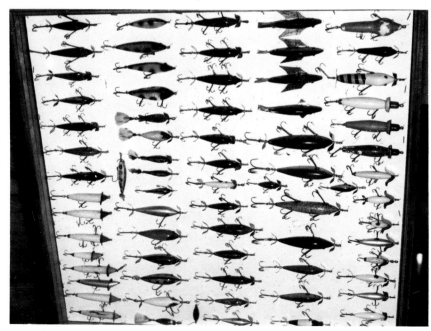

This photo is part of the old Heddon Collection
Photo courtesy of Clyde Harbin

Part of the old Heddon Collection
Courtesy of Clyde Harbin

Chapter Eleven
HIDDEN HEDDON HISTORY

Sometime around 1898, James Heddon started whittling a wood plug to be used for bass fishing in the lakes and streams around his home in Dowagiac, Michigan. James Heddon was the son of Richard Heddon, born in 1820, an immigrant from Devonshire, England. Jim Heddon decided, in the late 1800s, to carve frog shaped fishing plugs. Some of these exist to this day. These plugs proved to be very effective and, by the end of the century he was actively making plugs for the market

James Heddon and his sons, William and Charles, realized a potential business opportunity. According to the Heddon family, sometime around the turn of the century a $1,000 loan from William to his father was what really got the company off the ground. William (W.T.) Heddon would prove to be the "guts" of James Heddon & Sons Company, especially and more importantly, in the area of research and development for the products to be marketed by the company. Charles Heddon was the backbone of sales and marketing of the products for the company.

William Heddon's early years as an aeronaut or hot air balloon parachutist proved just how gutsy he really was. His 87 parachute drops attest to this fact. Luckily W.T., as William was later known, made it through his parachuting years in one piece, with only one serious injury being a broken ankle.

In 1903 William Heddon and his second wife, Laura, arrived in Ft. Pierce, Florida, 242 miles north of Jacksonville. "Combining business and pleasure" as William, himself, put it in a 1904 Field & Stream article titled "Bait Casting in Florida". With alligator shooting for variety, the two set out fishing the lakes of Florida and testing and developing the earliest Heddon plugs. The article in the 1904 Field & Stream goes on to say "Inquiry and correspondence finally resulted in my surrendering myself to the proprietor of the Jolly Palms Resort in Mohawk, Florida. It's located in Lake Country which is said to contain about 1500 lakes varying in size from a few acres to a hundred square miles. The first few days after my arrival at the Palms, in small parties we fished in nearby lakes and it was on one of these daily trips that I landed my largest bigmouth weighing, when taken from the water 10-3/4 pounds. I was high man for the season - and the demand upon my portable bait factory placed me so hopelessly behind that it became necessary to write for assistance".

James Heddon paddling W.T. Heddon, Taylor Creek - 1 mile north of
Ft. Pierce, FL, February 1903. Lure - the Dowagiac Expert

The Jolly Palms Resort in Mohawk, Florida was started in 1888 by
Charles Henry Stokes a commercial photographer from New York who enjoyed
the winter climate in this area. The rates at the Palms in those days
was $14.00 per week, $10.00 per week for the season included reasonable
use of dogs, boats, horse and Mr. Harry Stokes service as a guide. Extra
guides $1.00 per day with only a limited number of guests taken.

Will Heddon (Billy Bass) with Harry Stokes (Florida Harry) with
the Stokes boat and big string of bass ... 1906

The Jolly Palms Resort in Mohawk, Florida was accessible by railroad only. The Tavares & Gulf ran right past the main house of the Jolly Palms Resort. The Tavares & Gulf ran about 25 miles and arrived at the Holly Palms twice a week delivering ice, supplies, mail, guests and baggage.

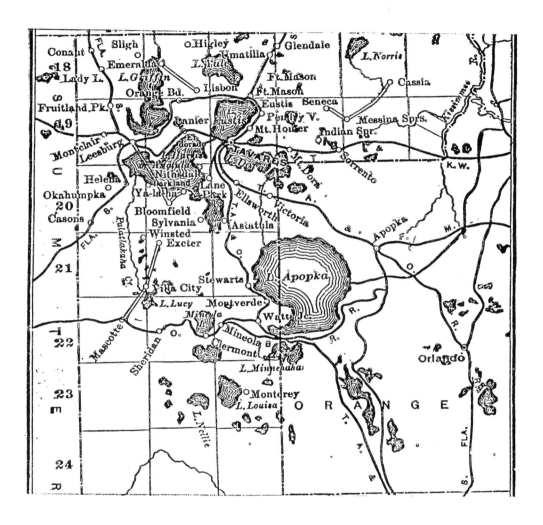

The resort was located on Plum Pond which was part of a nine lakes chain. Often one of two cypress boats owned by the resort would be loaded on a horse drawn wagon in order to access other lakes in the area, sometimes combining hunting and fishing on the same day. The great hunting and fishing and exclusive use of the boathouse as their bait factory proved to be deciding factors in Will and Laura Heddon's decision to use this as their winter headquarters for research and development of products in the early years of James Heddon & Son Company.

"The Boathouse"
Many Heddon plugs were developed here

William and Laura had a perfect place to make and test their plug, which were proving to be very popular. In a six page letter to his father Will writes, "the longer I stay the better I like it and so does Laura". One page 5 of the letter he wrote, "ask Charles if he has sent tracer of first shipment containing my 500 white cedar blanks"

William (or W.T. as he was known at this time) also wrote articles for sporting magazines sometimes under the pen name of "Billy Bass". His articles generally dealt with fishing, the use of plugs, bait casting, etc.

Dr. Walter Stokes, son of Charles Henry Stokes, guided W.T. Heddon and attests to his skill as an angler. "He was a top plug man, and was undoubtedly the most skillful manipulator of top water plugs that ever lived". He would cast it out in an appropriate place and, of course, he knew how to read the shorelines and where the bass were likely to be, and where the big ones were likely to be. When the lure hit the water he would seldom retrieve it at all, although he used every kind of technique. Sometimes he would retrieve it immediately and very rapidly, then he would stop it halfway and let it rest there. Sometimes not a minute but two or three minutes, particularly if he had sensed or seen a ripple, and thought maybe a big fish was around and approaching it. Then he would twitch it slightly like a frog resting on the water, and then he would move it toward him a little bit, and finally he would start it towards him just as rapidly as he could as thought it had spotted the fish and was trying to get the hell out of there, and at that point the bass would often strike it hard!"

Will's wife Laura was also an expert angler, hunter and possessed uncanny knowledge of the outdoors. She founded the Central Florida Chapter of the Florida Audubon Society. Laura and Will were inseparable fishing partners. According to Dr. Walter Stokes "she was a profoundly good ecologist before anybody ever heard of the word. She was one of my teachers in that respect. She was observant of everything she saw out there and the relationship of everything to the other things".

Laura Heddon

W.T. and Laura Heddon were ahead of their time in many ways. The precise, accurate records they kept were unheard of until years later. The time of day, sunlight, air temperature, water temperatures, riffles, moon phase as well as the distance the plug was cast and the distance at which it was struck by the fish were records they kept. Such accurate records are seldom kept even with today's scientific fishermen.

The Heddons gave up the use of the Jolly Palms in 1909. They continued to fish at Plum Pond but moved their factory to a shed behind the Straker residence in Minneola, Florida where they were to build a cottage of their own.

The summer months would bring them north. They had a residence in Chetek, Wisconsin where a rod and limited plug factory was started in 1907. They also fished Long Lake in Minnesota near Park Rapids. Research and development continued through the summer months in their northern stomping grounds.

W.T. & Laura Heddon bait casting Birchwood, Wisconsin
June 12,1910

The earliest fishing plugs developed at the Jolly Palms included the first plugs advertised by James Heddon and Son Company. The "Dowagiac" Underwater appeared along with a famous surface plug originally referred to as "Dowagiac" Perfect Casting Bait in 1903. By 1904 the "Dowagiac" Perfect Casting Bait was known as the "Dowagiac" Expert. The "Dowagiac Expert" is also referred to by the nickname "Slopenose". In 1904 a 4-treble hook version of the regular 2-hook "Slopenose" was added. This 4-hook version was not highly recommended by the manufacturer. Some fishermen apparently wanted more hooking power. The two hook "Dowagiac" Expert was later known as the #200. In 1904 a new version of the "Dowagiac" Underwater called the New "Dowagiac" Minnow appeared in an ad. By 1905 this version was standard being referred to as the #100 "Dowagiac" Minnow (underwater). The 5-hook version was called the #150 "Dowagiac" Minnow (underwater). These two plugs stayed in the line from 1905 until 1939.

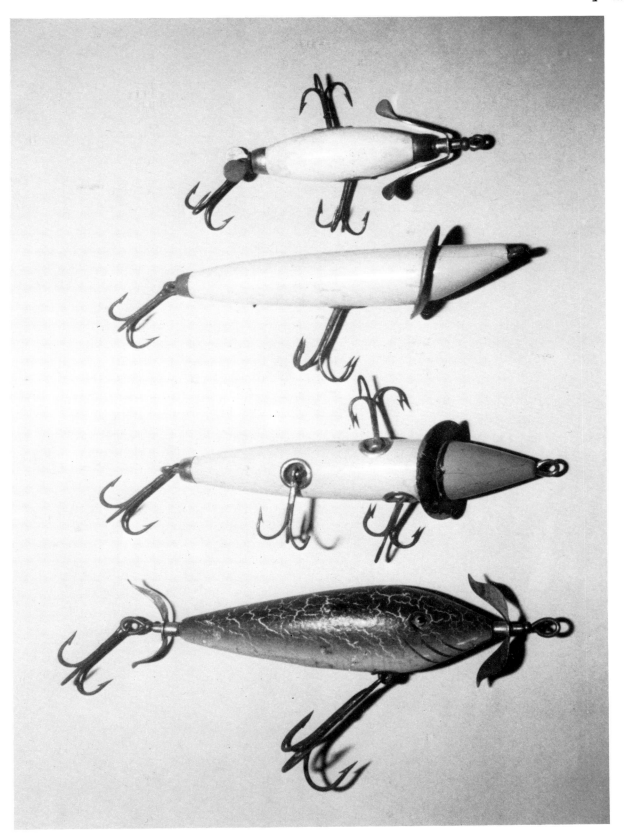

Top to Bottom: Underwater Expert, "Slopenose",
4-hook "Slopenose", #300

The #300 Surface Minnow was developed by W.T. Heddon primarily as a result of his experimenting with a surface plug to attract the huge largemouth bass that swim in fresh Florida waters. It is interesting to note that the #300 was in the line from 1905 to 1929 and later reappearing between 1937 and 1939 as the Musky Surfasser.

These plugs conceived of and developed by W.T. and Laura Heddon were stepping stones to the full and extremely effective line of fish catching plugs offered by the James Heddon Sons Company for decades to follow. Heddon plugs set the highest plug making standards ever achieved.

The information contained in this chapter is due to the ongoing research done by Clyde Harbin of Memphis, Tennessee. Clyde "The Bass-man" Harbin deserves the thanks and gratitude of all persons who either collect or are otherwise interested in old fishing plugs and their history. Most of the information contained in this chapter is from the highly informative Video Tape titled Volume 4: Heddon/Stokes Heritage. This tape is available from Clyde Harbin, 1105 Marlin Road, Memphis TN 38116 and/or VHS Tapes, Box 154087, Dept. NFLCC, Irvin, TX 75015.

The authors of this book are grateful to Clyde for his unselfish sharing of knowledge. Knowledge that was only gained by hard and diligent work over a number of years.

Photo Credits

In some cases the photographer will be listed first followed by a slash mark (/) and the name of the collector whose plug is pictured. When a number is given in parentheses it shows the same credit for that number of photos in consecutive order. Page number will be listed first and photo credits will be listed from left to right down the page.

1 - Ray Bangs, vii - Ray Bangs, 13 - John Beck, Bill Renneisen, 15 - Dudley Murphy, 17 - House, 18 - House, 19 - House, 22 - House, House/Tom Newcomb, 23 - Walt Blue, 26 - House (2), 27 - House, 28 - D. Murphy, 29 - D. Murphy, Color Section - A - Marc Wisotsky whole page, B - Kit Wittekind, House, Jim Bourdon, House, Jim Bourdon, House, C - Earl Glasshagel, Joe Georgetta, Bill Jones, D - Jim Frazier, D. Murphy, Arlan Carter, E - Arlan Carter whole page, F - Dudley Murphy whole page, G - Dan Butts, Bruce Dyer, Arlan Carter, H - Joe Courcelle, House, Joe Courcelle, 42 - House/Jim Frazier, 44 - Greg Mackey, House, 45 - Ray Carver, 46 - Marc Wisotsky/Al Munger, 47 - R. Bangs (2), 48 - R. Bangs whole page, 50 - House, 51 - R. Bangs, J. Bourdon, House, 52 - Karl White, Bill Jones, 53 - House/B.Jones, 54 - House, 57 - House, 58 - House/M. Wisotsky, D. Murphy, 59 - House, 60 - House, 61 - House, Clarence Zahn, 62 - D. Murphy, House (2), 63 - Tony Przybylo, John Swedberg, 64 - House (3), House/Bill Stoetzel,, J. Bourdon, A. Carter, House (2), House/H. Gerstenberger, 66 - House (4), House/Frank Baron, 67 - House (2), C. Zahn, 68 - House, House/W. Blue, House, 69 - House, D. Murphy, House (2), Bob Gorashko, 70 - House, J. Bourdon, Clyde Harbin (2), House, 71 - C. Harbin, House, D. Murphy, C. Zahn, D. Murphy, 72 - Dick Wilson (5), 73 - C. Zahn, C. Harbin, Rick Edmiston, House, C. Harbin, 74 - Dick Wilson, House, Clyde Marbin, A. Carter, 75 - House, Robert Gustafson, House, 76 - Dave Hoover (2), 77 - House, 78 - House/A. Carter (2), J. Bourdon, 80 - C. Zahn, House/W. Blue, House (2), W. Blue (3), 81 - A. Carter, D. Murphy, House (3), 82 - C. Zahn, C. Harbin, D. Murphy, 84 - House, 85 - C. Harbin, House (2), C. Harbin, 86 - House, C. Harbin, House/J. Bourdon, 87 - House, J. Bourdon, C. Harbin, M. Wisotsky, 88 - C. Harbin (2), J. Bourdon, 89 - House/M. Wisotsky (2), Dick Wilson (2), C. Harbin, House/M. Wisotsky, 90 - J. Beck, D. Murphy, 91 - House (2), 92 - W. Blue, House, J. Georgetta, Don Underwood/Jack Looney, House, 93 - House (2), Paula Popko, 94 - House, W. Blue (2), 95 - Russ Mumford, House, C. Zahn, 96 - D. Murphy, 97 - House (2), W. Blue, 99 - House, Paula Popko (2), House, 100 - House (2), C. Harbin, House, 101 - R. Carver, C. Zahn, 102 - House, C. Zahn, House (2), 103 - C. Zahn, House, A. Carter, 104 - D. Murphy, 105 - C. Harbin (3) 106 - House, W. Blue, 107 - House (2), 108 - House, C. Zahn (3), 109 - House, 110 - D. Murphy, House, House/ Bill Jones, 111 - House (2), 112 - R. Edmisten, W. Blue, K. White, 113 - A. Carter, 114 - D. Murphy, 115 - House (2), 116 - House (2), C. Harbin, 118 - C. Zahn, D. Murphy, House, 119 - D. Murphy, C. Harbin, House, 120 - House (2), 121 - House, J. Looney, House (6), 122 - House, Ed Weston, House/John Woodruff, House (2) 123 - J. Bourdon/F. Baron, W. Blue, House, W. Blue 124 - House (4), 125 - B. Jones, Bob Vermillion, 126 - B. Vermillion, J. Bourdon, House, 127 - C. Harbin, D. Murphy, 128 - House, C. zahn, W. Blue, House, 129 - C. Zahn (3), 130-House (5), 131 - D. Murphy, C. Harbin (2), 132 - W. Blue, C. Harbin, W. Blue, Tony Przybylo/ Rich Treml, 133 - Bourdon, House/Abe Eberly, House, W. Blue, House, Larry Bryant, 135 - D. Murphy, 136 - D. Murphy (2), R. Bangs/Bruce Wilsie, 137 - House, 138 - House, A. Carter, House (2), 139 - House, 140 - House, Henry Taylor, House, House/Jerry Myhre, House, 141 - Henry Taylor, 142 - House (2), 143 - C. Zahn,

Photo Credits (Continued)

143 (cont'd) – D. Murphy, B. Jones, House, 144 – House/W. Blue, House, 145 – C. Harbin, House (2), D. Murphy, C. Harbin, 146 – House, D. Murphy, 147 – C. Harbin, D. Murphy, 148 – House, C. Harbin (2), 149 – D. Murphy, C. Zahn (2), 150 – House, House/J. Myhre, 151 – House, R. Bangs, House (2), 152 – Russ Mumford, House (2), 153 – D. Murphy, House, T. Przybylo/R. Treml, C. Harbin, 154 – House (2), R. Mumford (2), 155 – R. Mumford, Tom Steele, J. Bourdon (2), W. Blue, House, 156 – Tom Steele, R. Mumford, House (2), 157 – B. Vermillion, House, 158 – House, D. Murphy, House, 159 – House(3), W. Blue, C. Zahn, 160 – C. Harbin, House, 161 – House, Dave McCleskey, House (3), 162 – D. Murphy, Randy Hilst, 163 – D. Murphy (2), House/Doug Lenichek (2), 164 – A. Carter, W. Blue, A. Carter, J. Woodruff, House, 165 – House (5), 168 – House/J. Myhre, House (5), House/ Ray Carver, House (2), C. Zahn, 169 – Jim Frazier (2), House (2), House/J. Myhre, House, D. Murphy, W. Blue, B. Jones, C. Zahn, Chuck Borst, House, D. Murphy, K. White, 170 – House/Malcolm Clark, House (2), 171 – House/ A. Carter, House (3), House/J. Myhre, House (2), 172 – House/Trig Lund, Joe Courcelle (3), 173 – Joe Courcelle (2), House (2), J. Courcelle, House, 174 – J. Courcelle (2), House (2), J. Courcelle, House (2), 175 – J. Courcelle, John Anderson, House, J. Anderson, House (2), 176 – J. Courcelle, House/Carter, House (2), House/Phil Byrne, D. Murphy, 177 – C. Harbin (2), Bill Renneisen, 178 – Marc Wisotsky, C. Harbin, W. Blue (2), C. Harbin, R. Bangs, 179 – W. Blue, C. Harbin, R. Bangs, C. Harbin, B. Falkenstein, A. Carter, House, 180 – W. Blue (2), C. Harbin, W. Blue, C. Harbin, House, C. Harbin, House, 181 – House, C. Harbin, House/Earl Knudson, R. Bangs (2), 182 – W. Blue, Jim Wisdom (2), C. Harbin, 183 – Rick Edmisten, House/B. Wilsie, R. Bangs, C. Harbin, R. Bangs, W. Blue, C. Zahn (2), 184 – Jim Wisdom (2), D. Murphy, J. Wisdom, W. Blue, 185 – J. Wisdom (2), C. Harbin, J. Wisdom, Ed Robison, W. Blue, 186 – C. Harbin, J. Wisdom, W. Blue, D. Murphy, 187 – C. Harbin, House, W. Blue, A. Carter, W. Blue, Ed Robison, D. Murphy, 188 – J. Wisdom, House/W. Blue, C. Harbin, House, J. Wisdom, House, J. Wisdom, House, 189 – C. Zahn, J. Wisdom, C. Harbin, House, C. Harbin, J. Wisdom, House, W. Blue, 190 – C. Harbin, J. Wisdom, House, D. Murphy (2), W. Blue, J. Wisdom, C. Harbin, House, 191 – J. Wisdom (2), House, 192 – C. Harbin (2), W. Blue, Jim Cantwell, W. Blue, 193 – C. Harbin (4), W. Blue, C. Harbin (2), 194 – House/A. Carter, J. Bourdon, House, A. Carter, House, 195 – Dennis Wolfe, House, C. Harbin, A. Carter (2), 196 – C. Harbin (2), House, House/J. Myhre, C. Harbin, R. Edmisten, C. Harbin, House (2), 197 – House/W. Blue, House, R. Edmisten, House, C. Harbin, House, 198 – C. Harbin, House, C. Harbin, House, W. Blue, J. Bourdon, C. Harbin, 199 – Bill Jones/Trig Lund, House, C. Harbin, W. Blue, A. Carter, House, W. Blue, House, A. Carter, 200 – House, W. Blue, K. Wittekind, House/Bob Essick, 201 – House (3), B. Jones, W. Blue, House, 202 – C. Zahn (2), House, K. Wittekind, A. Carter, K. Wittekind, 203 – K. Wittekind (5), B. Jones, House/Al Tumas, House/A. Carter, C. Zahn (2), House, 204 – W. Blue, C. Zahn, House (2), K. Wittekind, Bob Gorashko, B. Jones, House/W. Blue, 205 – House (2), John Beck, House (2), C. Zahn, 206 – House (3), House/Ongert (2), J. Bourdon, House/Bourdon, House/P. Byrne, House, 208 – House/P. Byrne, House, House/S. Ongert, W. Blue, House/P. Byrne, House, J. Bourdon, 209 – House/A. Carter, House/P. Byrne, House, J. Bourdon, 209 – House/A. Carter, House/P. Byrne, P. Byrne, House/S. Ongert, House, S. Ongert, 210 – House (2), House/S. Ongert, J. Bourdon, Bill Renneisen, House, House/P. Byrne, 211 – House/Ongert (2), John Beck, House/P. Byrne (2), 212 – Dudley Murphy, Tony Przybylo/Rich Treml (2), W. Blue, Ray Bangs, Joe Georgetta (2), 213 – Joe Georgetta, R. Bangs (2), J. Georgetta, 214 – R. Bangs (3), House, B. Jones, J. Georgetta (2), 215 – J. Georgetta, House (2), C. Harbin, 216 – Joe Georgetta (2), House, C. Zahn, 218 – Ray Carver, Karl White, Bill Renneisen (2), Karl White, 219 – B. Renneisen, C. Zahn, John Beck, Clyde Harbin, 220 – Clyde Harbin (2)